# MEN Are Like Wine

*Anne Violette*

First Edition

For information about wholesale orders, please contact:
Awesome Writer, LLC at:
www.AwesomeWriter.com
793 Main Street
Eliot, ME 03903

Cover Design *by Anne Violette*

All Photography *by Conrad Steward of Allure Photography*

Professionally Edited *by Raye Shelly*

Manufactured in the USA

ISBN-10: 0615684963
ISBN-13: 978-0615684963 (Awesome Writer)

# DEDICATION

*To Jason, my love.*

*For seeing the vision from the very beginning and preventing the tragic loss of great literature. Without your persistence and unwavering support and encouragement, this may have been the great idea that never came to be.*

*Thank you for your loyalty and love,*
*and for three beautiful sons.*
*I am truly blessed.*

# Foreword

Pope John XXIII said it well;
**"Men are like wine.**
**Some turn to vinegar, but the best improve with age."**

Wine is a passionate subject . Can you think of a more delightful way to enhance your libido, forget about your woes, and keep your heart pumping properly? Why yes... MEN will also do the same thing. Any wine connoisseur will tell you that certain characteristics of wine range between luscious and finicky; to deep and poetic. There are those that are best fresh and others that should be locked away in the cellar until they mature.

The "Keepers" are those bottles that we can still enjoy many years later. Young ladies tend to grab the mid-to-low grade wines just for the sake of staying within the budget. However, once they get older, women may awaken to the more expensive and mature wines that will bring greater value and longevity.

Women love wine and the feeling it gives them. Wine makes them giddy, giggly and sometimes buzzed. Wine is intoxicating, smells delicious and tastes nice for most any occasion. However, certain types can lead to headaches in the morning.

Sip, don't guzzle this book. It is meant to be enjoyed just like a great man and a delicious glass of your favorite wine, no matter what kind (he) may be. Whether you like sweet, strong, sugary, bland, expensive, cheap, dry or something good enough just for just a one-night rendezvous, you will find a type of wine to suit most everyone.

Just like a well-fermented bottle of vino, four years of research has gone into the making of this book to ensure the closest matching of the characteristics of the wine as best befitting with the personality types of men who share the same qualities. However, please note that these are only meant to be analogies and not taken too seriously.

Instead of a Table of Contents, you will find a "MENU". I hope you enjoy your selection(s). A good bottle of wine is an aphrodisiac; one to be relished and savored from the moment you pop the cork. May your glass always be filled to the brim with great wine and your heart always filled with love.

PS – In my book, the nice guy does not finish last.

# Menu

# Pinot Noir

## "THE BAD BOY"

P***inot Noir... you naughty, naughty wine; with your*** *wicked deliciousness and tempting blend of spices. Pinot Noir is one of the most complex red wines, with an intensified extra ripe sassy flavor that makes up its rather thorny personality. One may detect many exciting aromas and zesty undertones from this well known tablemate. It's bad to the bone with hints of ripe tomato, leather, cigar, sassafras and black cherries with a touch of cinnamon and peppermint. Hot, indeed. Smoke, toast and cedar with black olives can be noted in the background of a fine glass of Pinot Noir.*

*Some avoid this spicy wine after having an experience of heartache a time or two, while others embrace its high alcohol content. Its name 'noir' is fitting; in France, it means dark or black like the deep shades of grapes used to make the wine. The red berries and violet tints of raspberry, black cherry and other berries just beckon to be toasted.*

*From its very start, Pinot Noir is known as a difficult grape, from propagation to growth, to cultivation and even production at the winery. Its traits offer instability every step of the way, with the main vine often producing generations of berries that are completely unique from its origin. It can have bedecked smells, sourness or decreased production with many genetic variants – over 1,000 different kinds – whereas other wines produce much more consistently from one generation to the next. In other words, Pinot Noir is one-of-a kind and unique with each harvest. Its unpredictability is one of its most prevalent, yet decidedly frustrating qualities.*

*Even the fermentation process is difficult, straight to the bottle aging. Sure, Pinot Noir does mature, but only at about 7 to 8 years past its peak. Pinot Noir has a rare ability to lock in those same qualities that make it so different from other grapes, from its sharp beginning to last momentous sip.*

*Yet despite all of these seemingly complicated qualities, there is something entirely magnetic about Pinot Noir. It is sensual, different, and daring. The many variables are one of its main draws. Few wines can be quite as seductive as a rich glass of Pinot Noir. No two will ever taste the same. Each bottle has its own set of characteristics.*

*You can find Pinot Noir grapes in many wine-producing countries throughout the world. All of them have that same sensuality. Intoxicating, intriguing and temperamental with a finish that makes you yearn for more. Its allure is what makes it so dangerous. There is no stopping after you sip a glass of its overwhelming toxicity.*

*Ask any wine maker and he will tell you that Pinot Noir has a mind of its own. The grapes prefer cool climates. The vines must be carefully cultured with persuasion. Still, there are no guarantees. This naturally unpredictable variety will just stomp its feet and do exactly what it wants to do anyway.*

*It's not fair to generalize. There happen to be a few varieties of this delicious wine that will yield something similar every year. It depends on where they are grown. Some wine growers have learned how to tame this unruly grape.*

*Nevertheless, each fresh batch will come with its own round of excitement. Pinot Noir doesn't just sit on the shelf. And don't even bother trying to make sense of it or predict the outcome for another season. Doing so is a bit like trying to determine where and when the next hurricane will brew.*

*Oh yes, Pinot Noir can be a daredevil.*

*Rarely will you find this wine to be cheap; although, every type of wine comes with a less expensive option. Even the lower shelf bottles have a taste of liveliness that is always worth the price. From the table wine version to the bottle stashed away for later consumption, you will likely be enamored and smitten from the first minute your lips meet Pinot Noir. It is not so much a sought-after wine as it is one that often works its way into your heart unexpectedly.*

*Always surprising with its antics and tantrums, Pinot Noir elicits a charge of electricity. It's so bad, yet so good.*

❖❖❖❖❖❖❖❖❖

# NOIR ❣ Sienna

**The loud pipes of a motorcycle rumbled by Sienna's** house one day at 4:00 in the afternoon, as a muscular guy rode by on his jet black Harley Davidson V-Rod Muscle bike. As she snapped the last piece of laundry on her clothesline, Sienna wondered what a guy like that was doing in her quiet neighborhood.

Thinking nothing more of it, Sienna went about her business until the next day. Once again at 4:00 p.m., she heard the unmistakable roar of a tough bike headed her way. Sienna ran to her front window just in time to see the same guy on the same bike, except on this day, he rode slowly by as he passed her cottage. From her bay window, Sienna could see him a little better. She recognized him as a guy who had dated a friend of hers back in high school, but that was years ago and she had not seen the friend – or him – ever since. His name was Pinot Noir.

Although he was a notorious troublemaker, there was something about Pinot Noir that women were drawn to. The motorcycle was one aspect, but it was something more magnetically inexplicable. Most people called him by his last name, "Noir." Sienna wondered why he had gone by her house two days in a row at the same time, although she chalked it up to coincidence.

Until the next day, when it happened again.

This time, Sienna's curiosity got the better of her. She stepped out on her porch at exactly 3:55, just in time to hear the unmistakable growl of the bike in the distance. The sound grew louder as the motorcycle neared her house. This time,

Noir gave her a quick nod as he rolled by. *'Hmmmm.... That's really strange,'* she thought.

And so it went like this for about a week or so. Sienna began looking for reasons to be outside at the time she anticipated Noir would roll by. She would walk to the mailbox or rake the leaves or mow the lawn, often smiling as he slowly made his way past her house. The V-Rod gave her goose bumps. She wondered what it would be like to ride such a powerful machine.

Sienna was soon to get her wish. After a couple of weeks, Noir finally pulled into her driveway. "I just stopped to tell you that I like those frayed shorts," he said with a nod.

Sienna studied him for a minute. Noir was disheveled from the ride. A smirk came upon her face, as she coyly said, "Thanks." But then she turned her back, as if heading back into her front door.

"You're not going to talk to me? What, am I too rough around the edges for you or do you just not like my ride?" he asked, pointing to his bike.

"I like your bike. But I don't know you." Sienna said, as she kept walking.

"You might want to," he said. "Let me take you for a spin."

"Tomorrow." She acknowledged. "Same time." Then she closed the door.

Just as expected, Noir rolled up to her house the next day at 4:00 sharp. As Sienna came out of her house, he was sitting casually on his bike, waiting. Noir was chewing on a toothpick. He wore a ripped shirt that was cutoff at the sleeves. The first thing Sienna noticed was his tattoos. One said 'DEVIOUS' on his upper bicep. There was a tough-looking bulldog on the other arm and a swirling sword tangled in barbed wire on his shoulder. He wore diamond stud earrings and had a small scar over his eyebrow. Pinot Noir was roughly good-looking, and the scar and tattoos made him kind of sexy.

Her goose bumps came back. Actually, they had never left since the day before, as Sienna busied herself with nervous anticipation. '*What the heck am I doing?*' she wondered all day. '*This guy is bad news. I can just sense it.*' Yet, Sienna knew she would go. She couldn't help herself.

As Sienna swung her leg over the back of the motorcycle, their conversation was brief. It was a ride, and nothing more. Sienna gripped his belt as Noir revved up the throttle. He smelled like cologne. It was unmistakably Gucci Guilty, "*Intense.*" At least he was clean, even if he did look intentionally scruffy. Sienna savored the warm summer air hitting her face as they rode all over town. The rumbling of the bike made her legs tingle. It was clear she was enjoying herself.

And that was the first of many more rides on the back of Noir's motorcycle. The bike was one powerful tool of seduction, if nothing else. And Noir's eyes were set on Sienna. For now, she was his prize.

Certain people tried to spoil Sienna's fun by dishing the details of his past. It was a fairly small town, so people had nothing better to do than gossip and try to make other people miserable. While at the hair salon one afternoon, her stylist said, "You know your boyfriend used to be in jail for awhile, right?"

"Ya," said Sienna. "It was just for something dumb he did as a teenager, nothing to worry about."

"Are you sure? He looks like the kind of guy who might cheat on you," said the stylist. "I'm just looking out for your best interest, honey."

"No, you're just jealous," replied Sienna. Then she stood up. "Thanks for the trim. What do I owe you?"

"... But ... but .... We're not done yet, I still have to do the back!" exclaimed the hairdresser.

"Yes, we are done," Sienna added. With that, she left 25 dollars at the stylist's station and grabbed her purse to leave.

"Sorry!" the stylist yelled, although it was a bit too late for an apology. Sienna slammed the door of the salon, as the jingle of a wreath made of bells rang loudly behind her.

It was true; Pinot Noir had a reputation as a bad boy. Her friends warned her not to date him. Sienna didn't listen. The motorcycle was enthralling, but so was he. Noir was a daredevil. Each day was exciting and unexpected. Sometimes he took her to the pool hall. Sometimes it was the casino. Sometimes it was a rock concert, like Linkin' Park, Korn or System of a Down. Sometimes they showed up to his pals' houses just to hang out. They also rode the V-Rod with packs of other bikers. Going down the highway, they were all a fearful sight to see. Noir took Sienna with him as much as possible. And always, he made her feel like a beauty queen with constant flattery. She loved it.

Indeed, dating Noir was exciting. He was very athletic and worked out faithfully six days a week. Even doing nothing all that important was fun whenever Sienna spent time with him. Especially riding around on his Harley, with the wind blowing through her hair. It made Sienna feel alive and passionate about life.

Sienna loved his leather jacket and his rough hands. Noir was confident and dynamic. People noticed him. Some feared him. He often smoked cigars, the big Cubans with the crisp tips. He was quite sensual and physical in bed.

Sienna dressed the part, wearing sexier outfits that were daring and edgy. To some people, her attire was a little on the slutty side, but Noir loved her look and that was all that mattered. Her collection of Fredericks of Hollywood apparel got bigger and better. Sienna loved wearing 4" spiked heels and short lacy minis with her new boyfriend. She wanted to be just as edgy as he was.

After they had been dating for awhile, Noir hit her up with a request. "I think you should get a tattoo, babe. It would look hot on you."

Thinking about it for a minute, she said "What kind of a tattoo? I mean, where would I put it?"

"Maybe right here?" he said, gliding his pointer finger across the small of her lower back.

"I don't know... I think it might hurt," Sienna replied.

"You wouldn't do it for me?" Noir whispered.

"We'll see. I'm not sure what I would put there. I think a tattoo should represent something special about your life," she added. "I mean; I just don't see myself putting something like 'Devious' on my body."

"But you are devious, aren't you?" Noir kidded with her. She giggled.

"Let's drop it for now. We'll see. I'm not fond of needles, or pain," Sienna added.

"Don't be a wuss!" he egged her on. She kiddingly punched him in the arm.

Despite people's judgment of his character, the Bad Boy was a great match for Sienna. Sure, people talked. They tried to badmouth the bad boy and spoke of things he did in the past. He had been in jail in his late teens for about six months. He had been a bully in school, but in his defense, he had either stuck up for wimpier friends or just defended himself against other tough guy wannabes. He had lived hard and had a tough upbringing. This only enhanced his level of confidence, turning him into a guy who did not put up with BS. Noir had a bit of a chip on his shoulder sometimes, but deep down he was a good person with a big heart and a soft side. He was like the Teddy Bear in leather, with a grim expression and harsh laugh that bellowed across the room. His voice carried, which made him seem large. Noir's big muscles were even part of his character.

However, dating the bad boy did not come without the occasional drama. He was sometimes temperamental and moody. Sienna had even caught him flirting with other women a few times, although Noir wholeheartedly denied any wrongdoing. He was sweet behind closed doors, but had a tough exterior that covered the sensitive side that few people saw beyond the day-old facial scruff and bold tattoos. His playfulness and flirtatious spirit were what Sienna most enjoyed.

Even though Sienna had been contently single, the Bad Boy found a way to rile her. Therefore, she often caved in to his random whims and wants. He was a bit bossy, which was one trait she found annoying. Noir called her his "girl."

These conflicting personality traits were part of the adrenaline rush she experienced in being with him. To Sienna, Noir was a bad boy on the outside, yet not so bad on the inside. That was part of what she found so intriguing. Noir was a complex man. He was daring, unpredictable, and spontaneous.

Little did she know, Sienna had lassoed the proverbial stallion. Noir was the wildest horse and she was in for the ride of her life. Any other guy would have bored her to tears. The trick was to match his feisty wit and spicy character with equal adaptation. A guy like Noir would not be happy settling unless he had met his match; physically, mentally and enthusiastically. He had always searched for a sexy chick that could be cool and give in to his crazy ways, yet who was also a nice piece of arm candy. Oh, and with a brain to boot. The bad boy had to have it all or none at all.

Noir was never happy with a girl who cramped his style. Hence, he developed a reputation as one to "Love 'em" and "Leave 'em;" when in reality, he had just not yet found a girl who could hang without letting him have his way once in awhile.

And that was why she went to the tattoo parlor with him. He drew a cool design that he wanted her to get inked on her lower back. Despite her hesitation, Sienna didn't want to disappoint Noir with her own insecurities.

"Are you ready, Miss?" asked the tattoo artist. He was covered in tats from his neck to his feet, at least on every blank piece of skin that people could see from underneath his t-shirt and ripped denim Lucky jeans.

"Not really, but let's do this." Sienna took a big gulp and laid down in the chair, face down.

The needle hummed as she squealed a little bit the first time it touched her skin.

"You've gotta stay still, girl." The artist scolded her.

"I'm watching you!" said Noir. She blinked hard as a tear rolled down her cheek.

"Okay, I'm ready." She bit down hard, grinding her teeth. After a while, she didn't even feel it anymore. The needle felt like a nuisance but her body adjusted to the initial twang of pain.

After a few hours of chatting with the tattoo artist and listening to Noir taunt her, she stood up and glanced over her shoulder in the mirror. The tattoo looked pretty cool, if she did say so herself. It featured a tribal design with a blue moon in the middle. But upon closer inspection, there was lettering inside the moon. It read, "NOIR".

"What do you think?" asked the ink artist.

"Ummm, yeah I like it, but I didn't tell you to put any lettering on it." Sienna said with hesitation.

"What's wrong baby, you don't want my name on your hot bod?" asked Noir. "I'm the one paying for it! Now you're stuck with me," he said with a smirk.

Suddenly, Sienna regretted getting a tattoo. She loved her boyfriend but she wasn't sure if she wanted his name stuck to her body for the rest of her life. Silently, she hoped it was something she could live with. '*What if we break up someday and then I'm stuck with his name on my back?*' she wondered.

It was too late to change her mind. And then she realized that dating Noir meant that she didn't really have a mind of her own, because he was the dominant one in their relationship. Sienna always caved in to everything he wanted to do, everywhere he wanted to go and agreed with most everything he said. Her opinions, thoughts and expressions were a reflection of his.

But instead of complaining, Sienna hugged her man and said, "Thank you, sweetie," with all of the fake enthusiasm she could muster. "It's really nice."

Sienna put her shirt back on while Noir paid and tipped the tattoo artist. With that, the two hopped on his Harley and rode off. Now it was official. She was "his" girl, and a marked woman. Sienna hoped that one day Pinot Noir would not trade her in for a new model and that he would continue loving her as much as he loved his V-Rod. Wrapping her arms tightly around his waist, Sienna buried her nose in his leather jacket and enjoyed the ride.

# PROVISO

**We've all tried a glass of Pinot Noir. Or at least** noticed it. However, certain women find it just too racy and high in alcohol content to even attempt. It is inevitable that most women are turned on and intrigued by the Bad Boy. Men know this to be true, just as much as women. This is no secret.

Pinot Noir will lure you with its finicky and spicy flavor, but be forewarned that it will own you with its higher alcohol content than other wines. No two vineyards, bottles or brands of this randy wine are the same. The taste is daring, spontaneous and unexpected. The grapes are 'berry' delicious and ripe with a sensational flavor that will have you reaching for another glass. Pinot Noir is nothing shy of irresistible.

But don't mistake its distinctive spiciness as harmless. Pinot Noir isn't a "sipping" type of wine. It is meant to be drunk, enjoyed and savored. Once you try it, you are sure to drink the whole bottle and find it rather delicious. Honestly, a woman has not truly lived until she has fallen in love with a favorite Pinot Noir at least once in her lifetime.

Some may recommend avoiding Pinot Noir. There is a rumor of heartburn among those who consume too much. Of course you may come across a bad batch every once in a blue moon, but this should not keep you from experiencing all of the fun delights that Pinot Noir has to offer.

Many women reach for Pinot Noir more than once and often test many different brands, hoping for different or better results each time. Others find it disappointing. Unlike other wines, Pinot Noir is hit or miss as to whether it will become a favorite for life. Some ladies are able to capture its essence and lock it away for safekeeping. Others try Pinot Noir a couple of times and dislike its mood swings and unpredictability.

Either way, Pinot Noir could turn out to be one of the best wines worth testing. Don't let people taint you with their own opinions or experiences with it. It may be perfect for you and not so good for someone else, but that's what makes Pinot Noir one of the very best red wines on the planet.

As a word of advice – if you are curious about Pinot Noir and want to try it for yourself – at least choose a "good" Pinot Noir, one that's had a chance to mature for a few years. It won't take you long to discover whether Pinot Noir will become your favorite or if its precariousness and snippy disposition is worth having another round.

# Riesling

## "MR. INDEPENDENT"

R***arely will you find a Riesling wine that is blended*** *with any other variety, and that is because it is a wonder all on its own. It is varietal purity at its best, as an aromatic blend of peach, pear, apple and tropical undertones that deliver a sweetly independent flavor. This is only one of the reasons why Riesling is one of the world's favorite white wines. There is something people admire about Riesling, from its noble versatility to the pleasure it delivers. Call it the ultimate up-for-anything wine for those who prefer something dry, spicy and sweet all at the same time.*

*It's steely, soily, slate profile is expression-driven. You can taste the free-spirited nature within every sweet sip. Its zesty persona is able to accompany many types of cuisines, from Spanish to Mexican to Asian to Mediterranean. As a world favorite in white wines, Riesling is renowned for its individuality and vivid personality. Many admire Riesling as a successful choice, whether freshly made or saved for decades.*

*Most would give Riesling the title of a noble wine. Certainly it is within the top three white wines you can find around the globe. Actually, Riesling's ancestry dates as far back as the beginning of A.D. and originates from a centuries-old German grape. An aged Riesling displays a golden amber shade that resembles pure gold, making it feel very affluent to the palate. However, you may easily find an excellent late harvest batch that is just as cool and crisp as a crunchy batch of leaves that have recently fallen from an oak tree. Riesling is both daring and sentimental at the same time.*

*In comparison contests, Riesling is often crowned champion against many worthy rivals at wine festivals and wine tastings. It is a centerpiece wine that is just as pretty to keep on the counter and look at, as it is to consume. Keep Riesling on hand and you won't disappoint any surprise guests who might pop into your home unexpectedly.*

*Although most Riesling renditions are excellent not long after vinification, they do age rather well and can actually get better. Because of its high acidity and wide range of flavors, you can look forward to certain stages you might encounter as Riesling ages. Each phase is fun and more complex than the one before. Indeed, dry, semi-sweet, extra sweet or aged to a honey-like elixir, Riesling is excellent; with no residual sugar to speak of. It excels at every point from beginning to end of the dry to sweet scale. There are no grapes known that can match Riesling toe-to-toe in their abilities to transition into something so completely different than what they resemble on the exterior, yet equally compelling at both ends of the spectrum.*

*If you ask someone who loves Riesling why they do, they might just become overwhelmed by emotion. Oh yes, Riesling is awesome through and through! It hits every note, like a musician strumming his guitar in perfect harmony with the lead singer. Even the winemakers rarely mess with it. Most like to tweak favorite wine recipes, but hardly ever with Riesling. It is rarely blended with any other varieties, hence making it one of the only standalone versions you will find. That's because adding other types of grapes would cloud the underlying flavor and just make it either too sweet or too dry. Riesling is rarely oaked and most always stored in steel barrels during the fermentation process. You could call it the "Wine of Steel" since it is tough enough to endure most anything and still be good and resilient the whole way.*

*Sometimes the fact that it is not blended with other wines makes it more difficult to market Riesling to the masses. Every bottle tastes different, making it slightly unexpected. Because of this, Riesling may always be faintly on the backburner behind Chardonnay. At least, sales-wise.*

*Some Rieslings are quite classy and meant to be crafted as more of a late harvest dessert wine. This is done by allowing the grapes to hang from the vines and plucking them well past their peak. The water is then removed from the wine in an evaporation process to yield rich flavors and subsequently higher acid and sugar content. With fine Rieslings, you can see through the grape to the heart of the minerality and sun that display the characteristics of the soil in which it was produced. This peerless transparency refers to Riesling's ability to emit complex flavors and aromas reminiscent of its birthplace. Another point to its independence.*

*There is no denying that Riesling is remarkable. As far as white wines go, it offers succulent appeal and irresistible sweetness. Riesling is a loner of exemplary salute.*

❖❖❖❖❖❖❖❖❖

# RIESLING ❣ Scarlet

**After waxing his sailboat in the hot sun, Riesling** was in the mood for a late afternoon run. He didn't want to lose momentum on his upcoming 10k marathon, which was only a couple of weeks away. Last year, he came in fourth overall so he vowed to train harder for the next year to claim a first place title. Riesling didn't like to be second, third or fourth best at anything. Only first place would do.

Admittedly, Riesling was an overachiever. He had been that way for most of his life. Whether it was being the best with his career or with many of the activities he really enjoyed participating in, Riesling always strived to excel.

He was well-liked and wildly popular. There were many women who wished they could slay the alpha male; however, Riesling was much too busy for any serious commitment these days. He had races to win, waterways to sail, adventures to take and places to go. A woman would only hinder his ability to perform well, so Riesling flitted from one casual affair to the next.

Riesling liked to test his own prowess to see how far he could go. He was a black belt in martial arts and the MVP of the men's soccer league. He owned two exotic cars, a black Maserati GrandTurismo MC and a silver Audi S8, one of the first to come out in the New Year's models of fast cars. Riesling had been very successful the last two years in day trading. So well, in fact that he was able to work only a couple of days a week and earn well into the triple digits. Riesling liked to reinvest his money in other things, such as real estate properties that he could rent out. The market was full of great deals and Riesling took advantage of every avenue to snatch up the short sales and foreclosures in a buyer's market. He was smart and savvy.

To look at him, you'd never know he came from money. Riesling had blond longish hair and kept a nicely shaved goatee, which made him appear casual. He fit in well with the surfer crowd, which he liked to do a few times a month. Living in San Diego, Riesling knew of many great hotspots to catch some serious waves and other great places to go scuba diving. He was also a scuba instructor, or at least he had been before he got too busy day trading and real estate investing. Nevertheless, there were a few referrals for private lessons, but Riesling took them on an "as-available" basis.

Financial stability afforded him the means to do the things he always enjoyed. Riesling was really popular everywhere he went; however, he rarely stuck around long enough to have any real close ties – both in friendships and in dating prospects. He liked it that way. He was a loner and preferred the "acquaintance" types of friendships, rather than trying to tie up too many emotions in having close friends he truly cared about. He was "Mr. Independent," right to the very core.

Riesling took great care of himself physically and rarely showed the typical signs of aging. There were very few activities he hadn't participated in, from golfing to running, or basketball, soccer, drag racing or sailboat racing in regattas. He was physically fit throughout his 20s, 30s, into his 40s and even beyond. Riesling was the eternal playboy. He found it easy to pick up women, with his boyish smile and classy free-spirited, fun and funny character. All Riesling had to do was make them laugh, and the women easily responded to his advances.

In truth, Riesling once had a girlfriend when he was quite young. She was his first love and he fell head over heels. She was the first and only woman to ever hear the words "I love you" come from his lips. Riesling was sweet, very sweet. He picked her flowers by hand instead of buying them. He wrote her cute notes and happy messages. He even braided her hair. However, one day she broke his heart and told him that she wanted to go to college overseas and that she thought they should "see other people" instead of trying to manage a long-distance relationship. She wanted to have fun and be young and free.

After wallowing for a few weeks, he thought about how right she was. From that point on, Riesling adopted the "have fun and be free" attitude so that his heart would never be broken again. Instead of being vulnerable, Riesling learned to have power. He learned this important lesson: *The one who cares the least has the most control.*

He took this spirit with him both in relationships and in business. From that point on, Riesling adopted the 'shoulder shrug' mentality. In other words, he didn't care whether you did business with him or not because he would still make money with or without your deal, and he didn't care whether you loved him or not because he would never love you back the same way.

This attitude carried him well throughout his life, except in one respect. Although Riesling was virtually fulfilled and undoubtedly stimulated by all of his whirlwind adventures, there was something missing.

Riesling didn't even realize it until his early 40s. He met a woman who intrigued him. Scarlet was different from many of the women he had dated, although their relationship started out with the same intentions as they all did. Have fun while it lasted was his recurrent theme. There was no woman who could change his mind because he refused to take any relationship to the next level.

The last girl tried to get her digs in Riesling by getting pregnant. He was now the proud Daddy of a five-year old girl. Riesling was a pretty good dad and saw his daughter on the weekends and once or twice throughout the week, but the little girl lived with her mother. Deep down, he liked it that way. The thought of settling in to the home style family scene really scared him, so even though many people expected him to marry the girl after she found out she was 'preggo', he never asked her. In fact, Riesling never even told the girl he loved her.

So eventually, just like all the other women he dated throughout his life, they went away. They got sick of never hearing the words "I love you" from his lips. He was in a way, too selfish to say it and too afraid to be vulnerable. Riesling just wanted to have fun, fun, fun with no real commitments. He was a thrill-seeker.

Then when a dark-haired beauty stepped into his life in his early 40s, Riesling had a bit of a wakeup call. With Scarlet, the beginning went much the same as they all did. He got to know his women slowly. He liked to build up to the main attraction. Riesling was very sweet and creative at swooning them. There were many charming qualities about him that women liked, both physically and mentally. Just his stories and adventures alone were enough to make their hearts melt. To women, Riesling was the sweetest bachelor and a great catch. He was the type of guy all women hope to find. Handsome, in great shape, successful, adventurous, he seemed to have it all. But they didn't know what they were in for, and that was a dead-end relationship.

Riesling and Scarlet went over to dinner at the house of her friends, Jane and Joe. They were a couple in their early-

30s who were very much in love. The couple had only been dating a few months, but the love between them was strong and powerful enough even to pull at the heartstrings of a commitment phobic such as Riesling. Jane was gushing about a beautiful card from Joe, her wonderful soul mate, along with a dozen red roses he had given her that day "just because." When Scarlet read it, a tear rolled down her cheek. Deep down, Scarlet couldn't wait for Riesling to tell her that he loved her. They had already closed in upon the eight month milestone of dating and she didn't want to be the first one to say it. Unbeknownst to her, Riesling was never going to.

Eventually sixteen months went by. Riesling's beautiful brunette girlfriend was growing antsy and felt that their relationship had already surpassed the "getting to know each other" phase. "*Isn't this guy ever going to tell me he loves me*?" Scarlet wondered. He was not.

One day, she blurted it out. Scarlet had dreamed of getting married one day and having a baby. Time was ticking and so was her biological clock. She was in her late 30s and had been searching for the right guy. She thought that maybe Riesling could be that guy.

Even Riesling's daughter adored Scarlet. The little girl truly looked forward to her visits, which were only every other weekend when Riesling had custody of the child. Scarlet even went to church with them both and met his entire family, including Riesling's parents and siblings. Yet, after all this time, still no words of love.

So, after she said "I love you" to him as she put her jacket on to go home from a night out together, he stood there, stunned. Riesling didn't say it back. Scarlet looked surprised that he had nothing to say in return. Feeling hurt by having put down her walls, she then promptly added, "It's okay if you're not ready to say it."

Hastily, Scarlet left and got in her BMW to go home. Thinking about it afterwards, Riesling wondered if he would ever be ready. There were still many places to go and things to see, and races to win and planes to jump out of. Certainly, he could not be tied down and bothered by falling in love, could he?

He scratched his head, wondering. Then the next day, he admitted to Scarlet the truth. "Listen, about last night... I should tell you before you get your heart too tangled up in a guy like me, that I haven't told a girl I love her since I was in high school. I just want to be frank with you. It may never happen."

Saddened, Scarlet nodded her head. "That's quite ridiculous," she said.

"I just can't..." Riesling tried to explain. "Because I don't genuinely feel it, like I did then. I put my heart out there and it got stomped on. Like a bunch of grapes."

"Yeah, except in this case you might get something worthwhile," said Scarlet, trying to make light of his embarrassment.

"I'm sorry, I do really like you and enjoy spending time with you. I like having you as my girlfriend," Riesling murmured into Scarlet's ear, hoping she would fall for his sweetness.

However, after that moment, the dynamic of their relationship changed. Knowing she never had a shot – yet determined that she could be the one who broke the spell – Scarlet tried a different strategy. She had recently read a book by Sherry Argov entitled, "*Why Men Love Bitches*" and one of its underlying messages was to never let a man have the upper hand or he would walk all over you. This smart brunette was a clever cookie, so Scarlet abruptly broke up with Riesling.

Dumbfounded, he mused how such a thing could have backfired. After all of the previous attempts at finding a girl who he could love such as that of his high school sweetheart, Riesling was shocked when a girl dumped him instead of the other way around. Most often they would call and grovel a bit, hoping that Riesling would change his mind and love them back. He moved on to the next woman just as easily as he could land a dirt bike – effortlessly from one side of a stream to another – and with careful practice.

Instead, Scarlet had beaten him to the punch. It made her more mysterious. His own principles resounded in his head: "*Everybody wants what they can't have... everybody wants what they can't have...*" he repeated, over and over.

He called Scarlet several times to discuss and explain himself, but she refused to answer or take his calls. She disappeared. She deleted him from her Facebook and changed her relationship status to "Single". Scarlet did not respond to his emails or texts. Riesling became frantic. Even though nothing had changed, the fact that she would not even talk to him truly bothered him in a big way. It made him crazy, in fact.

That Saturday, he was supposed to have run in a marathon. Instead, he woke up bright and early and went straight to the florist. He picked out a nice $99 bunch of flowers that were so big; he could barely carry them alone. There were gorgeous tall daffodils and orchids nestled perfectly in baby's breath, with a few colorful gerberas, carnations and calla lilies. If these flowers didn't win Scarlet over, nothing would.

As the doorman buzzed her apartment for him, he wondered if she was alone. "*Had she met someone else?*" he wondered. Not hearing from her drove him insane. "*Would she say no and not let me come up?*"

Scarlet buzzed him in. He rode the elevator to the eleventh floor, as he had done whenever they had stayed at her place. That had been rare. She had most often stayed at his. He liked having his creature comforts close by. After he walked down the corridor, Riesling knocked on Scarlet's door, nervously holding the giant bouquet.

"Wow! These are amazing!" she said as she opened the door, wearing a cute tank top and pajama pants. "It's so early, what are you doing here, Riesling?"

"You wouldn't take my calls." He reminded her.

"Oh, you know," Scarlet brushed her hand in the air, as if to shrug him off. "It's nothing personal. I didn't want you to waste your time by falling in love with me. I was doing you a favor."

"Well, I wanted to see if we could work something out?" he asked. "I come bearing gifts."

"Look, maybe we should have determined this earlier in the relationship. I really want to meet "*the one*" and maybe have a family someday. You clearly don't want that. I'm not trying to hold you back. Look, don't you have a marathon to run in today?" Scarlet said, pointing at her watch.

"Yeah, I missed it. Well, I should say, I missed you." Riesling said as he hung his head apologetically.

Her plan worked. Most women had gone about it the wrong way. To snag this type of man, Scarlet knew that she had to play his game. So she started dating him again, but did not tell Riesling she loved him. Scarlet spent another few months with him, still hoping in the back of her mind that he would eventually give in. Still, he did not. Deep down, Riesling was just an adrenaline seeker. That was true in love, money and activities. He liked to ride big and give little, but with great taste.

Finally, Scarlet ended things again after spending a few more months waiting to hear the magic words she always hoped Riesling would say. When she broke it off the second time, Riesling left her alone. He knew he was the reason Scarlet went away, but his heart missed her. After a couple of months, he called her out of the blue.

"Hi Scarlet, I was hoping you would answer," he stammered.

"Sure, why wouldn't I? How are you doing?" she asked.

"So, do you still love me?" Riesling blurted out.

"No, I don't Riesling." Scarlet answered.

"Well I don't understand that," Riesling spat, acting put off. "How can you love someone and then fall out of love with them, just like that? If you love someone, don't you love them forever?"

Scarlet paused, and then said, "Not if they don't love you back."

Hanging up, Riesling felt dejected. He realized that he had been holding on to the idea of what he thought true love should be. The kind that lasts forever, as he had thought would be with the girl who had broken his heart so many years ago. Even though he should have thanked her – because perhaps he would never have done so many fun things over the last twenty plus years. He had a sudden epiphany. Maybe, just maybe Scarlet was right. Maybe it was possible to love more than one person in a lifetime. Maybe certain people come into your life through a short window, whereas others come in through the doorway. And then there is one special someone who makes themselves right at home.

After sulking for a few more days, Riesling came to the conclusion that he felt much the same with Scarlet as he had felt back in high school with his braided first true love. It had taken him a full 25 years to mature. He reached for the phone several times and then pulled his hand away, trying to resist the temptation to call her again.

Finally, the urge was too great to bear.

He picked up the phone and quickly skimmed through his favorites to find Scarlet's phone number. As he waited for an answer, his heart raced. She did not answer. Her voicemail came on.

Stumbling for a moment, Riesling said, "Scarlet, please call me when you get a chance. I have something really important to tell you."

❖ ❖ ❖ ❖ ❖ ❖ ❖ ❖ ❖

# PROVISO

**Let's all roll our eyes about Riesling now and get it** over with. C'mon, it's one of every woman's favorite white wines. It's so sweet and fascinating and delicious! There's a lot to love about Riesling. So why are we rolling our eyes?

Being sweet and affectionate only goes so far. Eventually, the other person likes to feel love and hear the words spoken. Honestly, what's the harm? Even if you've loved in the past and been hurt by someone, you just have to keep trying. And even if you never get it right, well at least all of the attempts will be enjoyable along the way.

Raise your glass to Riesling. Embrace someone who loves you. At least if you're unprepared to love each other fully, you can both agree on loving this fine choice in white wines. Love is tough to come by these days, in a world filled with hate. Making someone else happy is not such a bad thing, as long as you don't have to sacrifice your own happiness to do it. You'll never have to with Riesling. This is one wine that stands alone exceptionally well.

Yes, this brilliant overachiever is a keeper. Especially after Riesling has time to mature. Yet, no one could have foreseen its growing – and glowing – popularity. Even within the past decade, Riesling sales have skyrocketed. In all price points, Riesling has moved away from being a shy heartthrob to a trendsetter. You will find styles in all categories of Riesling, from bone dry to sugary sweet. More and more people have discovered the love it can bring, once it finally comes into its own skin.

But don't be fooled by its wild popularity and good looks just yet. Riesling must be tamed! It can be, but only with patience and persistence.

If you do fall in love with Riesling, you're not alone. Its intensity is refreshing and enthusiastic. Riesling is mouthwatering and satisfying when consumed young, but a well-made Riesling can age for decades with great vivacity. Riesling is much too independent to share the spotlight or to profess its need for a partner of any kind.

If you're not ready for Riesling, you can save it in the wine cellar. Riesling is age-worthy and freethinking. It's no wonder so many people are reaching for this newfound wine of stature. Riesling's zesty taste and determination for success is impressive and will certainly find a place in your heart!

# Rosé

## "THE CHEAPSKATE"

***Rosé is a wine made up of leftovers, like the best*** *halves of red grapes blended prematurely with white. Merlot, Syrah, and even Pinot Noir or Grenache grapes can be used to create Rosé. At first glance, Rosé seems likable with its light, pinkish color. However, this blush bluster is the same color as the cheeks of embarrassment.*

*It is a wine one might buy as an afterthought, with a spare ten dollar bill. And if you have the ten bucks to spend, Rosé is not a bad wine. It has very good intentions, though marked with an off-colored reputation as a wine that looks much better than it really is. Most known wine connoisseurs will crinkle their nose with the mere mention of it. Rosé wants to be up there with the more popular choices, but alas, its tincture is less favorable.*

*Some say that Rosé has very little taste. You can dress it up, but you shouldn't take it anywhere in which dignity is required. It is a great wine to have on hand to give the host of a party, in the event of an unexpected invitation. Although first impressions are crucial, it would be better to show up at a stranger's house bearing a bottle of pretty Rosé, rather than to show up empty-handed. However, it may be perceived as distasteful among certain circles of wine snobs. These are people who perceive Rosé to be at the bottom of the cheapness scale as far as quality wines are concerned.*

*It is distinguished in façade with its pretty packaging, yet not quite the flavor you'll be expecting, considering the showy first impression. Red grapes are the primary ingredient, despite the opaque result of this blush beverage. Red Rosés are more luxurious; however the lack of character and presence among its peers is a red flag – with no pun intended.*

*By all accounts, Rosé plays the part of a rich-looking wine. The off-colored blush is delicious in appearance, dressing nicely for all occasions from the lunch date to the evening outing. Playing the role of sophisticated, it may not be obvious at first glance just how cheap this wine really is. Rosé is dapper, with a fine aroma in knock-off designer wear. Anyone looking for a great deal will find enjoyment in Rosé wine.*

*Because the grapes are peeled shortly after they have been harvested, they are very sweet in the beginning. As a matter of fact, Rosé wine is delightfully sweet-tempered. With its deeper color than a true blush, Rosé is just as palatable as it is a pretty companion. However, the blended melody of authentic red wine and early disassembly of the grape skins can leave mighty tannins. And the longer that the skins of the fruit remain in contact with the juice, the bolder the shade of red. Bleeding the vats in the early process of fermentation will decrease the percentage of red coloring that is typically derived from making Rosé wine. In essence, the pink shade is created from the leftover remnants of that winemaking process. Depending on the winemaker, Rosé can also be made in shades of purple or peach.*

*Rosé wine is light, crisp and fair in texture. Its strange fragrance and weird after-flavor can only be described as dry and arduous, like hand-me-downs that seem worn and outdated. The dry taste of Rosé is intense. This comes in unexpected contrast to its off-colored appearance.*

*It's no wonder Rosé is blushing. Maybe it's a little embarrassed not to have made it to the finish line among the classifications of fine wine. Regardless of sugar content, sweetness level, flavor, and its confusing marketing ploys, Rosé wine continues to be a choice of both ladies and men. Just don't make the mistake of ordering Rosé at an upscale restaurant. Or for that matter, bringing it along on a first date.*

*It is best to drink Rosé right after buying it, rather than keeping it as a collectible for the wine cellar. Rosé's value is not high, even though its intentions are. If you're lucky, you might actually find a handful of 'mom and pop' sized vineyards that produce high quality blush wines. They are made traditionally, and well. However, the majority of mass marketed Rosés are distributed as a simple, tasty and affordable option for wine drinkers who are on a budget.*

*It seems a bit ironic that a wine with such a beautiful name happens to be one of the less superlative choices. Considering a bouquet of "Roses" is synonymous with beauty and romance, the wine version of this namesake is a bit of a disappointment. It's like thinking your Hyundai is as nice as a Mercedes.*

*But you could always upgrade at a later date. Rosé is good enough for now. It will get you slightly buzzed and giddy, but not be the happy ending of your wine sampling adventures. Just enjoy it for what it is: a beautiful wine that is diligently working its way into a position of respect.*

❖❖❖❖❖❖❖❖❖

# ROSÉ ❣ Misty Moss

**From rim to base, one might wonder what Rosé did** for a living, because his "put together-ed-ness" was initially enticing. That is, until she learned what he was really all about.

Misty Moss met Rosé the day before Valentine's Day. She was with a group of friends who had invited her to hear a musician sing at a local pub they frequented. One of the girls in the group knew the singer. They may have been dating. Regardless of the connection, Misty went because she was bored and didn't have any other plans.

While walking back from the pub, a bunch of men came from the opposite direction. A few people in both cliques knew each other. So, both the herd of men and the pack of ladies stopped to talk. Rosé happened to be among the group.

He was rather tall, with gorgeous skin that was a nice blend between light and dark. Rosé was neither white nor dark complected, he was blush. His eyes were hazelish, at least in the dim light of the street lamp. His leather jacket was crisp. Or was it pleather, like the plastic leather that was designed to look real? It was difficult to see. By first impressions, Rosé appeared distinguished.

The flirting began with a few compliments, followed by a conversation. Misty Moss gave Rosé her phone number as the groups parted ways, only to have him call an hour later.

"I just wanted to make sure you got home okay," said Rosé after Misty answered.

"No, I think you just wanted to make sure I gave you the right phone number," Misty said.

"Maybe in part," he admitted, "but I also wanted to see if you'd like to go out with me tomorrow afternoon or evening. It's Valentine's Day, you know?"

"I guess that wouldn't hurt anything. My other plans fell through." Misty fibbed.

"Great, what time?" asked Rosé.

"How about 5:00-ish?" she said. He agreed. So, Misty Moss went to bed smiling, thinking about how cute Rosé was.

The next day, he texted her. It said, "Hey. I have a great idea for a first date. How about a couple of bottles of wine and we go sit somewhere on a park bench?"

Misty thought about this. What an unusual request. She thought dinner might be better. Sitting on a bench, drinking wine out in public, was not her cup of tea. So, Misty texted Rosé a reply. "What if I have to go to the bathroom? I think dinner would be better."

His response was surprisingly honest and strange. "Really? You think dinner would be better? Well in that case, our date will have to wait until Tuesday after I get paid."

Misty rolled her eyes, a little stunned. Great. A broke guy. So she did what most women do when faced with a dilemma. Misty called her friends for advice. One answered. She explained the whole text message and her analysis of it. "What should I do?" Misty Moss asked her friend.

"Well Misty, you could suggest something else if you really want to go. Otherwise, you'll have to blow him off," advised her friend. "It depends on how much you like him."

"I don't know yet. Today is Valentine's Day so I was hoping to go out and do something," Misty argued, mostly for her own benefit.

"Then, suggest coffee. Surely he can afford that!" laughed her friend.

Misty texted Rosé back after speaking with her friend at length about the pros and cons of meeting him. "How about a coffee date then?" said the text. He agreed. He even offered a movie afterward.

Rosé picked her up promptly at 1:00 p.m. It was an afternoon date that began with the typical cliché dialect and trite compliments. Perhaps genuine, but not all that original. Rosé took Misty to a local coffee shop, where she ordered a fluffy latte and sipped it slowly throughout the conversation. Rosé ordered a plain black coffee. No frills. Part of their discussion was deciding on a movie, following coffee. Again, it was not so original. Yet, Misty went along with it.

The first indication of Rosé's cheapness was the tip he left the waitress at the coffee shop. Although she wasn't much to look at, the petite, wrinkled waitress provided really outstanding service. Rosé gave her 50 cents.

*"Hmmm..."* Misty thought. *"Was he really that cheap, despite his fancy Ralph Lauren polo sweater and nice LL Bean jacket?"* She let it go as insignificant, but not without making a mental note to bring spare dollars on the next date to avoid embarrassment on behalf of the wait staff.

After they arrived at the movies, the two spent a few minutes choosing which one to see. Well, Rosé did. Misty's movie suggestions were ignored. He chose a war movie. Not exactly a romantic first date choice. Nevertheless, when they got to the ticket counter, Rosé began haggling with the box office attendant.

The cashier said, "That'll be $28 today, sir."

Rosé replied, "Is that the best you can do?"

Shaken up, the ticket agent was silent for a moment. "Well, sir I could actually give you both tickets today for $19.50."

Rosé begrudgingly parted with a twenty dollar bill. Stunned, Misty Moss whipped her head around and gave him a look of disbelief. "Did you really just dicker with the movie ticket girl?" Misty asked him.

"You never know unless you ask," he replied. Meanwhile, throughout the entire movie, Misty shook her head in disbelief. Rosé didn't even offer to buy popcorn!

After he took her home, Misty avoided his calls for a few days. Giving Rosé the benefit of the doubt, she eventually returned his call after enough time had passed, citing excessive work as an excuse for not returning the call sooner. After a brief conversation, Misty agreed to another date. She made it for a Thursday so that she could still keep the prime weekend nights free, in the hope of a better offer.

The second date was better. Misty hypothesized that perhaps Rosé had just hit a tough spot that first time, and maybe she had been too judgmental. She was embarrassed for him but still liked him. After all, Rosé was polite and not hard on the eyes. However, Misty maintained a distant coolness by avoiding any meaningful conversations that would require emotional development. It was better that way.

The only strange thing she noticed about their second date was when she dropped her phone on the ground next to Rosé's foot. As she bent down to pick it up, Misty caught just a glimpse of silver stuck to the sole of his shoe, just below the heel. She would never have noticed it because it was barely visible, but her phone had landed just to the right of his ankle.

Not daring to say anything, but finding the urge to be much too great to bear, Misty asked, "What is that on your foot?"

"OH, that..." his cheeks turned a light shade of pink. "Um, well just the other day I caught my shoe on a crack in the pavement and it snagged a little bit. I just put a little piece of tape on it for now."

"You duct taped your shoe?" Misty Moss burst out laughing.

Seeming annoyed, Rosé said, "Well, just until I can get to the store and get a new pair." She could tell he was not amused, so she dropped the subject. The rest of their date went fine with no real red flags, except for the shoes.

Congratulations Rosé. He made the cut to a third date.

The next time, Misty let Rosé take her out on a weekend night. He asked her to dress up for a fancy dinner, at a dimly-lit restaurant by the river. She noticed that people were staring at them, although she had no idea why. It seemed they rose more than a few eyebrows. Was there something obvious that Misty didn't see?

At the end of dinner, the bill arrived at a more than friendly price of $120 after drinks and a palatable gourmet lineup. Rosé glanced expectantly up from the check, questioning Misty's contribution to the portion without officially asking. Horrified, she shrugged her shoulders and said, "I didn't bring my purse. I guess next time."

"*What a freakin' cheapie*," Misty whispered under her breath. So, Rosé put the meal on his credit card and they left.

On the way home, they stopped at a well-known department store. “I need to return something,” muttered Rosé. “You don’t mind, do you? It will just take a second.”

She thought it was unusual timing. A sort of mood-killer, if you will. *‘Who does that sort of thing on a date?’* Misty wondered. It seemed that shopping should be the last thing on his mind, especially after a nice dinner.

Naturally curious, Misty asked Rosé why he had an urgent need to return an item while on a date. “I don’t come over this way very often. It will save me an extra errand and even more in gas. You don’t mind, do you?” He asked. Misty shook her head in disbelief. “Plus, I found this very same tool at another store and its $10 less,” Rosé added.

Misty rolled her eyes. ‘*Go figure*,’ she mused.

A few days later, she was bothered by the whole incident. Aside from his cheapness, Rosé wasn’t such a bad guy. He had brought her flowers once and always called her whenever he said he was going to. He was good looking and intelligent. He had aspirations, at least on the surface. After all, he was going to school to become an engineer. So, Misty could see the potential and thought that maybe he was just going through a rough patch, being a poor college student and all. She thought that maybe if there was something there between them, that one day when he was finally an engineer he would have a lot more money to spend on dating. Hence, Misty wondered if she was the one being unreasonable.

On the flip side, how could a guy possibly have the nerve to take a girl out for a nice dinner, tell her to dress up and then expect her to fork over half of the bill? Misty found his suggestion utterly repulsive. Poor college student or not, that was just in bad taste. That was it; she decided to write Rosé off.

Her friends laughed as Misty retold the story later in the week. One friend said, "Maybe you're not giving him a fair shot. Maybe he really likes you and wants to impress you, but he just doesn't have any game. Do ya think?"

Thinking about her friend's advice, Misty questioned her own behavior. Maybe she had been too shallow. Maybe she was letting a good guy go who really liked her, but who had financial challenges, get away. Or maybe her friend just had lower standards. Nevertheless, Misty decided to call Rosé back to thank him for the dinner date the prior weekend.

When she did, Misty heard an automated message on the other line. "Doo.... Dooo.... Dooo! I'm sorry, but the party you are trying to reach is unavailable. Please check the number and dial again. If you need help, please call the operator for assistance."

This was not a good sign. Either Rosé didn't pay his bill or he skipped town. Option A was Misty's first inclination.

A couple of weeks passed. Rosé called one day from an alternate number that she didn't recognize. Misty was surprised to hear from him, yet somewhat inquisitive once she heard his voice. "I called you a couple of weeks ago to thank you for dinner", she said. "But your phone wasn't taking calls."

"Sorry about that," he offered. "Someone stole my phone so I had to shut it off."

"Don't they usually just report it lost and give you a new one?" Misty asked. "I mean, you do have insurance on your cell phone. Don't you?"

Rosé avoided answering by changing the subject. "Listen, I want you to come over one night this week for dinner." He asked her in a low, sweet voice. Rosé had always been very sweet both on the phone and in person. He was very polite and opened the car door for her, as well as pulling out her chair as she sat down at a table. These cordial acts and sweet compliments were his underlying redeeming characteristics. They were also the reason Misty kept going out with him, despite the many red flags.

"That sounds nice," she finally said after a few moments of silence. "Is there anything you would like me to bring?"

Typically, when an offer of dinner at someone's house was on the table, it was just a polite thing to ask. Kind of like asking someone, "*How are you?*" and expecting "*Fine*" as a standard response. However, there were always those rare individuals who proceeded to tell you everything in their lives that were far from fine.

The offer of adding something to the meal, such as a bottle of wine, loaf of bread or a small dessert was just Etiquette 101. But Rosé's response threw Misty for a loop.

"Yeah, that would be great." Rosé said enthusiastically. "Why don't you bring a chicken?"

"A chicken?" Misty Moss looked at her phone, bewildered. Did he mean a live chicken, with feathers intact?

"You know, I like those rotisserie chickens under the warmers at the supermarket," he interrupted.

Baffled, she thought maybe Rosé was joking. So she played along. "Anything else?" she said sarcastically.

"Yeah, how about a couple of salads and a loaf of French bread? And maybe a bottle of wine," said Rosé.

"But, that sounds like the whole dinner!" Misty gasped. "I thought you were inviting me for dinner because you were going to make it!" Her face was now contorted.

"I don't live near the grocery store. It would be an hour drive to town and another hour back. That's a lot of gas to use up." Rosé explained. "Plus, it's your turn. I bought you dinner the last few times."

Staring in disbelief, Misty was speechless. Then she responded with, "UH... well we only went to dinner once, but whatever." Then she slammed down the phone. Immediately, she blew up three of her friends' cell phones, telling each of them of the unbelievable nerve of Rosé and the even more bizarre turn of events.

Her friends laughed. "I think you should go," suggested one friend. "Maybe he'll pay you back when you get there. Give him the benefit of the doubt."

After she calmed down, Misty called Rosé back. "Sorry about that," she lied. "My phone died. When do you want to do this?"

Excited, Rosé asked her to come the next day. So she foolishly went shopping and drove an hour to his house, with all of the prerequisites in hand. Rosé seemed thrilled to see her. His eyes lit up as he opened the door. He had prepared a candle-lit table with a small pink carnation placed strategically in the center. Fitting. Carnations were one of the cheapest flowers. Although Misty was really annoyed, she summoned enough fake enthusiasm for a smile and a hug. "Thanks for inviting me," she mumbled.

They sat down to dinner. Rosé looked at his salad, pushing the onions and the tomatoes off to the side. "If I were going to make a salad for myself, I would make it with spinach, diced cucumbers, olives and ranch dressing."

"Well, I didn't know what you like in your salad. So... I put what I LIKE," Misty retorted, raising her voice. "And why don't you crack open that bottle of wine? I think I'm really going to need it." She huffed.

He got up and popped open the cork, bringing one glass of wine back to the table for her. "Where's your glass?" she questioned.

"I don't like this kind," he replied.

Misty sighed. "Is there anything you do like?"

"Sure, I like you," he stated.

"Of course you do. You like me because I'm gullible." With that, Misty stood up from the table. "You know, I think I've gotta go. I just remembered somewhere I have to be."

"Aren't you going to stay the night? We've been dating for a while now, and I thought it would be nice if you stayed here with me," said Rosé with a look of anticipation.

"You have to be kidding me!" Misty yelled angrily. "You have a lot of nerve inviting me over here for dinner and asking me to bring all of this stuff! And all you've done is complain about everything you DON'T like. You are a cheapskate. There is *NO WAY* I am spending the night. Besides, we haven't been dating 'awhile'. We've only gone out a few times, spread out over an entire month. And your phone has been shut off for half of that time, which made it pretty hard to get to know you. Did you forget to pay your bill or something?"

Rosé appeared shocked by Misty's outburst. "Have you lost your mind, woman? I've spent $167.85 on you so far."

"You're counting?" she asked, grabbing her coat. The hair on her arms stood up in fury. She left, slamming the door behind her without looking back. Misty Moss peeled out of the dooryard as fast as her tires would burn. '*He's counting! How much he spent! Are women some sort of an investment these days?*' she pondered, shaking her head the whole way home.

A month or two passed. Misty came home one day to find a gift bag outside of the entrance to her apartment. It was right next to the potted cactus. Inside the bag was a bottle of Rosé wine. A small card was attached. It read: "*A peace gesture. Would love to see you again.*" ~ *Rosé.*

*"I don't think so,"* Misty thought to herself. She placed the bottle of Rosé right where it belonged in the kitchen. On the bottom shelf.

❖❖❖❖❖❖❖❖❖

# PROVISO

**Rosé can be found most anywhere, from the** neighborhood convenience store to the supermarket or wholesale club. No one can deny it's cheap. However, you may have good luck with Rosé if you lower your expectations.

Although women these days are much more independent, the majority still have old-fashioned values regarding men paying for a date. The first few times are within the critical *'getting-to-know-you'* phases of a relationship. Going "Dutch" with a lady is not in good taste, especially if the invitation was given by the guy. How embarrassing. Most likely, she will shoot down the offer to split 50/50, anyway.

Beware of Rosé on a first date. Rosé should be reserved more for a couple who's been dating for awhile and then decides to stay home and watch a movie together. With a big pizza. Rosé is only a small step above beer, although some would disagree. At any rate, a bottle of Rosé would implicate a cozy night at home.

Rosé is often a lonely wine. It's the perfect add-on to an evening of the History Channel. You buy Rosé when you have nothing better to do.

It's a shame, really. There are a lot of good qualities about Rosé. It's attractive, mildly entertaining and will give you a pretty good buzz. Unfortunately, the buzz will be short-lived and could lead to stomach problems or gas. This can be a wine that does not digest easily, even though it looks good. The pretty packaging can be misleading.

Rosé doesn't have a long shelf life, which can give you a hangover if you drink too much. That is because of the cheap tannins, whereby the grapes are squished up and then bubbled during the fermentation process. Finer wines undergo a longer period of fermenting, which eliminates the probability for gastro-intestinal reactions. Of course, this varies depending on the quality of the wine.

And headaches? OH MY. Drink too much Rosé and you may feel like you've been struck directly on the forehead with a pick axe. This is because of the sulphites and additives in the wine, which are used to enhance its color.

Another word to the wise, just in case you do choose Rosé: Drink it while it's fresh and read the date on the bottle. Spend a little more for a good bottle to avoid the headaches and repercussions later. And whatever you do, make sure to use Rosé up within one to three days after opening it. After the oxygen hits the open bottle, the wine may begin to deteriorate. Duct tape is not a great solution.

Finally, for every glass you do drink ... plan on drinking one glass of water in equivalence. Or just lower your expectations. For those who like Rosé, sometimes the headaches are worth the price you pay.

# Zinfandel

## "THE COMIC"

T***here's a reason why Zinfandel is on the Top 5 list as*** *one of America's favorite wines. You might even say that it's "America's Grape." What truly sets Zinfandel on the top of that list as compared to many great types of wines are the berries used to make it. They're so darn finicky. Most of the grapes ripen unevenly. So you might get some that are not quite ripe enough, some that are perfect, and then others that are on the verge of dehydration. The latter can make the wine taste "raisiny." All of these variables can be found within the same grape cluster, which leads to a dynamic and unique flavor, although difficult to achieve.*

*Zinfandel yields vibrant acidity from the faintly unripened areas and perfect juicy and fruity flavors from the ripe ones, as well as depth and complexity from the berries that are slightly gone by. This makes Zinfandel grapes challenging to pick. You have to wait for the precise moment to achieve acceptable proportions out of all the miscellaneous variables. With all of this effort just to determine the quality of Zinfandel's characteristics, is it worth it? You bet!*

*Zinfandel is a great wine. And it knows it. As a worldwide favorite, you will find Zinfandels both in the red and white category. However, not all Zinfandels are alike. The difference between a bad and good bottle depends on the grape, the wine region in which it is made and the recipe for the end finish. Even then, it's not definite.*

*The roots of Zinfandel can be traced back to Long Island, when a grower in 1820 began selling the vines. By the mid-1830s, a nursery in Boston started advertising "Zinfendal" (as it was then spelled). A vineyard in Massachusetts was credited with introducing Zin grapes to California, all within the same decade. Since then, winemakers have put a great deal of effort into making Zinfandel well known, and with great success.*

*This wine was also popular during the Gold Rush and, when wire and timber were hard to come by. This made growing and harvesting the grapes difficult, so Zinfandel winemakers adopted a technique called "head pruning." Some vintners of today still use this same style.*

*Rich and ripe with blackberry, raspberry and plum, and just a smidge of tobacco, Zinfandel tastes unusual. The distinctive kind of unusual, that is. Not the weird kind. Its full tannins are primitively simplistic, yet clever. Those who drink Zinfandel will do so with enthusiasm, for it evokes enchantment with a spirited stance. Undertones of black cherry or pepper work to stimulate the senses. It's sweet and spicy at the same time.*

*The grapes of Zinfandel are mindful and fresh, like an eager wine with aspirations yet to be met. Its full-bodied crispness is fastened with a bright cedar afterthought, just waiting to be sampled. The smell has a countrified mixed scent of earth, leather and pepper, with swift tannins. Zinfandel has mouthwatering persistence, right to the finish.*

*In fact, "Zin" is often asked for among the reputable vineyards of California's wine region. Versatile and vain, it's a wine that can be found in a horde of flavors. What a clever chameleon! Zinfandel's widely varying taste yields exuberant personality and character.*

❖❖❖❖❖❖❖❖❖

# ZIN ❣ Cerise

**The windshield wipers monotonously swayed back** and forth as Cerise tried parking her car at the mall. She had driven around the entire building twice, searching for the perfect spot; one that was close to an entrance and that did not have two feet of water waiting for her feet as she stepped out of her car. Finally, she spotted a place to park that was not too far from the food court. It was within running distance of the steady downpour lurking outside her vehicle. Nevertheless, she was committed to do what she needed to.

Fortunately, she had brought her umbrella along. It was quite fashionable, too, with a bright coral and pink paisley pattern. After she parked and opened the umbrella just outside her door, she heard a voice shouting at her through the rain pellets. "Scuse me! Excuse me.... Miss! Miss!"

As she squinted through the raindrops, Cerise saw a guy in a preppy looking shirt – looking rather drenched – running towards her. “Hey, that’s a nice umbrella!” he said, yelling through the rain.

“You came running over just to tell me you like my umbrella?” Cerise looked at him.

“Well, I was hoping you would let me stand under it with you to walk inside,” he asked.

“That’s pretty nervy of you,” she said, while he walked beside her. “How do I know you’re not some crazy killer?”

“Cuz if I was, I would have grabbed you by the waist and dragged you over there to my van!” he joked, as he pinched Cerise’s waistline just a little bit to get his point across.

“That’s your van?” Cerise asked, pointing at a funny-looking Jeep.

“Yup,” he said proudly. At that point, they had both made it to the entrance by walking briskly together under the umbrella. “Well, thanks for the lift! Maybe I’ll see you around,” he smiled and went off about his business at the mall.

After a half an hour of shopping at the Bath & Body Works store to replenish her supply of Pink Chiffon body lotion and a basket full of other smelly-good treasures, Cerise was feeling rather hungry. She paid for her bag of girly delights and went to the food court in search of the perfect salad. Well, at least as perfect as a salad from the mall could be.

“Since you shared your umbrella with me earlier, why don’t you let me do you a favor in return and buy you lunch?” A voice startled Cerise from behind, as she looked up at the menu. It was the umbrella-in-the parking lot guy, again.

"Are you following me?" she asked, pretending not to be shaken up.

"Yes, I'm trying to steal your identity," he joked. "Except that people might not believe me when I tell them my name is Samantha."

"But that's not my name," she said.

"You see?" he said. "Already people don't believe me."

Cerise laughed. "You're quite the jokester, aren't you?"

"It's better than being too serious," he replied. "My name's Zin. So, will you let me buy your lunch?"

"Well, do I have to eat it with you?" she asked.

"OUCH!" Zin grabbed his heart, pretending to rip it out of his chest. "You're a cold one, aren't you?"

"Not really, I'm just teasing you back." Cerise smiled. "I guess that would be fine."

So she ordered herself a delicious pecan and raspberry salad with spinach leaves and raspberry vinaigrette. Zin ordered a sandwich and the two searched for an empty table at the food court.

While they were eating, Zin had Cerise laughing up a storm. She hadn't laughed so hard in years and had tears rolling down her cheeks from all of his jokes. By the end of lunch, Cerise thought Zin was actually kind of adorable. He had a playful personality that was magnetic.

"So, what do you do for a living, Zin? You have a pretty good sense of humor. Is that your real name?" she asked.

"Wow... and she's pounding the questions at me!" Zin said, animatedly trying to catch imaginary rocks in the air, as if Cerise were throwing too many questions all at once.

"Well... I...," she stammered.

Before she could finish, Zin said, "Although I've retired from my dream of becoming the next winner on the "Last Comic Standing" – mostly because it was cancelled – I do have a backup job as an English teacher at the high school. And Zin's short for Zinfandel. If you must know." Then he looked at her expectantly, as if waiting to hear what she did for a living, as well.

"I'm an editor. At a magazine. It's just a regional publication," Cerise said, taking the pause as a hint.

"Oh, then we have something in common," he winked, raising an eyebrow. "We both have a fondness for the English language." Zin puckered up, as if kissing the air.

"Indeed, we do," she agreed. With that, Cerise took out a business card and handed it to Zin.

"Alright! Digits!" he exclaimed. "But this is your work number. I'd rather date you than do business with you, quite honestly."

Cerise smiled. "I've gotta go, but let's see how things play out."

For the next few days, Zinfandel courted her on the phone. They both had moderately busy schedules, but after almost a week of flirting they finally went on a "real" first date.

Zin took her to a Thai Restaurant. The waitress came by their table carrying two small shot-sized cups that looked like toothpick holders. "Do you like Saki?" asked Zin.

"Sure, I guess so," Cerise replied. She was unfamiliar with Asian food, actually. So, she picked up the

Saki and guzzled it, tilting her head back as she downed the entire cup of hot wine.

"It's not a shot. It's Saki," explained Zin, laughing. "You're supposed to sip it."

Her face turned a bit red. Cerise couldn't think of a comeback. "Oh..."

Throughout dinner, the two had a great time laughing over many things. About their jobs, especially. Zin was full of great stories about the lazy kids at school. He was one of the few teachers at the school who believed in giving homework. He told her a number of great examples of the famous excuses he heard whenever the kids failed to complete their assignments on time. Zin called it his "Top 10 Excuses" skit.

"You know, you really should be a comedian," Cerise complimented him. Being a wee bit vain, Zin pretended to feather his tail like a peacock. He even had a special noise he used, although it sounded more like a pigeon than a peacock.

After dinner, Cerise decided she liked him. The chemistry was there. She had always been more of a serious person, but she liked the way Zin brought out her bright side. He was very intelligent and able to come up with witty retorts for most any part of the conversation. Even though some of his jokes were cheesy, he always played them well and bounced back effortlessly. Cerise imagined that he was funny in the classroom, too.

Of course, after that dinner date, it wasn't the last of Zin. A few days later, he showed up on Cerise's doorstep with a bottle of wine and a small cactus. One in each hand. The cactus had a flower protruding next to it, with the whole ensemble tied neatly with a small white ribbon around the plant pot.

Cerise opened the door after looking through the peephole to see who it was. As she let him in, he handed her the bottle of wine and the cactus. "I brought these for you," said Zin.

She replied, "Thank you.... But, a cactus? Now that's quite original, I must say."

"Well, I don't know you that well, so I think a cactus is perfect," Zin explained.

Cerise asked, "Why so? Am I a prickly person or something?"

"Hardly," Zin answered. "But a cactus lasts much longer than flowers. Even if you forget to water it for a long time, a cactus is very resilient. And this flower on the side gives it just the right touch of romance." He pointed at the little flower. "Wouldn't you agree?"

"Well, I've gotta give you points for originality," Cerise smiled, setting the cactus down on her entertainment center. "I don't have much of a green thumb, so perhaps a cactus will suit me just fine. Then again, the poor thing might not stand a chance against someone like me."

"Somehow, I think you'll remember to water it." With that, Zin moved in and kissed Cerise unexpectedly on the lips. They kissed for what seemed like three or four minutes.

When their lips broke apart, she said, "I'll write it on my calendar."

"The cactus?" asked Zin. "Are we still talking about watering the cactus?"

"I think I'll have to keep it awhile and get to know it. We'll see how well the cactus and I get along," Cerise offered, coyly implying that Zin could stick around in her life, as well. And so it was on that day – the "Cactus Day" – that they began dating officially.

This was only the first of many inside jokes between Cerise and her new boyfriend. Zin made her laugh all the time, which translated into many other aspects of her life. She became happier at work and people noticed a "glow" about her that was different than the serious side they had often seen. Cerise started joking around with people and coming up with great ideas for new articles for the magazine. Her writing became flavorful and the readers were pouring in with letters of praise. Was it because Cerise was falling for Zin?

As she learned more about him, Zin revealed to her a difficult childhood that he had tried to overcome by becoming the class clown. In this way, he earned attention with his natural sense of humor. It was just part of his persona. In Cerise's eyes, this made Zin even more authentic.

But at times he was slightly immature. Zin's brilliant acidity came from faintly un-ripened areas; although the mature side of his personality outweighed the deficiencies. He had raisiny wisdom from reading avidly. Cerise, too, loved to read, which gave them much to talk about, laugh about, debate about and share with one another.

So, even though Cerise had been single for a while, she found herself thinking that maybe Zin would be a good fit for her. He was funny, witty, smart and somewhat adorable. He wasn't drop dead gorgeous, but he was attractive enough to be noticeable. Zin's face had character. He was thinly built, like a runner. His hair was brown with a few touches of blond from the sun. What was most striking about him was his smile, including a nice set of teeth that were as white as a ream of paper.

Cerise played it by ear and decided to just have fun and see where things went with Zin. There had to be something bad to find out that she was unaware of, but after a couple of months of seeing each other, she had still not seen any red flags. She wondered if maybe it was time to bring Zin home to meet her family, or if it was too soon.

Cerise had not brought any guy home for a few years that were special enough to meet her folks, who were a very sweet couple in their $38^{th}$ year of marriage. These days, that was an accomplishment. Cerise had not been able to find someone worthy of bringing home to them for quite some time; although, they often asked and hoped their daughter would meet their future son-in-law very soon. However, the last couple of men Cerise had dated for any length of time turned out to be duds and their relationship did not go anywhere.

She figured she would get her friends' advice on the next "Chick Night" that she faithfully attended every Wednesday. Chick Night was a core group of five or six friends who planned a girl's night away from the guys. The system was to rotate houses every week, so that one person did not get stuck repeatedly doing all the cooking and cleaning. Plus they got to try a lot of different dishes, depending on what the host decided to make. Sometimes new friends were introduced by one of them bringing another girl along from the "outside." It was kind of like a 'Guys Poker Night' except without the guys. And without the poker. ,

Cerise had brought up Zin's name on several occasions. This time, she asked her friends, "Hey, guys... Zin seems to be a pretty great guy so far. Do you think it's time to introduce him to the family?"

"Have you slept together yet?" asked Carrie, who was one of the girls.

"Oh, no.... not yet. But we're getting there, I'm thinking about doing the deed this weekend." Cerise giggled. The women all talked about any and every topic imaginable. Sex was always one on the list of favorites.

"Girl!" shouted Carrie, who was one of her louder friends. "Don't you know you gotta try it before you buy it?"

"What are you talking about?" Cerise asked.

Carrie said, "I mean, how do you know he doesn't have a small wanky or something?" Some of the other women busted out in laughter.

"Well, we've fooled around," Cerise admitted, a little embarrassed.

"Fooling around and doing the naughty are two completely different things!" debated her other friend, Deedra.

"For you, maybe," Cerise agreed. "But I like to build up to the main attraction. I like to have chemistry with the person, not just bonk till your eyeballs fall out and then call a cab the next day."

One of the other girls chimed in. Rachel said, "YA! Don't you remember Shiraz? That happened to Jenny not too long ago."

"Well, at least I know he's not a P-L-A-Y-E-R!" Cerise retorted. "Look, you repeatedly keep choosing men like Chianti! I think you like that sassy type. But to each their own. Zin is funny..."

"Whoa, whoa, whoa!" her friend Deedra smiled. "Uh-oh. I think you like this guy. You're gettin' defensive."

"Ya," said Carrie. "It's always great in the beginning. Cerise, you know this! Then after a few months, the guy goes off his probationary period and his true colors come out."

Deedra added, "I think you should wait another month or two before you bring him to the family. Rachel has a point. You're not thinking clearly, cuz you're in 'Ooo-Ooo Land' right now, plus you're probably horny since you've gone Lord-knows-how long since the last time you got any..."

All the girls cracked up. The wine was getting to them. "*Maybe they're right,*" Cerise wondered. "*I should wait. But not to find out these things.*"

After Chick Night, for the next few days Cerise was worried. She was paranoid that they might be right. What if Zinfandel DID have a small one? Then what would she do? Even though some guys used the "it's not how big it is, it's how you use it..." line, everybody knew that those remarks were just plain BS. The only people who said it were those who had boyfriends with small ones and who wanted to feel better about the situation.

In reality, women did notice the difference. And they cared, too. It was a big let-down whenever significant time was devoted in getting to know a man, only to discover that he had this problem. What then? How to duck out afterwards?

On the bright side, there was always BOB to come to the rescue. Yes, "Battery Operated Boyfriend" was always there in a pinch, with his perfect bedside manners and quick response time. So, Cerise decided not to stress anymore about it and just see what would happen between her and Zin. Maybe her friends were blowing this out of proportion. They liked doing that. It made Chick Night more fun to stir up controversy.

Actually, Cerise was quite pleased about the pace of their relationship. Zinfandel had never pressured her to put out and she had been proud of her willpower, considering how long it had been since she had been intimate in her last serious relationship. Unlike some of her friends, Cerise was a girl who liked to wait. Even though it was more uncommon in today's all-too-hasty-to-get-naked-society, there were still some couples who liked to get to know each other on a deeper level before giving in to their lustful desires.

Besides, things were going along awesome between Zin and Cerise. So, she decided that before she brought Zin home to meet her family, maybe Carrie was right. Bedroom performance was the only thing left that Cerise was still uncertain of; although, there was definitely a strong attraction between them. By then, Cerise had been dating Zin for about three months and things were getting hotter by the day.

That weekend, she figured it was "time." Cerise didn't want to be the one to seduce Zin; although, it had never proven difficult for Cerise or any of her female acquaintances to get a man to agree to such a wonderful thing. So, she did what she thought best. Cerise called Zin while she was still at work. It was about 4:00 p.m., so she knew he would be out of school by then.

Zin answered on the second ring. "Good afternoon. And to what might I have the pleasure of speaking with you so urgently today that it couldn't wait until I see you tomorrow?"

For a moment she hesitated. "Well, I've been thinking..." said Cerise.

He interrupted, "Thinking about ME! Oh I am the luckiest guy in the world!"

Cerise said, "Well, that's just it... the lucky thing..."

"Please tell me you're not breaking up with me," Zin said, half joking. He knew Cerise liked him enough. He would have been caught off guard if she had changed her mind.

"No, silly," she reassured Zin. "I was thinking about how fun it would be if we went somewhere this weekend. Alone."

He got it. "Ahhhh... you're feeling frisky, then? I knew it would only be a matter of time before you were putty in my hands. What brought on this sudden thought? Do you have a sexy co-worker there or a magazine spread about Brad Pitt that got you all hot and bothered?" Zin was kidding, of course.

Cerise felt awkward for a second. "No, I mean... uh well I just.... You know..."

Zin said, "Or maybe I was way off base and you just wanted to go away for the weekend and stare at each other instead? Or bake cookies? Play with dollhouses? I'm up for whatever, sweetie. But please don't choose the latter. It would really smash my macho man image."

She laughed, "You know, I just was thinking it would be nice to..."

"Shhh... everything in due time." On the other end, Zin fought hard to contain his enthusiasm. However, he couldn't resist the urge to try to make Cerise laugh. That was just who he was. Zin was a jokester. "I should probably tell you that having sex before marriage goes against my religion."

Cerise was silent on the other end. "Ummmm... what? You're religious?"

"Yeah, I've taken an oath of celibacy," Zin said in his most serious voice.

"Well, that certainly puts a damper on things, doesn't it?" Cerise said, snidely.

"Yup, you'll just have to wait for the goods," Zin still tried to play off his prank.

"Are you being serious or just funny?" she asked.

"Well, don't tell me you just want to date me so you can have your way with me," said Zin. "What kind of girl are you?"

Again, Cerise was quiet. She couldn't tell if he was joking or not, but suddenly she was having doubts. She didn't know if she could be with a man who didn't want to have sex. Ever. She didn't mind waiting, but...

"We can still go away together!" Zin waited to hear her reaction. It wasn't as he had hoped.

"What's the point?" Cerise said, feeling suddenly frustrated with Zin's latest news. She surmised that perhaps she didn't know him as well as she had thought. It was the first Cerise had ever heard of Zinfandel having any religious beliefs that went against premarital sex. In fact, he had never even mentioned going to church before, ever. How would she be able to "*Try it before you buy it*?" as her friend had so eloquently recommended?

"Whoa!" Zin said, on the other end of the line. "Now this is a reaction I did not expect."

"Well, maybe I should find a boyfriend who actually LIKES being intimate!" Cerise said, hastily. Then she hung up. But after she did it, she felt sick to her stomach, as if someone had punched her in the gut. Cerise knew she had overreacted.

But to some extent, the damage had been done. Zin was a little shocked by his girlfriend's behavior, even though it had been a joke. He thought about it and wondered why people put so much precedence on sex, when it seemed like other things were more important. They already had the chemistry together and a lot of things in common. He enjoyed hanging out with Cerise. She was a "nice" girl, at least in the time Zin had come to know her.

The last girl he dated had been a head trip. Now he wondered if all women were. *"Are all women just as nutty as the rest?"* Zin wondered. He needed time to think about this.

Zin waited until late that evening to call Cerise. She answered after a couple of rings. "Hello?"

"OKAY! I changed my mind!" exclaimed Zin. "I decided to quit my religion and go away with you for the weekend! We can bonk until our eyeballs fall out. And if you don't like it, then you can just call me a cab the next morning and send me packing. What do you say we just get in the Land Rover and be spontaneous? We won't bring any maps or any plans or any Smartphone with us. Just you and me, and a few bottles of wine and a box of condoms. Whattya say?"

Cerise laughed. At least Zin could always bring a smile to her face. And this time, an extra few flutters to her heart. He was funny, intelligent and suddenly, Cerise didn't even care if he had a big ding-dong or not. She knew it in her heart... she was falling for him.

"Alright," Cerise said after thinking for a minute or two. "But I hope you don't have any unpleasant surprises for me."

"Like?" Zin replied, wondering what she meant.

Cerise thought quickly on her feet. "I don't know... like maybe you had a sex change operation a few years ago that you are trying to hide. Or maybe you're a one-minute man. Or maybe you have a small...."

"Cactus?" Zin interrupted. "I can assure you, I am not a woman in disguise. I can last all night long. And I can provide you with a package that even UPS cannot deliver due to weight and height restraints."

"Okay," she said, satisfied with his answer and with their plans. "Then it's settled. We're going away for the weekend." Cerise smiled, feeling warm and tingly just thinking about Zin. She knew they would have fun. Even more importantly, Cerise knew that she loved him. And that was going to make the weekend even more memorable.

❖❖❖❖❖❖❖❖❖

# PROVISO

**With Zinfandel, you do have to "buy it before you** try it," rather than the other way around. Any given brand doesn't reveal its goodness until you have already made the commitment to give it a whirl. Only then will you discover if he's a dud or a wine worthy of bringing home to meet your friends and family. Zinfandel does try hard to please drinkers.

Right from day one, you'll never know if you grabbed a spicy bottle or a dud. If you stick around long enough, you're sure to find out eventually. Just ask a group of cackling girls who are all in a room together, and you're sure to get many answers about Zinfandel's likability. Some women love Zinfandel, while others find him annoying.

But despite its rising or falling popularity, Zinfandel is resilient. He can either take the stage with a standing ovation or leave the room sitting there staring, waiting for the punch line.

Until you're sure that you grabbed a good one, don't bring Zinfandel to give the host of a party. They may politely offer it back in return. Zinfandel's sarcasm is not always appreciated in certain circles. Especially with people who just don't understand Zinfandel's off-colored and non-traditional approach. Some circles may even find Zinfandel's unconventional taste to be a bit offensive, but it's a matter of being subjective. Others can appreciate Zinfandel's remarkably zany outlook and unusual style.

If you do find a keeper, you are truly lucky. This wine will treat you right if given the opportunity to do so. It will make you laugh with its good taste and witty, unrefined attitude. A well-made Zinfandel may take a while to develop its best character. Once it does, you will get a great buzz and a lot of satisfaction.

# Shiraz

## "THE FLING"

***Richly enthralling and full-bodied in texture, Shiraz*** *is a wine of overpowering seduction. It has a ripe, fruity palate with subtle tannins, showing layers of exotic spiciness like toasted vanilla, plum or blackberry. Often it produces hints of licorice, plum or pepper with a smidge of mocha or blueberry. Shiraz is deep. It can be eloquent in nature, but always with a soft touch.*

*To avoid any upcoming confusion, Shiraz and Syrah grapes are one in the same. It was Australia who first began calling Syrah "Shiraz" and the name took on a life of its own with wine lovers. Depending on the grower and the region in which they are raised, Syrah or Shiraz grapes are harvested in nearly every wine-bearing part of the world. The style and region will predicate the grape's flavor and whether it will be better for just a one-night rendezvous or saved in the cellar for future swooning.*

*Some wineries that prefer to exude more sophistication or restraint will opt for the name Syrah, whereas those with boldness will go with Shiraz. Either one will snap the pants off an unprepared consumer. Shiraz's full-bodied characteristics have even been described as hedonistic.*

*Common traits of Syrah – Shiraz are its brazenness, texture and higher tannins than other wines. Oh yes. With that kind of in-your-face meatiness and kick, it's no surprise that this flavorful blend of white pepper, blueberries, chocolate and currant will get you drunker than other reds. It does have higher alcohol content, so look out!*

*As an unrelated tidbit, Shiraz doubles as a fine wine and the namesake of a famous city in Iran, which is also called Shiraz. It is known internationally as the city of poetry, flowers, beautiful gardens and fine wine. Several famous poets, scientists, artists and astronomers were born in this city of expressive essence.*

*The world became reawakened to the opulence of Shiraz, as other countries began to grow the fruit. It thrives within a magnanimous range of climates. The spicy characteristics have brought Shiraz into the limelight because of its ingenious lyrical brilliance and artistic nature. Shiraz can sweep you off your feet even without words. It yields layers of intoxicating density accompanied by a luscious and long-lasting flavor.*

*Shiraz is ethnically diverse and culturally savoir faire. It is world-worthy and savvy, blending well with many other wines around the globe to create a wine with fascinating complexity. The depth of Shiraz is always considered to be intellectual and spirited. It is versatile enough to be opened and enjoyed immediately, or to save for many years in mark of a special occasion.*

*Either way, prepare for a mouthful of zesty bouquets that linger, with a grand finale. Whenever Shiraz comes into the picture, it will surely be a dazzling display of intrigue and charisma.*

❖❖❖❖❖❖❖❖❖

# SHIRAZ ❣ Silver

**There was nothing Silver loved more than dancing.** She loved to salsa dance, line dance, break-dance, ballroom dance or any type of dance that allowed her to feel uninhibited and free. What Silver lacked was a partner; although, sometimes she met men who were good enough to keep her toes alive for an evening.

Wondering how she might be able to meet more people who shared her hobby, Silver enrolled in a dance class. She was a little nervous about signing up for it solo. Most of the people who took dance lessons were couples. But when she called the studio, she was assured by the receptionist that many of the people were like her and just wanted to learn how to dance better, whether or not they had a partner. Therefore, there would be plenty of people to practice with if she chose to come. Silver did. Not only would it be a great way to meet new people, but she would be able to dance to her heart's content at least two or three nights a week. As a bonus, the studio often had special events that allowed the participants to show off their new skills.

Silver signed up for salsa dancing, which was her favorite. She loved the Latin music and the rolling of their hips as they moved to the rhythm. None of the men she ever dated liked dancing all that much. Most of them only danced to slow songs or moved their hips a little bit back and forth to pretend they were "into" it, when they would have rather been making idle chit-chat or sitting.

When she arrived for the first time at the dance center, there was a group of about fifteen people dressed in yoga pants and leotards. Some took their dancing very seriously, whereas Silver did it more or less for fun; although, she enjoyed the challenging aspects of it and the exercise, too.

The first person she spotted was the dance instructor. He was really hot and exotic, with a sexy Latin look and spicy attitude to match. "Good afternoon, everyone. Welcome to our first class. It is my pleasure to teach you salsa dancing. My name is Shiraz."

Silver was smitten. His worldly accent had a hint of Spanish. Was he Puerto Rican, Peruvian or Columbian? She couldn't tell, but whatever it was, just his voice made her skin tingle with excitement. He noticed her, too.

Everyone in the room was standing in a half circle. They all took a step forward to tell the rest of the class their names. They also stated the reason for participating, upon the suggestion of Shiraz. "I'm Silver. I'm here because I love to dance, but none of my friends share in my enthusiasm," she volunteered when it was her turn.

"Welcome, Silver!" said the class, in unison. But the only voice she heard was Shiraz.

Salsa lasted for an hour. Shiraz called on her a lot to show the rest of the class a move they could try with a partner, since she had come alone. Silver was glad she had not brought someone else along. Whenever Shiraz's cool hands touched her palms or twirled her around, she forgot about the rest of the room.

Shiraz smelled luxurious and masculine. His white tank top and loose sweatpants were rolled up at the bottom, making him stylish even within a casual environment. A couple of dog tags on a silver beaded chain hung around his neck. Since she didn't speak Spanish, Silver didn't know what they meant. But the way they jingled when he danced made her giddy.

At the end of class, Shiraz beckoned her. She had purposefully packed up her towel, water and sandals slowly so that she would be one of the last to leave. It worked. His obvious flirtations showed promise. "Silver, you did great today. I can tell you have danced the salsa before. Why did you sign up for the beginner's class?" His accent was smooth and sing-songy.

"I've never had any formal lessons. I just like the vibrations of salsa. It's so quixotic," Silver explained, with wide eyes of praise.

"I can tell you are a very passionate woman," he smiled. Silver returned the grin. "How about you be my partner for a fiesta this Saturday? I'm supposed to be one of the hired dancers, but I have yet to find a partner. Would you like to be my other half for that evening?"

Inside, she wanted to jump up and down and do cartwheels. However, Silver maintained her composure and upheld a calm exterior. "That sounds like a lot of fun, but I've only had one lesson. What if I mess you up?"

"You won't," Shiraz reassured her. "Just follow my lead and you will look like a contestant with the *dancing with the stars*!" His English was not so flawless, but apparently his dancing was. To illustrate his talent, he grabbed her hand and whirled her around perfectly – twice – whilst finishing off with a dip so low that Silver's hair gently brushed the floor.

"Wow, you're good!" said Silver.

"I could give you private lessons if you like?" Shiraz winked.

"Oh ... I bet you could!" she replied.

"But, you see it would look very silly if I were to go to the fiesta without a beautiful date," he flattered her.

"It sounds like fun. What should I wear?" asked Silver. She had never been to any dance competitions and did not want to look out-of-place.

"Wear anything that makes you feel sexy and feminine. You will dance better if you let the music flow through your whole body," Shiraz implied, as he traced an imaginary outline of a woman's physique in the air for descriptive purposes.

"Shall I meet you there?" asked Silver.

"Yes, yes, Cariño. Let us meet and become one on the dance floor ... you and I." Shiraz was dramatic as he gently lifted Silver's hand and kissed the top of her knuckles, sending goose bumps throughout the entire length of her arm.

Silver chose white to wear to the fiesta. It was a Spiegel classic that never went out of style, featuring a daring crocheted back that showed off a lot of skin, with a white wavy skirt that was just short enough to be mysterious, yet long enough to be covered adequately. The white enhanced her long blonde hair and suntanned skin. To bring out the blue in her eyes, she wore a turquoise necklace and big, dangly hoop earrings. Silver was satisfied with perfection.

When he saw her, he pretended to have a spot-on heart attack by grabbing his chest and leaning backwards. "Wow! Me vuelves loca!"

"I don't know what you said, but it sounds wonderfully exciting," Silver replied.

"Vamos! Let's go!" said Shiraz, grabbing her hand and leading her straight to the dance floor.

"Where are you from?" yelled Silver over the music.

"Here and there. I lived in Spain, Venezuela and Puerto Rico. Mi Mamà is from Puerto Rico and Mi Papà was from Brazil. But he was in the Brazilian army so we moved a lot. And we have been in the United States now for 18 years," Shiraz summarized.

Just then, he dipped her low to the floor and pressed his nose against hers. Silver was breathless. They danced all night long, as crowds gathered around to watch them. She felt like a star, but it was Shiraz leading her with such professional dancing skills. It was no wonder people called Shiraz '*Rey de la Danza*' – the King of Dance!

There were people there who had taken Shiraz's class. He knew how to do the flamenco, rumba, calypso, salsa and many other high-energy styles. Shiraz also danced with some of his students, who were women that brought a date or their husbands along for a night away from the kids. Some of the women seemed envious of Silver; although, she did her best to ignore it since she was purely there to have a great time.

Just after midnight, Shiraz pulled her close to him and said, "It's really hot in here and we have danced the night away. What do you say we go to the beach and take a look at the full moon as it looms across the ocean?" She couldn't refuse.

They walked to his car. Shiraz escorted her to the door of his Mercedes Benz SL550 silver convertible. "Oooh... my favorite color!" she cooed.

The car roared as Shiraz shifted through the empty parking garage. "You won't be too cold with the top down, Muñequita?" he asked Silver.

"No, it feels great," she replied. "I'm still hot from dancing."

They drove through the streets of Miami, lined with palm trees and flamingo mail boxes. Shiraz knew a perfect spot to take her. The soft white sand felt cool on her feet as she stepped onto the beach. He laid down a quilt and gave her a hand to sit. "I brought Champagne," said Shiraz.

"How charming," she smiled, as she reached for the glass he poured.

For the first few minutes, they sat and talked. Shiraz was a financial analyst by day. He analyzed numbers for Fortune 500's that were considering mergers and acquisitions. His job was to tell the companies whether or not the decisions were sound and viable. Shiraz was also working towards his Master of Science in Finance. On the nights he did not have dance, he could be found studying through online classes. Silver loved listening to him talk and found his profound Hispanic accent to be quite arousing. There was something about the way Shiraz rolled his "R's". He folded up the sleeves of his designer dress shirt and his Hollister Jeans were rolled up at the cuffs.

"And what about you, Sirenita?" asked Shiraz. He brushed Silver's long stray strands out of her eyes, ever so gently. She melted.

"I.... Me... I'm an art gallery director and curator." She stammered a bit, still jolted by his touch.

"I see... so you are cerebrally challenging, as well as beautiful," whispered Shiraz, as he leaned in to kiss her. They made out for the longest time. Shiraz was an unbelievable kisser. When he tried to creep his hand up her leg, she stopped him.

"Not yet," she whispered. But she did let him get to first base, as they lay on the quilt for hours watching the glorious light of the moon as it danced across the ocean.

He didn't call her, but Silver saw him again at their dance classes. Shiraz was still flirtatious as he called upon her to show the rest of the class certain moves with his instruction. Everyone had a great time. At the end of Thursday's class, Shiraz said, "Last Saturday was so much fun. Let's go again, Mi Querida!" Silver agreed. "We're going to a different place this week."

This time, Silver looked stunning in a cobalt blue sarong with fringes, which went well with the festive music of the steel drum band playing in the tiny hideaway that Shiraz had chosen to take her. With the top down in his silver Benz, Silver felt uninhibited and full of life. The breeze was invigorating as it gently pulled her hair back. The leather seats were just warm enough to send a tingling sensation through her pelvis. Shiraz had turned on the seat warmers just enough to make her comfortable.

After another fun night of dancing, Shiraz asked the band to play a slow number. He grabbed Silver's hand and pulled her tight against him. She made out a hint of 'Agua de Colonia 1916' original Spanish cologne intertwined with sweat. It was an erotically masculine combination. "Mmmmm... you smell so sweet, Florecita," Shiraz murmured into her ear.

"I was just thinking the same thing," replied Silver. He squeezed her.

"Do you want to come to my penthouse tonight and have a '*nightcap*'?" Shiraz asked, after kissing her for what seemed like a full minute. Silver looked down and then into his eyes.

"I don't know if that's a good idea. I may not be able to control myself," she jested.

"Then, let's go! Vamos!" Shiraz eagerly replied. With that, Silver trotted through the door behind him as Shiraz made a beeline for his car.

They made out on the way to the car, in the car and some of the way back to his place. They could barely keep their hands off each other. Silver was already half undressed before they even got there. "Keep your eyes on the road!" she scolded.

"I can't... you are soooo wicked. Quiero hacerte el amor," he said, looking intensely into her eyes.

"I don't know what you said," Silver said, breathlessly. "But it sounds amazing."

Shiraz smiled. "It will be!"

And it was; although, Silver did not get one single wink of sleep that night. Shiraz was just as skilled at lovemaking as he was at dancing. He was seductive, tantalizing and passionate. Their lust for each other was reciprocal.

Once again, Silver went home feeling buzzed by Shiraz. She didn't hear from him again until class the following Tuesday. It was her third week going and so far she was having the time of her life. Every weekend on Saturday she met up with Shiraz to go dancing and then saw him again on Tuesday and Thursdays at class only. The rest of the nights he was too busy to get together. His work and education took up much of his time. But on Saturdays and sometimes Sundays until early afternoon, Silver was his escape.

Their relationship was purely sensual. They were both enthralled by dancing and looked forward to that weekend release from the obligations of life.

One weekend, they went to an art festival late in the afternoon, followed by dinner and another night of dancing. As they stepped out into the street to walk back to the car, Shiraz and Silver were really hot and bothered. The tents had closed up for the night since most of the vendors were coming back the next day. They couldn't wait to get back to the car, so Shiraz pointed at one of the tents. "Are you thinking what I'm thinking?" he asked Silver.

"You mean... in the tent?" she said. "Ooooh, you're naughty!"

He unzipped the tent and they went inside, just as many of the dance clubs were closing. All of the people that left were walking by, none of them knowing there was a couple in the tent getting busy right in the middle of the street. Silver did her best not to make any noise, but it was difficult. She was in a precarious position, especially when they finished, trying to leave the tent with so many crowds all around them. Their hearts pounded loudly from the adrenaline of the fear of being caught. She had never done anything so outrageous before and it was exhilarating.

Their fling lasted for about eight weeks. Shiraz never called Silver during the week, nor did she. They were both too busy with work and other things. But both of them looked forward to their weekly rendezvous.

Then one day, Silver showed up to dancing lessons a little later than usual. She never missed a class, but a client had detained her at the art gallery. To her surprise, Shiraz was not there. Instead, there was a woman who was in the midst of illustrating a few new dance steps to one of Silver's classmates. She dropped her satchel off in the back of the room, wondering where her Latin lover was.

"Hi," the dark-haired instructor said, as she reached a hand to Silver. "I'm Wendy. I'm your new dance teacher."

"What happened to Shiraz?" asked Silver.

"Oh, he had some family obligations at the last minute and will be unable to finish the last four weeks of classes," explained Wendy. "I'll be taking over where he left off. Usually I teach the Monday and Wednesday classes."

Trying not to hide her disappointment, Silver fell in with the rest of the group and was not herself for the rest of the session. She just wasn't "into it" and her dancing steps were off. She could barely concentrate. The following Thursday, Silver didn't even bother to go. She hoped everything was okay with Shiraz.

There was no way to know where he would be that Saturday, either. Silver and Shiraz always went to different hot spots to dance, never the same place. She would have had to cover a large territory if she wanted to locate his whereabouts. Plus, Silver had a feeling he wouldn't be out dancing anyway if something had happened.

After a couple of weeks, Silver tried to recall any information he may have revealed to her in the time they spent together. However, they had done very little talking and mostly their relationship had been more about action than words. She did remember that Shiraz had pointed out the office building where he worked one time when they drove by. However, not having heard from him first, Silver was hesitant to drop by. He worked at a prestigious firm and was not sure if a surprise visit would be welcome.

Of course, her curiosity got the better of her. Still dressed in her business attire from the art gallery, Silver drove there one day on her lunch break. She found the name of a company that sounded familiar on the sign in the office lobby and pressed the elevator button to get up to the fifth floor. As she waited, she was nervous. Silver had never gone past the boundaries of their comfort zone. She wasn't entirely certain that she was even going to the right place. Nevertheless, Silver had a burning urge to find Shiraz.

As the numbers made their way down, the elevator doors opened in slow motion to reveal a couple who were in the farthest corner. Hearing the 'bing' as they arrived on the main level, the couple gathered themselves together and faced the lobby. Silver was standing there with her mouth open in astonishment just in time to see Shiraz looking rather disheveled and un-tucked. There was bright red lipstick all over his neck and the pretty brunette next to him appeared rather smitten as his hand rested casually on her rump.

Embarrassed, Shiraz looked down as he walked past her. He couldn't even look into Silver's eyes as she repositioned her crossed arms from her chest to her hips. The two of them walked outside and Shiraz must have excused himself from the brunette, most likely telling her that he had forgotten something back upstairs in his office.

Shiraz walked back through the glass doors of the lobby, where Silver was still standing by the elevator. "Princesita, what are you doing here?" asked Shiraz.

"Well... I... was just worried about you after not seeing you in class. The new dance instructor said you had family issues to deal with... but it looks like you are fine, so I will go," said Silver.

"Oh, well that wasn't what it looked like," he tried explaining, pointing to the elevator. "She is a client."

"From what I can see, it looks like you treat your clients very well here at this company," Silver said, sarcastically. Then, not wanting to waste another minute hearing any lame explanations, Silver stormed off. Over her shoulder she shouted, "Thanks for the dance lessons!"

And when Silver passed by the woman in the red suit who was waiting for Shiraz by the curb, she couldn't resist. "By the way, you have lipstick all over your face. Those private dance sessions are wonderful, aren't they?"

❖❖❖❖❖❖❖❖❖

# PROVISO

**Keep Shiraz in mind for a good-tasting, good feeling** wine. Be careful not to fall in love with Shiraz in haste, for his flavor changes with the seasons. Each new crop bears grapes that are a slightly different than in years past, making this type of wine very finicky and not something to become obsessed with. Enjoy Shiraz while it lasts. He is passionate, yet sporadic.

He will make you blush with his good looks and seductive beckoning. He will notice things about you that others may have passed by. Shiraz is all about romance, but with certain spontaneity that triggers naughty thoughts. It's a wine that is nonetheless enjoyable, intoxicating and memorable. The exotic sensations of Shiraz can be enjoyed right away; yet with a soft and supple finale that will be memorable, to say the least.

In all likeliness, Shiraz will be more of a fling than a forever kind of relationship. He is a wanderer and yearns to spread the love around the world. He must experience all that life has to offer, including women. He flourishes in the three-to-six month shelf life, and with vivacious energy right from the very first sip.

Later on in life, Shiraz does mature very well. In fact, a fine bottle of Shiraz has a very long shelf life. The layers of complexity increase with age, only after Shiraz realizes the virtues of a stable relationship. However, due to its high energy and passion, there will never be a guarantee of monogamy. Its full-bodied intensity is too filled with character, expression and finesse to ever settle. When he's gone, you can be content in knowing that the intrigue and mystery of Shiraz is something unforgettably delicious.

# Pinot Grigio

## "THE NETWORKER"

*C**all it the Conversationalist, the Intellect, or the** Brainiac. Any of these descriptions will suffice the personality of Pinot Grigio. Even its blue-grayish color reflects the fine line between fascinating or incredibly uninteresting; depending on the bottle or brand you happen to come across. The fascinating type might be crafted from a rich strain of worldly vintage grapes – whereas the less interesting variety – made of leftover remnants.*

*Pinot Grigio will talk your ears off with its fruit-laden character, light and dry personality and whining hint of freshness that keeps you long engaged for an evening. Most varietal Pinot Grigios have a level of sweetness; hence, they will lose acidity quickly, after becoming ripe. Also known as Pinot Gris, this wine's undertone is a bit dull, yet somehow "bright" enough to be entertaining.*

*Maybe not surprisingly, Pinot Gris is widely collected throughout wine social circles, even more so than wines like*

*Merlot or Chardonnay. It goes well with most any dinner event, perfectly partnered with any great meal as a wine that will be undeniably stimulating. Beware of its ability to corner you at a cocktail party and then never let you go. Pinot Grigio insists on being heard. Before you know it, the evening will be over before you've had a chance to mingle with other wines.*

*The fact of the matter is Pinots have a fair amount of complexity. That's the thing we love about them. Many variations of Pinot Grigio are capable of great depth and intellect. Although they may be lacking enough pizzazz for anyone to become deeply smitten, this wine has a deep desire to be known and admired. It possesses a number of great characteristics that may not be fully appreciated until maturity because Pinot Grigio becomes even more thrilling as it matures. The longer you keep a bottle in the wine cellar for a later date, the more palatable it becomes. Younger versions of this wine could merely bore you to tears.*

*If you are looking for an engaging conversation about the scandals of governors, or the goings on in foreign countries, or the melting iceberg crisis, or the possibilities of an asteroid hitting Earth, or the endless highlights of last week's NFL game, or the advantages of choosing Canon over Nikon, or the likeliness of getting the bacon-and-eggs flu, or whether flying bicycles will be the next transportation solution of tomorrow, or any other meaningless banter; then Pinot Grigio is the wine to choose.*

*Oh, and Pinot Grigio is a rather know-it-all, to top it off.*

*Pinot Grigio is more on the conservative side, making it able to set well with anything from a backyard cookout with burgers and corn chips; to a fancy gala with a five star dinner. Certain people greet Pinot Grigio with a warm smile of forged cordialities. Yet surprisingly, it can grow on you, becoming more fascinating with every sip.*

*Pinot Grigio is not a heartthrob. It won't take your breath away like one of the many other varietal white wines, but you certainly won't refuse it if offered a glass. It can leave you gazing off into a daydream as it drones on... and on... and on. Grigio's flinty and crisp character has a hint of lemon rind and butter, which can be pleasant, but never superb. It is said to have a thought-provoking tang with a lingering freshness.*

*An uptight wine, Pinot Gris can leave you overwhelmed or even bloated with its high yeast content and aroma of dough. Even still, Pinot Grigio is an undeniable favorite among wine lovers around the world. Pinot Grigio is well-rounded, versatile and wise, like the tasty rinds of an apple that reveal an enriched flavor. Its dry air is expected and consistent. Without it, there would be less table banter and conversations would be brief. It has a fairly common taste because it takes less effort to produce than other wines; however, Pinot Gris does possess a pragmatic structure that is welcome and surprisingly deserved.*

❖❖❖❖❖❖❖❖❖

# P.G. ❣ Blue

**Pinot Grigio was decidedly brilliant, like the** harmonious lull of an orchestra quietly transitioning from one song to the next; without missing a note. He could easily shift into the next topic just as easily as the stick shift of a 5-speed high performance automobile. His blatant disregard for time was a nuance, yet somehow the mesmerizing qualities of his presence were accepted. One would have thought of P.G. as rude, if not for the sake of being misunderstood.

Listening to Pinot Grigio tell stories led some to believe he had lived a hundred lives before. He told them with much the same wisdom as a young boy who believes himself to be a Great War hero, professional athlete, or at the very least, a bazillionnaire. P.G. seemed to know everything about anything and never ran out of words, or topics. He was the type of guy who could talk twenty minutes about anything... from simple toilet paper to the complex sophistication of NASA projects. Initially, people thought P.G. to be a yuppie. His similarly crisp character was a little on the fruity side. Alas, P.G. was a different blend all on his own.

Looks-wise, P.G. was neither attractive, nor unattractive. He was of average height, build and there was nothing truly distinctive about his features. He looked like "any guy" you might encounter at the supermarket, on the crosswalk, or opening the door for you at a hotel.

Despite what people perceived, P.G. had many friends. He stayed in touch with everyone that he came across; going back from elementary, junior high, high school, college, graduate school, and every job he had ever worked at, as well as those who he met at trade shows and other networking events. P.G. was the ultimate networker. "New people" were his specialty because it gave him the chance to have another long-length conversation about the topic of the day with a complete stranger.

At a big convention one day, P.G. walked through the trade show from booth to booth with his plastic yellow bag filled with advertising pamphlets and business cards. P.G. also enjoyed dropping fistfuls of his own cards into every fishbowl giveaway at every booth of every vendor who was there. He was a business consultant who looked for any and every opportunity to meet new potential clients. As he approached the pet supply booth, P.G. spotted a nice-looking lady who was representing the company. She held a handful of brochures about special, all-organic dog food. "Well, hello there, sir," she smiled. "Do you have a pet?"

"No, I don't," P.G. replied.

The woman stood there and blinked. On her lapel label, the name read "BLUE BELL." People called her Blue. Most of the people who stopped at Blue's pet supply booth were pet owners.

The company positioned a huge banner with the name OPW – Organic Pet Wholesale over the booth that was decorated like pet land. They even brought a doghouse and dog dish filled with the special organic pet food they were selling. There were silver bags filled with samples for the customers who stopped by, as well as a fishbowl for people to drop in their business cards for a chance to win the free doghouse that was on display.

"But, I was thinking about getting one someday," P.G. added, after they had a pause in the conversation that was long enough to size each other up. "You know, a dog would be nice to have when I get ready to do the *'family thing'*... down the road." He swooshed his pointer and middle finger together in the air with each hand as he reached the 'family thing' statement, as if to imply a quotation.

The girl blew a small bubble, as she kept chomping on her gum. "I see," said Blue. "Well you can take a free sample, but I'm not sure how fresh it will be by the time you want to use it."

"It's quite alright, I already ate some lunch a few minutes ago," P.G. said, patting his belly.

"Kay," she said, trying to maintain a stoic expression. "Good luck with that."

"You really dislike your job, don't you?" asked P.G., changing the subject.

"Ummm... it's okay," she blushed.

"Well, you're certainly not doing a good job at '*engaging the customer'*," P.G. said, again using quotes around the words he spoke with influence.

Embarrassed, Blue's cheeks turned warm and bright. She wondered if P.G. was a secret mystery shopper. Some of the other employees at OPW had encountered those stealthy undercovers who came in to evaluate the service; although, it had never happened at any trade shows. Quite honestly, Blue had never aspired to become a dog food saleswoman. Those were just the cards she was dealt, as a single mom who was trying to pay the bills to feed her kids. Blue had two children, who she left with her mother, sister and sometimes daycare while she worked full time. The money was decent and paid a commission for sales on top of an hourly wage.

"Sorry, it's been a long few days at this convention," Blue apologized.

"It's okay," he replied and dropped his business card in the fishbowl. Figuring it would make her day pass faster, P.G. asked Blue every trivial question he could think of about the ingredients, the flavor, and the packaging of their brand of dog food. That was how he came to be so smart, by asking so many questions.

After he finally left her table an hour later, Blue took P.G.'s business card out of the bowl. She planned to call and apologize because of the comment he had made regarding her performance. However, Blue had her chance even sooner. They ran into each other at the grocery store later that evening.

"Fancy meeting you here," P.G. said, as he tapped Blue on the shoulder. "Are you looking for a tomato or a tomA-toe?"

"Oh, it's you..." Blue said, surprised.

"Ahhh, yeah... it's me! From the trade show, remember?" P.G. questioned.

"Of course. How could I forget? You are a chatty fellow, aren't you?" asked Blue.

"C'mon, am I bothering you?" he replied.

Blue thought for a second. "No, I guess not." Truthfully, she had been lonely. Blue was not very outgoing, especially for a salesperson. She lacked the confidence to talk to men. She didn't have good radar when it came to whether a man was married, had a girlfriend or if he was single. And in her type of job, there was not much opportunity to meet single people. Most of her customers were families with kids and pets. And since she had kids of her own for whom she was solely responsible, Blue rarely trolled the bar scene.

In a way, Blue liked the attention from P.G., although she pretended to be annoyed. She was not good at flirting. It was a skill she had never used much, especially within the last seven years since her divorce.

So, Blue just listened as P.G. went on, and on, and on. Just when she thought she had a break in the conversation to leave, he snagged Blue in another lengthy dialogue about something totally irrelevant, making it near impossible to duck out. To P.G., the natural desire to connect with anybody who would listen made leaving a little hazy. Even looking at your wristwatch didn't work with him.

Finally, she said, "It's been great meeting you, both times today. But I really do have to go and pick up my kids soon. I left them with my neighbor."

"Oh, I'm sorry! You must go. How many kids do you have?" he asked, nearly starting another conversation.

Blue didn't take the bait. "Two.... Gotta go!"

P.G. stood there, perplexed. "Wait, I wanted to ask you if you want to do lunch or dinner or coffee or sit by the pool sometime?"

"Sure, sure, whatever," said Blue, hastily scrawling her number on his wrist with a Sharpie she took from work. As she walked to her car, Blue questioned why she had done it. *Why do I want to bore myself by going out with him*? she wondered all the way to the car.

Nevertheless, Blue found herself sitting across from P.G. a couple of weeks later, as he had been persistent in leaving messages on her voicemail. She had put him off a couple of times by telling him that she couldn't find a babysitter. Finally, P.G. called and told her about a friend of his who was a professional nanny and who had agreed to come over and watch her children for free. Well, P.G. was taking care of the tab, anyway. Now Blue had zero excuses.

Their first date was at a rotating restaurant at the top of the city. The whole restaurant spun around slowly as people dined overlooking the bright skyline, with the sun just setting over the purple and blue horizon. It was romantic and Blue had not been out on a date in a long time, so she was actually quite pleased with herself for getting back out there again. The ordeal with her ex-husband hadn't left Blue in a mood to experience heartache again anytime soon, so she remained content simply raising her kids and spending most of her days doting on and caring for them. Yes, at times she was lonely. But never lonely enough to want another headache from love gone awry.

As they dined, P.G. never ran out of tales to tell. His multifarious knack for keeping Blue entertained was oblivious to her staring out the window sometimes, especially when his topics reached the cusp of boring. He rarely asked Blue much about her interests; although every once in a while, she piped in to tell a brief tidbit or two about her life. P.G. had never learned to listen as much as he liked to talk.

Blue studied him a couple of times. P.G. didn't really have any striking features that made him a "lady killer," but he was at least modestly handsome. His hair was thinning and his eyes were kind. He had a couple of laugh lines from smiling. He was a little shorter than average but not shorter than Blue, which was okay with her. At this stage in her life, Blue put more emphasis on a man's personality than in his appearance.

As he drove her home, P.G. expected to hear the same non-committal avoidances he often heard after dates. Girls said things like, *"I'm really tired and I have to get up early. So I'll see you again sometime soon."* Or, *"I had a nice time; we'll have to do this again one day."* These phrases were often accompanied by a big yawn. And '*one day*' never came again.

Instead, Blue surprised P.G. "You know, that was the most fun I've had in a long time." The non-telling expression she had carried on her face for most of the evening did not give P.G. the impression that she had been having fun. "Besides, after spending so much time talking about crayons, soccer games and imaginary dragons under the bed and things of that nature, it's actually refreshing to hear some 'adult talk' every now and then. You know what I mean?"

P.G. nodded. "Yes, well I'm happy to hear that. I'd like to see you again, too."

With that, she kissed him quickly on the cheek and practically slammed the door on him, saying "Thank you for dinner. Call me to arrange something." She didn't want to get trapped into another lengthy chat.

The next day at work, as Blue was helping a customer learn about the amazing macrobiotic ingredients in OPW dog food, a skinny kid strolled in through the front door of the pet supply store. He was holding a pretty vase with yellow roses. The manager went over to greet him and then looked straight back toward Blue, pointing. The skinny kid started coming her way, as Blue's cheeks grew a light crimson and the blood rushed to her cheeks.

"Excuse me for one second," Blue apologized to her customers.

"Are you Blue Bell?" asked the kid. "These are for you."

Blue took the bouquet and thanked him. She hadn't received flowers from a man in at least eight years, back when she was dating her husband and before he had gotten her knocked up. On a small card read, "Something to brighten your day." – P.G.

'*How lovely.*' She thought. And it did brighten her day.

And so it was that Blue and P.G. began dating, although he did nearly all of the talking in most of their social situations. She was soft-spoken. He wouldn't shut up. When out in public, people often shot her glances of apologetic, unspoken compassion, as if feeling sorry for Blue that she had to endure such lengthy conversations day in and day out. Even though she found his excessive talkativeness rather annoying, Blue liked many other things about P.G.; although she couldn't pinpoint any one thing in particular.

Up until that point, P.G. had been unable to find a girl who could tolerate his hours-long conversations about anything. From the shocking statistics of every MLB player – dating back to the debatable first invention of baseball; to the full explanation of 1001 ways to use duct tape – P.G. was like a human encyclopedia. Many girls just did not have the depth to withstand it, nor the patience to listen without a chance to talk about their own needs in return.

Except someone like Blue, who was complacently natured. Yes, she would have been more content staying home most evenings with her kids and watching "Toy Story" than to rub elbows with all of the random business people P.G. knew. They were complete opposites, yet enjoyed one another simply for the companionship. It was nice to have someone to talk to and care about. Another plus was the extra business he got for Blue at OPW, just by talking about her store to everyone they came across.

One day as they were sitting on the couch together, P.G. was astonishingly quiet. Just as she was enjoying the moment of silence, he asked, "You know, I've often wondered why you work at a pet supply store if you don't even have a pet. That's what you gave me a hard time about that day when I stopped at your booth at the trade show. Remember? Doesn't that make you a hypocrite?"

"Well, I suppose. But I like animals, so it gives me a chance to be around them sometimes without having to own one. Besides, I was thinking about getting one someday," Blue added. "A dog would be nice to have when I get ready to do the *'family thing'*... down the road." She crooked her pointer and middle finger down as if to mimic P.G.'s imaginary quotes.

"Funny girl," he said. "You are pretty witty when you do talk, which isn't very often. I'd like to know more about you... but you're so closed up."

"That's not entirely true," Blue huffed. "Who can get a word in when all you do is babble on and on about nonsense?"

"Nonsense?" he repeated.

"I've never met anyone who could talk for hours about nothing at all!" she exclaimed.

"Well, if that's the way you feel, then why are you with me?" asked P.G.

"I don't know!" Blue said. "You're steady. You're faithful. You're fascinating sometimes and definitely a smart cookie. There's a lot I do admire."

"What a relief," P.G. said. "For a minute I thought I might have to add another use to the 1001 uses for duct tape and stick one over my mouth.

"Could you?" she laughed. But then Blue thought about P.G.'s question long and hard. *Why was she really with him, even though P.G. wasn't exactly a perfect fit for her?* She pondered. *Was it for the same reason she settled for everything else that came her way?* Her job that was good enough but not her dream job, and now a boyfriend who was good enough but not her dream guy.

She was a settler. Blue was content with good enough and finding something to be satisfied with, even if they wouldn't have been her top choices. Blue also felt stuck with whatever she was given in life, although she had grown to care for P.G. a great deal. After all, he was not so bad. There was nothing special or great about him, but there was also nothing wrong with him. That was good enough for now.

After these thought-provoking reflections, Blue went to work the next day with questions in her mind. She was up on a ladder working on the store's inventory when the skinny kid came back through the door. This time, he walked straight up to Blue with another nice bouquet. The roses were light orange colored, almost coral. The card read, "Please take a moment to go outside."

She did. There were enough associates on the floor and the store was dead. As Blue followed the kid outdoors, he led her just around the corner of the store. P.G. was standing by his car waiting for her, holding a puppy. Instead of talking this time or even saying one word, P.G. placed a piece of paper in the puppy's mouth just before Blue came around the bend. He nodded to her and waved his arm down to the dog's mouth, signaling to take the paper.

Still a little shocked, Blue removed the paper from the doggie's jaws, opening it at the crease. Inside it read, "My name is Coral. I'm looking for a nice family to adopt me. Do you know of one?" Blue smiled as the puppy wagged its tail. P.G. smiled, too.

Then she reached up and hugged P.G. "I just happen to know a great pet store where we can buy Coral's doggie food."

"Does that mean you will keep me?" P.G. asked. "I mean... her?" He pointed to the puppy.

"Well, before I say yes, I need to know if she barks a lot. I can only take so much yapping before it gets a little tiring." She hinted.

"She might bark sometimes, but all you have to do is get a few pieces of duct tape. Weren't you listening when I told you about its 1001 uses, or do I have to repeat all of them to you again?" P.G. kidded.

❖❖❖❖❖❖❖❖❖

# PROVISO

**There is nothing truly glamorous about Pinot** Grigio. It remains delicious in its own way, in spite of a rather unexciting entrance. Pinot Grigio can be dry, with calculated precision. Its characteristics bear naturally arid grapes that give the wine depth and enhanced wisdom. Pinot Gris simply desires to share his worldly insights with all who will listen.

On the bright side, this chatty type of wine makes a delightful companion for any woman who is lonely. If you order Pinot Grigio, you are not likely to be nodding off; rather trying to get away from many overly detail-oriented stories that go nowhere. Pinot Grigio offers a thorough description that can bore the pants off the average listener. Hey, and maybe that's his entire strategy with women. Quietly, some people wander away from Pinot Grigio right in the middle of a great conversation. Especially if they spot a "more exciting" wine from across the room. Some ladies find Pinot Grigio much too dull compared to sweeter white wines like Riesling or Zinfandel.

For more ambitious women, Pinot Grigio is only appreciated in lieu of less vibrant wines. It's often difficult to distinguish Pinot Gris or Grigio from others because he may be guised as a waiter or a writer; a guidance school counselor, a tennis player, an automobile detailer or even a brilliant archaeologist. Variations of Pinot Grigio are everywhere, just like a popular name like Michael, John or Ron. Its ready availability and presence make ordering Pinot Grigio an easy thing to do.

These natural-born storytellers are abundant and can be found most anywhere, but the true gems are those bottles of Pinot Grigio that have fully matured. The best ones have a youthful energy and lively acidity, balanced by a smooth complexity and refreshing aftertaste. By then, your Pinot Grigio may have also developed a keen sense of humor that is lively and charismatic.

Women who date Pinot Grigio should not expect to get a word in edgewise, however the prospect for an entertaining evening is promising.

# Red Burgundy

## "THE CELEBRITY"

***You will find Red Burgundy to be anything but*** *ordinary. It exudes high class and prestige from first sight, with its incredible taste, color, shape and flavor. The dream of any girl would be the accompaniment of Red Burgundy to someplace public, where the cool people hang. You will always have a blast with this wine, since it loves to be in the limelight.*

*Red Burgundy is recognizable and exclusive. Made with special grapes that are grown only in a specific region of France, as the name implies, there is only one place on the globe that makes this type of wine. Burgundy. Its distinctive rearing is culturally divine. If the wine could speak, Red Burgundy's sexy French accent would make women swoon.*

*You must know the three classifications of Red Burgundy to understand its complexity and diversity. The Grand Cru Red Burgundy is the rarest, coming from only a handful of the best vineyards on the Cote d'Or. Less than 2%*

*of those produced here ever make it to this caliber. Grand Cru should have a star on the Hollywood Walk of Fame.*

*The Premier Cru is the second type. These Red Burgundies are also highly recognizable. Even though they might not be quite as exclusive as Grand Cru, they are very expensive and revered. Less than 12% of the Red Burgundy produced will become Premier Cru. You could compare it to a superstar athlete or man of exceptional stature. Someone who has "made it."*

*Finally, the Village – also known as the Regional Red Burgundy – is a kind of celebrity widely sought after within its region. These make up approximately 35% of all Red Burgundy. Celebrities are everywhere, from the local recognizable hometown celebrities who deliver the evening news, to the rising celebrities who are just on the brink of discovery. People love to follow celebrities and keep up with what they are doing at all times. Celebrities are the source of great conversations, and Red Burgundy is destined to be the talk of the town.*

*Its flashy characteristics are what make Red Burgundy intriguing as a wine that people find curiously brilliant. It smells of wild berries such as raspberries, cherries or blackberries and denotes fresh fruit in both very young and well aged versions. The older wines also reflect notes of floral bliss, such as roses and violets. Young Red Burgundies have an aroma of fresh jam, figs or cut grass, such as those young starlets who develop into something magical.*

*If allowed to mature longer in the barrel, Red Burgundy can become spicy and charismatic. It takes center stage with such delicious notes of ginger, cinnamon, licorice, and coffee. How could one not want to drink more than one glass? Each of these star studded characteristics yield a very rich and complex wine that is mysteriously captivating.*

*Since it is crafted almost exclusively from the Pinot Noir grape, Red Burgundy has a very complicated list of characteristics. Its colors range from brick or purplish red to ruby, garnet, bright clay or cherry. The darker reds often reach their prime between five to nine years of aging. These vibrant shades and luscious smells have been known to attract a fan base of global magnitude, including the paparazzi. Even Premier Cru and Village Burgundies cannot avoid the whispers of the media and the attention of the ladies. Once discovered, these wines can cost a great deal to buy and their value keeps increasing as they mature and become even more dynamic.*

*Oh yes, Red Burgundy is met with great enthusiasm everywhere it goes. When faced with occasional criticism, Red Burgundy simply shrugs it off. It is confident, poised, exciting and flavorful. While it is true that many types of wine have their fanatical supporters, there are no other wines signing autographs like Red Burgundy. Only a wine with such awe-inspiring power can tantalize and mesmerize such a broad audience. However, only a handful of people will be fortunate to taste the figment of goodness in a bottle of Red Burgundy. Because many of the high priced versions are held in reserve, only true collectors can shell out the cash to buy this starlet. Therefore, Red Burgundy may be more of a special guest appearance wine for those who can afford this desirable commodity.*

*Red Burgundy has an ability to captivate. Roll out the red carpet for this gorgeous wine that displays an always tasteful and magnetic personality. Its cultural-savvy, gorgeous color and aroma, rare upbringing and inherent sex appeal make this a wine of celebrity caliber. From the Mom and Pop growers to the biggest Vineyards, the grape growing and winemaking standards of Red Burgundy go beyond anyone's expectations.*

❖❖❖❖❖❖❖❖❖

# RED ❣ Winter Sky

**As he stepped out of the limo, Red Burgundy was** blinded by the flashes of cameras that surrounded him. The paparazzi were waiting for his entrance and encircled him like bees flocking to a single flower in an apple orchard. Red's entrance was nothing shy of spectacular. The media were always curious to follow his every move and judge every detail of his life. From the buttons on his Armani sport coat, to the gorgeous blonde who gracefully adorned his arm, people scrutinized every quality of Red Burgundy.

He was confident, handsome and successful. Having six blockbuster movies under his belt and hundreds of TV appearances, magazine interviews and many more who were calling his agent, Red was booked solid. Although he loved the attention, Red appeared somewhat modest and down-to-earth in person. Whenever people ran up on him with a pen in hand to ask for an autograph, Red Burgundy simply brushed his wavy black hair back with his left hand and casually grabbed the writing utensil,. Red made women melt.

Quite honestly, Red Burgundy liked the attention most of the time. Having already been engaged four times and married twice, Red was always the recipient of hot gossip and curious questions whenever the microphone was placed in front of his face. It wasn't that he didn't enjoy having someone in his life, it just seemed like as he changed and became bigger and more famous, so too did his taste in women. Becoming older and more into his own, Red Burgundy was considering offspring. He had never wanted kids in his younger days because he was too busy making movies; creating a legacy for his name. By traveling all over the world, Red Burgundy had made it to the upper echelon of A-Listers as one of Hollywood's golden boys.

He paused on the red carpet with his date for the evening. Winter Sky was also very successful, although notoriously scandalous in her own way. "*Red Burgundy ... are you and Winter dating now?*" someone yelled from the media circus. The lights were too bright to see the face of the voice who yelled. Squinting, he looked out among the sea of cameras.

"We'll see what happens. I'll get back to you on that," he said, in a charming French accent. Winter smiled with her cute dimples and abnormally white teeth. Indeed, she was the envy of many women, both those right in front of her and the millions who were watching the awards ceremony.

Because Winter Sky was still a young star, she had not yet earned the same level of prestige as that of Red Burgundy. However, as many stars and starlets understood, it's not "what" you know, it's "who" you know in this business. Winter felt empowered by his presence, knowing it would lead to even more people talking about her and searching for her name on Google.

Winter Sky met Red Burgundy at a dinner engagement a few nights prior. Both of their agents were friends and invited Red, Winter and several other

Hollywood stars. As the table of eleven gathered merrily, Red gave Winter several winks throughout the dinner.

Red had casually walked up behind her as the Maitre de took Winter's sparkly gold sweater to hang it for her. "Would you like to go to the GeeGee Awards Friday? My date backed out at the last minute and I think it worked out for the best. You are a much better candidate," he flattered her.

"Ummm, sure," Winter said, melting into a putty of goo. The guy whose poster she had hung on her bedroom wall as a teenager just asked her out. She tried to resist the urge to jump up and down eagerly, as if she had just been called up on stage to sing with her favorite rock star out of a crowd of thousands of hungry fans.

Quickly, Winter reached into her Prada handbag for a pen. "Here's my number," she scrawled on a napkin.

Red called Winter later that same evening. "I just watched the movie you were in. Very impressive. I am lucky to have your presence for the award ceremony on Friday," he said.

*"Wow!"* she thought. *"Red Burgundy watched my movie! He really likes me!"*

"Well, thank you Red!" she blushed. Of course, Red could not see this through the phone.

"Listen, I don't want to keep you up too late. At least not this time," Red chuckled. "I'll text you tomorrow with the details about the awards ceremony. You can ride with me. I'll have my driver pick you up in the limo. Be ready by 5:30 p.m. sharp babes, okay?"

Winter didn't question his authoritative tone. Any girl would have jumped to be in her shoes, so she wasn't about to balk or play the role of difficult Diva. Playing it cool was what Winter needed to do, even though it was difficult to contain her excitement. She had stared longingly at his gorgeous face every morning on her wall and dreamed of seeing him in person one day. Now, Winter's dream was about to come true.

Here she was. Winter had a surprising break, by sheer luck. She had tried out for a local TV program that had taken off and become national. Then she started getting other offers based on her performance and likeability by the audience. Now in her young 20s, Winter was finally getting a lot of name recognition.

Winter would have been lying if the thought hadn't crossed her mind that going out with Red Burgundy might even help her career. He was so famous and adored by everyone. He was always surrounded. Everyone wanted to sit by him, talk to him, take his picture or even touch his sleeve. And here she was... Red Burgundy's date for one of Hollywood's biggest galas!

The next day, Winter called her bestie. Gray had stood by her throughout Winter's rising career benchmarks. "Guess who asked me to the GeeGee Awards?" said Winter.

"WHO? WHO?" exclaimed Gray.

Winter sighed, "Red Burgundy."

"Red Burgundy, the famous actor?" Gray asked, surprised.

"Why, yes. The man himself," she said.

"Well, this calls for a shopping excursion," replied Gray. "I'll be there in an hour."

The two spent the entire day on Rodeo Drive, trying on glamorous dresses and accessories that were overpriced, yet oh-so-sensational! Finally, Winter Sky found just the perfect dress to wear for the red carpet. A sizzling red Valentino; with ample boob lifters and revealing cleavage.

"You know this is going to look hot in *People Weekly Magazine*!" said Winter.

"You know it girl," Gray agreed. Then they spent the rest of the afternoon picking out accessories and shoes and sipping lattes at the *Perky Persimmons Cappuccino Shoppe*.

On the Friday of the awards gala, Winter Sky spent the entire day at the salon. A makeup artist and hair designer worked their talented hands on her until she looked stunning and magical. By the time the limo came to pick Winter up, she looked perfect. Red Burgundy noticed.

"You look ravishing in red," he said, upon sight of his sexy date. "Please, come sit. I have a glass of my favorite red wine waiting. It's a burgundy, specially imported from France."

"How nice," Winter smiled. The limousine was amazing; with high-end Italian leather seats and built-in luxury surround sound, lighting and a dance floor with a pole in the center. "What's that for?" Winter asked Red, pointing at the pole.

With a big grin, Red said, "Oh, that's just something to hold onto if the ride gets a little too... bumpy." He winked.

By the time they rolled up to the red carpet, Winter was thoroughly buzzed. The wine was intoxicating in every rich sip, just like Red Burgundy's cologne. Winter's head felt giddy and surreal. She felt like the luckiest girl in the world.

The awards ceremony went well. Red was nominated for three awards, one of which he won. He was also elected as a host to introduce one of the female award recipients. After all of the hoopla and whispers of whether Winter was now Red Burgundy's girlfriend, she wondered what would transpire.

"Would you like to go to an 'after party' with me?" Red asked Winter when the awards ceremony ended.

"Sure, that would be fun," she batted her long eyelashes. They couldn't talk much that evening because of all the cameras in their faces. Winter was still somewhat of a newbie to the paparazzi, although Red was fairly annoyed and flamboyant at the same time.

The next day, on her morning walk with her poodle Fee-Fee, Winter spotted the magazine rack. The gossip newspapers and magazines had her photograph splashed across the cover, wearing her sexy red dress and looking beautiful next to Red Burgundy. The titles ranged from "*Who is Red Burgundy's Mystery Woman?*" to "*Will Red Finally Settle or is This the Next Big Fling?*"

Winter Sky rolled her eyes. *Great. They think I'm just a fling*, she thought. *We'll see about that.* She commenced texting.

"Had fun with you last night. Thank you for the invitation," she wrote to Red.

The day went by with no response from Red Burgundy. Winter was paralyzed with anxiety. *Did he get my message? Does he like me? Did he have fun? Am I trying too hard?* After all, Red Burgundy was known to be a playboy and not a guy who could be taken seriously in matters of the heart. His reputation of being a 'Love 'em and Leave 'em' type of guy eroded her thoughts. Winter Sky was young; therefore, still a bit immature and underdeveloped. One day, she hoped to become a famous Hollywood star with many great movies and performances on her resume.

Finally at the end of the day, Red Burgundy responded with a text. His messages and conversations were always straightforward.

"Would like to take you out again. I have Wednesday free next week. In production until then." It was brief. Nevertheless, it was enough to keep Winter's hopes alive that he was definitely interested.

But on the very day that Winter was to go out with Red Burgundy again, she took Fee-Fee on their morning walk. It was their ritual. Upon passing the magazine stand, Winter spotted a bunch of magazines with Red Burgundy's picture plastered all over them. He was at yesterday's Lakers game, sitting in the first row amongst some other well-known Hollywood celebrities. Sitting next to him was a well-known model, a brunette to whom Red had been engaged years prior. The headlines read, "*Red Burgundy. Back Together With His EX? Or Just Friends?*" and, "*Game On! Red Burgundy Spotted Swooning Ex.*"

Suddenly, Winter wanted to vomit. Speculation swirled around in her head like an overcooked cinnamon roll. Red Burgundy was a celebrity. What did she think would happen? *He's just going to break my heart, anyway.*

Winter picked up the magazine and looked at the pictures. She was tempted to text Red, but instead she called her friend Gray.

"Should I go out with him tonight, still?" Winter asked, after describing the headlines and the situation. "Will Red just make me look like a fool?"

"He is Red Burgundy. Just don't fall for him," Gray recommended. "Date him for a while; it could help your career. Who cares what he does? It will only make him like you more. You can't be too available."

So Winter did go out with Red again, and of course the next day she appeared on the covers of tabloids. "*Sugar or Spice – Is Red Burgundy Dating TWO Hollywood Beauties?*" It seemed that everybody wanted to know who

Winter Sky was and whether she was dating Red Burgundy. Suddenly, the production companies began taking notice of her, too. Calls started flooding Winter's agent.

The beginning of the whirlwind romance began, as well as the offers pouring in for new appearances and film offers. The more she went out with Red Burgundy, the more people became interested in Winter Sky. She began falling for him. He liked her, too. Since he was 15 years older, the tabloids certainly had a heyday with the story lines for their relationship.

Secretly, Winter never planned on becoming so attached to this man. Celebrities were notorious for failed marriages and relationships, in part because of the stress caused by tabloids, gossip magazines, and the paparazzi. It seemed that no one in Hollywood was immune from the constant shine of the spotlight, highlighting everything from the style of sweatpants worn to the supermarket or the other intricacies of their not-so-personal existence.

Life with Red Burgundy was no exception. As Winter's relationship with him progressed, Red stopped courting other women, including his ex. His loyalty and adorable French accent were irresistible qualities. Not only did he look good, he was genuinely a good person, often supporting humanitarian causes and showing up at schools to speak to kids about the importance of education.

"He is too good to be true," Winter beamed when she talked about their relationship to her parents. They too, had seen their daughter's picture on the covers of magazines and across the web.

"Well in my experience, anything that seems too good to be true usually is," warned Winter's father. Mr. Sky was a practical guy and guarded. He was not one to appreciate the tabloid stories about his little princess.

"I think what your father is saying," interrupted Winter's mother, "...is just to be careful. Hollywood is a different scene than you were raised in. Mr. Burgundy is fifteen years older than you are. That's quite a gap."

Winter rolled her eyes, only half listening to their hesitations.

After getting hot and heavy for the better part of a year, Red Burgundy asked Winter to marry him. The gossip magazines had a field day. Everybody wanted to know, "Who was this up-and-coming girl, "Winter Sky" who had stolen the heart of America's most sought-after bachelor?" She transitioned from a rising star to a superstar.

However, Winter's fame didn't come without the price of sacrificing her personal life. The paparazzi now stalked her. At the gym, at her studio, at the supermarket, or even on her morning walks with Fee-Fee, Winter Sky's picture was plastered across America. She got offers from prestigious media stations like E! and MTV. This caused Winter some anxiety, especially when she felt the pressure to stay thin and beautiful.

Meanwhile, after Red Burgundy made his spontaneous proposal to Winter, he became more withdrawn. He liked the "chase" but never liked the "catch." Hence, why he had been married four times. He second-guessed his decision to marry Winter. Maybe she was too young after all. Sensing Red's withdrawal, Winter tried harder to please him, yet it only caused him to step further away. He started working more and spending more time at his flat in Malibu, which Red kept even though he and Winter had moved in together.

Instead of just being honest with Winter, Red Burgundy did what many celebrities do when they no longer wish to be with the person they are with. He cheated.

Having Pinot Noir in his bloodline, Red was prone to be devious.

Winter Sky showed up at Red Burgundy's trailer one day on the set of the action movie he was working on. It was due for release by the following summer. Ironically, it was scheduled to hit theaters around the same time as Red's wedding to Winter.

At any rate, Winter's plan was to surprise Red with lunch, along with maybe "a quickie" for dessert. Then she hoped he would give her a quick tour of the set. As soon as Winter put one foot on the steps of Red's superstar camper, a voice said, "I wouldn't go in there right now." It was one of the makeup artists who was sitting under a nearby tree, sipping a Diet Coke. Her head was buried in her Kindle Fire. "Red has company."

"Uh, do you know who I am?" replied Winter.

"Yeah, I do," said the makeup artist, unimpressed. "You're his fiancée. But I'm telling you for your own good; just don't go in there right now."

"When you say, 'company' do you mean he is meeting with the producer or the director and they are practicing their lines or something?" Winter asked, half hoping it was true.

"No, I mean it's probably not a good idea for your own good to see what you might see if you step foot in there," the makeup artist replied.

So of course, Winter opened the door to find Red Burgundy in a rather precarious position on the sofa with his co-actress, right in plain sight. The expression on his face was priceless. Both Red and the well-known famous actress who was sitting on his lap – unclothed – looked at each other and at Winter. Embarrassed and furious, Winter turned back and left the trailer crying.

"I told you not to go in there!" yelled the makeup artist, as she slurped her fizzy beverage.

After a good night of bawling her eyes out and talking for two hours with Gray on the phone, Winter slept. She got up the next morning with Fee-Fee and walked by the dreaded magazine stand. The headlines flashed in front of Winter just as brightly as a red stoplight. They were "red" from the very beginning of their relationship. "*Fling with Co-Star! Red Burgundy Cheats.*" And "*Naughty Burgundy Caught Red Handed!*"

Winter Sky then realized that nothing had changed, except her hope that somehow their love affair would have a fairy tale ending. She was young and naïve to think that "Happily Ever After" can actually happen in celebrity relationships. Yet that's how it had always been portrayed in movies. Fall in love, get married, and live happily ever after.

As she stared at the magazines, it was at that moment Winter realized that Hollywood was mainly a place of fictional stories and roller coasters.

"C'mon Fee-Fee. Let's blow this place!" Winter told her poodle.

❖❖❖❖❖❖❖❖❖

# PROVISO

**Living in a world of instant gratification, Red** Burgundy is versatile. Young Red Burgundy may be arrogant until it matures. Then it truly becomes considered fine wine, which takes less time to achieve with Red Burgundy than with other types of wines. Quite honestly, it can be enjoyed right from the barrel and will still be delicious.

Red Burgundy loves the passion of a new relationship. In the beginning, the adrenaline kicks in but then subsides after a few months together. Just remember this is Hollywood where the expectations for career success outweigh the propensity for success in love relationships.

In its peak, Red Burgundy is rich and robust. Many other red wines wish they could be in the same class as Red Burgundy, with its rich effervescence and ability to attract a global audience. The demand is high, while supply little. The best Red Burgundy is never cheap. Beware of poorly made imposters.

By all means, get your hands on this exquisite wine. In looks, taste, charm, smoothness and spirits, this nostalgic red has a brilliance that can be appreciated by a worldwide audience. Keep in mind that Red Burgundy is a rare wine that can exit out of the picture just as unexpectedly as he arrived, leaving you yearning for its next appearance.

# Moscato

## "THE GAY GUY"

***The fruit forward and perfume-laden freshness of*** *Moscato will have you skipping through fields of melons, citrus blossoms and peach trees. Along the way, your buzz to cheerful goodness will be guided by sparkling rainbows and soft candy. But beware of its crisp bite. This fruity delight has a hint of sassiness, with spicy undertones that blend naturally into every bottle.*

*Not to be mistaken, Moscato is a fun, sophisticated wine that is rarely complex. Confectionary sweetness dominates the palate with every sip. Moscato ripens late, becoming evenly balanced with a light, fruity character and sun-kissed pastels of pink, pale yellow or straw. Its effervescent elegance is reinforced by generous streams of bubbles that seemingly never end. How delightful on a hot day, with a bowl of strawberries and a can of whipped cream!*

*You may find yourself giggling as the fun bubbles make their way to the top of the glass. Sparkles range from naturally bubbly to fizzy. The carbonation is captured during the process of fermentation and stays tightly sealed until you pop the cork off this cheerful contender. Moscato's spritzy character and lower alcohol content often appeal to newbie wine drinkers or those who just want a quickie glass while on a picnic at the beach.*

*If you didn't know it was Moscato, you may not be able to detect this sweet wine right away because of its many variations. Compared to other straight whites, Moscato comes in hundreds of different shades, colors and tastes, making it challenging to discern the real thing. Even Moscato itself is confused, having many different names that fall under the umbrella of Moscato. Muscat, Muscadel, Muscatel, Moscatel, Moskately, Moscatel, Moscarello, Moschetta, Moschini, Muscas, Moscon and many, many more. In fact, there may be as many as 200 different names under the Muscat family tree. Every single one is unfettered, mind you. Even those within the same family are spread out in many different directions. Red, blush, white and other sparkling wine variables can all be found under the name of Moscato. No wonder this wine is so confused ... and confusing!*

*Not many main course food selections complement Moscato. It is more of a standalone wine or dessert wine, perfect with summer fruit rolled in sugar or dark chocolate. Medium to sweet desserts can be enjoyed with Moscato, as long as they are not too strong, or intense. Nutty or berry-laden salads, pies or lemon-poppy breads and angel food cake are downright delicious with Moscato. Beyond that list, Moscato's categorically thin-skinned grape sucks the flavor out of other food pairings.*

*Now popular throughout the world, Moscato's ubiquity has risen as a fun and festive wine to sip with friends from all circles. It's difficult to trace Moscato's origin; although, many believe it to be Mediterranean in descent. Growers have found the grapes to fare better in rich soils, avoiding terrain that is too sandy, dry, or too shallow.*

*Even if Moscato is not the type of wine for you, there's no harm in tasting this vibrant and grapey party-goer. You may find it to be a refreshing alternative to the finicky dispositions of other well-known choices. Certainly Moscato's lingering finish and fragrant foreplay will bedazzle those who are clueless about its wild side. It's best to serve and drink chilled Moscato at its peak of ripeness when the grapes are young. When the bud first breaks, that's when the flavor reaches its fullest place of enjoyment. As it ages, the supple grapes of Moscato become like raisins, deemed by some wine drinkers to be less preferable.*

*Moscato gives new meaning to the eat, drink and be merry adage. Whether you agree with it or not, Moscato will undoubtedly have you frolicking with anticipation of the next cheerful glass.*

❖❖❖❖❖❖❖❖❖

# MOSCATO ❣ Copper

**As Copper came into the office one Monday** morning, there was a new guy sitting at the desk across the hall from her. The desk had been vacant ever since the troublemaker of the organization had been fired for stealing petty office supplies. It was more or less an excuse to let her go, since everybody else at the company despised her. She was always gossiping and crossing the line with her anger issues. Nevertheless, the car dealership had not been able to find an adequate replacement for many weeks. Until now.

Copper always shuffled into work carrying an oversized, yet colorful Prada bag on her left elbow and a Starbucks latte in her right hand. They were two things she couldn't start the day without. The bag harbored all of her "must-haves" and "just in cases," so that she could be ready for anything.

For example, she knew she "must have" her L'Oreal Majestic Mauve lipstick and her wallet and debit card. However, the extra things, such as a spare pair of pantyhose, miniature emergency sewing kit and corkscrew were in there too, "just in case." The bag weighed a lot because of all the stuff she carried, including gobs of store receipts that had accumulated. It was basically an attractive garbage bag.

As she settled into her office, Copper snuck a peek at the new guy out of the corner of her eye. The manager was talking to him, most likely showing him the ropes. He always liked to act like a big shot whenever new people started, but after the newness wore off, most everybody knew that he didn't really do all that much except saunter around the showroom all day, pretending to be busy. *What a card*, she thought.

Meanwhile, she was happy to see that the new guy was easy on the eyes. Okay, he was downright HOT. Copper was pleased not only that she didn't have to sit across from that annoying girl anymore, but that she now had a legitimate Hottie as her new work partner. Crunching numbers in the finance department was quite boring sometimes, unless she got some great customers to work with. These days, not many people had good credit, which made her job more difficult than it had been in years prior.

Another thought shot through her mind, almost at the same time. *Uh oh. Now I'm going to have to spend more time getting ready in the morning so that I can look cute and irresistible.* Copper wondered if he was married. From her vantage point, he was not wearing a wedding band. These days, that didn't mean anything, though.

She dug through the Prada garbage pit, wading through the stacks of receipts. Copper knew she had a compact mirror somewhere. Her lipstick was always readily available in the sneaky side pocket that zipped on the inside. After freshening up her lipstick and snapping a couple of Tic-Tacs to the back of her tongue, she walked up to Mr. Cutie's door, trying to appear nonchalant.

"Knock, knock!" she said, pretending to rap her fist on the imaginary space where a door would have been, if the company had not been so cheap.

"Why, hello there!" answered Mr. Attractive. He was so pretty and polished. His jaw line was every photographer's dream. His hair was perfectly layered and clipped in the back, with two dashing sideburns that lined his face perfectly. His blue eyes were mesmerizing. She probably looked like a fool, just standing there staring for what seemed like minutes, which was more like seconds.

Shaking out of a daydream, Copper pointed across the hall and said, "OH, I just wanted to introduce myself. I work just across from you, so if there's anything you need, just holler. Okay?"

"That's nice of you," he smiled. As he did, his bright white teeth gleamed in the fluorescent lights. "I'm Moscato." He stretched out his hand.

After wiping her sweaty palm on the side of her skirt, she shook his hand. "Great to meet you. I'll be just over there." She pointed at her desk, knowing that she looked foolish, since he had probably already seen her sitting at her desk. He just smiled and nodded in acknowledgement.

Lunch came and just like a giddy girl when the school bell rings, Copper bolted down to the break room. There were four other women who shared lunch at the same time, so every day they met up at the small table in the back. Sometimes they would gather there and carpool to a nearby Mexican restaurant they all liked, but other days they stayed in. It all depended on their workloads. Spring and fall were the busiest season at the dealership, but holiday sales also brought in more customers. Until she worked at a car dealership, she never realized just how important Presidents Day and Labor Day and Columbus Day really were.

At any rate, Copper met up with the ladies in the lunch room. Immediately, she initiated a conversation. "Did you guys see the new guy they hired in finance?" she beamed.

"No way!" another lady exaggerated. "Who is he?"

"He's you-know-who's replacement," Copper said, rolling her eyes. "And let me tell you, ladies. It's a step up!"

"Thank gawd," said another co-worker. "Is he married?"

"You ladies are so bad. You know the company frowns on employees dating," said one of the married women.

"So what? We don't even know if he's married yet!" piped in a third girl.

"Easy for you to say, you old married hag!" Copper said, laughing and kidding with her friend. She knew the married ladies had a sense of humor and liked living vicariously through the two single girls of the group.

"I'll ask Pinot Grigio in the customer service. He talks to everybody. Maybe he knows the scoop." The fourth woman offered.

"I call dibbs! That is... assuming he's not married," Copper added.

For a week thereafter, everyone was curious about Moscato. He seemed really, really nice. He was very funny and witty, as well as exceptionally bright. He had a bubbly personality and dressed nice. Moscato wore nice cologne, sexy ties and crisply pressed shirts. He was well-manicured and took pride in his appearance.

Unfortunately, no one knew that much about him. They knew he was punctual and a sharp dresser. Even Pinot Grigio didn't know anything. Moscato wasn't a corporate referral from another employee; he was just someone who had either been recruited or who had applied for the position on his own.

Determined to get to know him better, Copper struck up conversations with him whenever there was a lull. Sometimes she had ten customers in one day, whereas other days there were only two. Car shoppers were not consistent; although, there were certainly buying patterns.

After making idle chit chat for a couple of weeks, Copper finally got the nerve to ask Moscato the burning question of the year. "So, Moscato... what's your story? Are you married? Have a family? Couple of kids, maybe?"

"Nope. None of the above. I guess I just haven't met the right one. What about you?" Moscato asked, politely returning the gesture.

"Me neither," she said.

"That's surprising," Moscato said. "You're a pretty girl."

Copper just about fainted as her knees suddenly gave out from underneath her. "You are so sweet! Thanks. I could say the same about you. Well, except for the girl part. Clearly...." She said, as her cheeks turned as pink as a Mary Kay Cadillac.

After the ice had been broken, Copper said, "Say, a bunch of us are going to El Cha Cha's for lunch. They have some great quesadillas and tiramisu. Do you want to join us?"

"Oh, I don't know..." Moscato replied, hesitantly. "I have to watch my girlish figure, you see?" He patted his perfect six-pack through his shirt.

She laughed. "You're so funny! C'mon, it'll be fun. You can skip the tiramisu then and just get a taco salad."

"Alright, you twisted my arm." As he smiled, Moscato's cute dimple protruded on the left side of his laugh line.

Copper rounded up her lunch buddies and brought Moscato along. All through lunch, Moscato had the whole table full of girls laughing uncontrollably. The married women had tears rolling down their cheeks. "You have to stop!" cried one of them. "I'm seriously going to pee myself from laughing so hard!"

Indeed, Moscato was dreamy and charming. He was charismatic and animated when he told stories and jokes. As they all went back to the dealership, some of the other men in the sales department watched jealously as Moscato had all of the ladies swooning over him. They all looked like they had just had the time of their life.

"Who's this guy think he is?" muttered one.

"Yeah, how come they never invite us to their little Mexican rendezvous?" whispered another.

Meanwhile, Copper looked better than ever. She started going back to the gym faithfully every day after work and went tanning three times a week. She knew that in order to attract a classy type of guy like Moscato, she had to step it up a notch.

She had a hunch that he liked her, too. He was quite flirtatious some days, especially when there was nothing to do or when there were no customers to wait on. Moscato and Copper often threw paper airplanes with notes on them across the hall to each other. Occasionally they even hung out after hours; although, she thought it was strange he never made a move on her romantically. *Maybe he already has a girlfriend*, she wondered. So, Copper continued perfecting her appearance.

Moscato became one of her great friends. Deep down, she thought it might be better that way than to just jump into a physical relationship. She liked the "getting-to-know-you" approach. They went shopping sometimes and Moscato often joined her at the gym. It seemed that a lot of people knew him there. A lot of good-looking guys, too. Copper loved having Moscato as a bestie, but she wanted more.

She began thinking of a way she could tell Moscato how she really felt about him, without offending him or shying him away from her friendship. In her mind, the reason why he had not tried anything romantically was because of their work connection. It was not entirely against company policy to date co-workers, but some of the employees frowned upon it just for simple legality issues. The last thing anyone wanted was a sexual harassment suit; although by now, she didn't think Moscato would be worried about her stance on that topic.

One day a paper airplane came gliding into her office. Her head was bent down, looking at a customer's credit report. Copper was shaking her head. The numbers didn't look good. When she saw the paper airplane, she looked up. Moscato was sitting at his desk across the hall, smiling.

As she opened the paper airplane to reveal the message, Copper was slightly tickled to see what it said. "Go to the holiday dinner party with me this Saturday?"

Trying to appear unfazed, she looked up with a sexy grin and flipped her beautiful strawberry blonde hair over her shoulder. Copper nodded and lipped, "What time?" as if she was sending a message across a mountain.

Moscato said, "I'll pick you up at 7:30."

With only four days before the party, she set out to prepare that very evening. She skipped the gym and went to Macy's instead, trying on at least six dresses before deciding on a very sexy red cocktail dress with a satin finish. It was short and even a hint of slutty, yet with great taste. "*Perfect!*" Copper decided, looking in the mirror. The time at the gym really paid off. She had dropped an entire dress size since Moscato first started working at the dealership. She already had a sparkly pair of gold shoes and a pair of dangly gold earrings that would be perfect accessories. Satisfied, Copper left the mall feeling good.

When she arrived in the lunchroom the next day to meet her co-workers, she couldn't wait to tell them the news. "Guess what, ladies? Moscato finally asked me out!"

They all knew she had a crush on him. “Really?” they asked. “That’s great!”

“Yes, but don’t mention it to anyone just yet. I don’t want to appear too eager,” Copper added, with a wink. “You guys are all going, right?”

Most of them nodded, except one. “I can’t. I don’t have a babysitter,” said the one who couldn’t go.

“I know a girl in my neighborhood, do you want me to ask her if she can babysit for you?” asked another.

While the two arranged it, the rest of the ladies clucked like hens, talking about their outfits and their husbands and what to wear and what time to go. Everyone was excited for the holiday hubbub.

As Saturday rolled around, Copper spent the entire day getting ready. She went and got a manicure and pedicure in the morning, followed by a visit to the tanning salon and then to have her roots touched up and hair done in the afternoon. It was a day of pampering.

Moscato knocked on her door at 7:30. He looked so handsome in a silver and rust colored sport suit. Very “GQ-ish”; complete with a paisley vest and vintage Bogart Fedora. For a second, Copper was breathless.

“Hi sweetie, don’t you look lovely?” he praised her. “Are you ready to PAR-TAY?”

She was.

As they arrived, Copper was pleased by the turnout. The party included staff members from all of the company’s dealerships from the entire region, of which there were five. It gave the employees a chance to meet people they often talked to on the phone, such as when a customer was referred to them by a salesperson or manager from another lot. Many brought spouses or dates, too. The entire convention hall was filled with about 1,500 staffers. Not a bad turnout, indeed.

"Do you want me to get you a drink?" Moscato asked Copper, after they had chosen a table next to their friends from work. The husbands were engrossed in conversation and the ladies were looking around, pointing at people they knew.

"Sure, I'll have a glass of wine," she replied.

"What's your favorite?" asked Moscato.

"Oh, anything sweet. How about a nice, bubbly white? Surprise me!" she said, enthusiastically. Copper knew there was something there between them. She knew the chemistry was boiling. At least on her part, it was.

After a few glasses of wine and some dancing, she knew it was time to give Moscato the green light and to let him know that the feelings brewing between them were mutual. She figured that the reason he hadn't already done so was because he was still fairly new at work and perhaps he didn't want to overstep any boundaries or make anyone feel uncomfortable.

"Hey, do you want to go outside and get some fresh air?" Copper asked Moscato, after a rigorous half hour of dancing. Moscato had great moves. He had taken dancing lessons somewhere along the way. He knew how to swing her around perfectly, as if he was a natural-born leader on the dance floor. Moscato could dip her so low that Copper's hair touched the ground and many of the other guests on the dance floor crowded around, watching them. She knew they were envious, especially the men who only wished they could dance so well. Their wives stared, too, wishing that their husbands could swing them around like that.

"Yeah, I think we need a quick breather," Moscato cheerfully agreed. "Let me grab us a couple more glasses of wine."

"I'll meet you out on the patio. I'm soooo hot," she exaggerated, fanning her face with a leftover menu from dinner.

As Copper waited for him outside, she spotted Moscato at the bar talking to a fellow she knew at another dealership. Moscato wrote something down on a napkin and handed it to the guy before grabbing the two glasses and paying the bartender. She thought nothing of it, wondering how they knew each other.

Moscato came outside and delivered her another fresh glass of bubbly white wine. It was sweet and delicious. She licked her lips. "Thank you," Copper said politely. They stared over the city skyline as the full moon shone brightly overhead. "The fresh air sure does feel nice, doesn't it?"

"Yeah, this view is amazing," Moscato agreed.

As the buzz from four glasses of white wine came over her, she suddenly felt a surge of confidence. "You have something right there..." she said, pointing at his lips. Then she reached in and gently brushed her lips against his.

Moscato stepped back, not reciprocating the kiss.

"I'm... I'm sorry...." Copper stammered. "I thought...."

"It's alright." Moscato stood squarely, staring into her eyes. "You're a beautiful girl. It's just..."

"If you're worried about us being coworkers and this affecting our relationship at work, don't be!" she interrupted.

"No, it's not that." Moscato looked uncomfortable. "I mean... I don't know how to tell you this... I didn't realize you liked me that way."

"What is it, then? Do you have a girlfriend already? I'm so sorry, then," Copper apologized.

"Listen, I don't like to discuss these things at work but you've become a really, really good friend of mine and I hope that doesn't change," Moscato explained. "But you should know that I go the other way." His cheeks turned rosy in the moonlight.

She still didn't get it. She looked puzzled.

Moscato blurted it out, "I'm gay!"

"OH!! Of course!" she half-laughed in embarrassment of the rejection and for blatantly throwing herself at him. "I didn't realize it," Copper said, disappointed.

"I really like you, and if I was a straight man, I'd be all over that." Moscato tried to make light of it. "You're gorgeous. Any man would be lucky to have a sweet and sexy girl like you."

"Um, thanks," she said, feeling like an idiot.

"I hope we can still hang out? I really enjoy your company. It would be a shame to let this silly thing come between us." Moscato told her.

"Yes, of course. Consider it forgotten already." She smiled, wishing she could crawl in a hole somewhere in the ground and bury her head like an ostrich.

Somehow, Copper didn't feel any better. Instead, she felt like a fool. How could she have not realized that Moscato was gay? He didn't act gay; although, he was a lot more polished, manicured and put-together than most men she knew. In hindsight, the clues were there all along. The men who knew Moscato at the gym... the occasional comments about a good-looking guy as they shopped... the way Moscato dressed and the not-so-obvious mannerisms.

"*That figures*," Copper thought out loud as she lay in her bed that night, thinking about what a dummy she was.

*All of the good ones are either married or gay. How could I have been so clueless?*

*At least I got in shape again*, she mused.

❖❖❖❖❖❖❖❖❖

# PROVISO

**Let's set the record "straight." If you're among the** millions who love Moscato, it does not mean you are gay. It means you love a wine that is sweet, bubbly and aromatic! Admittedly more of a chick drink, Moscato is a wine that is rising in popularity, in part because of a few recent rappers who have mentioned it in their songs. And none of these rappers are gay (that anyone knows of). They simply like Moscato!

It's amazing how a simple gesture can influence sales. If that's the case, buy Moscato if you enjoy a refreshing summer wine that will quench your thirst. There are many great varieties of Moscato worth trying and most are quite delicious.

And who doesn't *LOVE, LOVE, LOVE* having Moscato as a bestie? Moscato is fun to be with and will help you with your wardrobe, shopping, and visits to the salon. Moscato will give you advice on which pair of shoes to wear with which dress and will make a great date for any party. He can also help you decorate your home and give you a shoulder to cry on whenever Pinot Noir or Chianti breaks your heart.

# Chianti

## "THE PLAYER"

***Invariably, you will find diverse opinions about*** *Chianti. Its ever-changing complexity is one that makes it one of the most popular red wines of the world. Not only is it beautiful to look at, but the taste of a nice glass of Chianti is irresistible. It beckons to be chosen among the many other great wines, and this strong and bold red will do whatever it takes to become the prize of your eyes.*

*As a wine, Chianti is still evolving, perhaps faster than any other type. The grapes are finicky and free-spirited, often never the same from one brand to the next. There are a number of variables, from the season in which the grapes are grown to the weather during their development and cultivation. Even the way they are handled during harvest.*

*A lovely characteristic of bright red Chianti is that you can enjoy it most in its youthful years, as well as later once it eventually matures. Some never do, but Chianti does age well compared to many other wines. It depends on how dignified and cunning it is crafted. How ironic that Chianti's current marketing efforts feature a symbol of a Black Rooster. When this cock crows, you best take notice! Building brand recognition is something Chianti strives for, and it rarely misses its mark. In fact, once you become familiar with its distinguishing (and exciting) characteristics, you may be able to spot a luscious glass of Chianti from across a room.*

*It is a pretty wine, named for the region in Italy that is one of the most pleasing and picturesque landscapes of the world. The grapes of Chianti span the countryside of Florence to Umbria, North to South and Livorno to Pisa, East to West. These vibrant vineyards evoke warm moods among the wine tourists, leaving them with a desire to live life to its fullest. The sun, food and wine of these lands can entice even the most level-headed individuals to be seduced with their magnificence.*

*Chianti is versatile and confident. It can be as romantic as a checkerboard tablecloth under a picnic basket in a field of daisies, but it can also be as bold as a lion on the prairies of Nairobi. Each bottle is made up of at least 80% Sangiovese. A good bottle of Chianti will charm you with its spicy aromas and salacious tastes of strawberries, black cherries, cranberry, raspberry, and plums. It's not jammy, but definitely sensational. Even scandalously enjoyable.*

*There's no denying that Chianti is bright, in two ways. Bright as in attractive, with all of its 'berry delicious' colors that resemble fun discos and sexy clothes. It is also bright in its ability to bedazzle, with often cunning attempts of aspiration. Chianti is a crowd pleaser and lady teaser. You can find good bottles that are either expensive or cheap. In general, Chianti is easygoing, fun and casual by nature.*

*Chianti also hides well as a blend within other wines. You may be surprised how well it mixes with Merlot (the Nice Guy) or Cabernet Sauvignon (Mr. Right). However, most women would cheer for the Chianti that is less tamed. Nevertheless, Chianti is much loved, whether it is loved for one night, or many. Its love may be short lived by those with high of expectations that Chianti will mature within a reasonable time frame. However, those who enjoy this sassy red will undoubtedly be smitten, albeit briefly... until the next glass.*

❖❖❖❖❖❖❖❖❖

# CHIANTI ❣ Mauve

**Chianti had more women hanging on the line than a** fishing pole. He was an evident player from the very first glance, but only to trained eyes.

In hindsight, Mauve mused about all of the red flags she had seen in Chianti the whole time they were dating. Mauve refused to acknowledge them because Chianti was just so dreamy, polite and flattering to her. He seemed like the perfect guy.

Right from the very beginning of their liaison, Chianti was a status symbol as the most eligible – and most handsome – doctor at the biggest hospital in Dixon County. All of the female nurses, X-ray techs and lab assistants at the hospital were in love with him. They gossiped about Chianti in the hospital cafeteria. Every one of them had a secret crush on him, even some women who were married. The fact that

Chianti was intelligent and also held a powerful position as a head physician only enhanced his magnetism.

Chianti played it cool, always pretending to be modest. He had a magic spell on women. It was a combination of his complex personality, winning sense of humor and strength. His eyes were like mesmerizing cobalt pools that stared through you. They gazed from behind long eyelashes and a pronounced jaw line. He was tall with a dark complexion, which made him seem mysterious. Chianti's clean cut hairstyle with a tightly trimmed fade implied a man who was not too busy to spend time caring about his appearance. With a brilliant white smile to match his white lab coat, Chianti fit the role of many women's fantasies of marrying a rich, handsome doctor. He knew this, and loved the attention. Chianti flashed that gleaming smile or wink at nearly every girl he passed in the hall or talked to throughout the day.

Mauve was also beautiful and worked at the hospital as an X-Ray tech. She was the best at what she did and was the one who trained all the newcomers. Mauve was extremely gifted and adored by both her patients and the other staffers. Not just because of her naturally nurturing personality, but because of her sense of humor and thoughtfulness. She was very pretty, with shoulder length blonde hair, fair skin and bright brown eyes.

Within Mauve's position in the hospital's busy ER, there were many occasions to flirt with Chianti. Being fairly new to the hospital, Mauve wasn't familiar with Chianti's reputation as a ladies' man. She started there with the intent of being a traveling tech; however, the nice offer she got to sign a two year contract was simply too good to refuse, hence Mauve decided to make her roots within the city.

They met up for lunch one day in the cafeteria. Mauve was eating, taking a quick break before the stress of the afternoon. "Is this seat taken?" said Chianti, as Mauve looked up to see the tall and handsome doctor talking to her.

"Ummm, no. Go ahead." She replied.

"Are you sure?" he asked again. "I don't want to interrupt your alone time."

"It's no problem," she smiled.

"I noticed you in the ER today. You're a go-getter. Thanks for your help with that motorcycle accident," said the handsome doctor.

"Oh, thank you," she replied. "Just doing my job."

"Say, you wouldn't want to go out with me later. If you're not tied up already?" A cute laugh dimple outlined his face as he smiled.

Mauve agreed, and that was the beginning of her roller coaster ride with Dr. Conniving.

Even on their first date at a classy restaurant on the Ave, Chianti's cell phone kept ringing and dinging with multiple texts and missed calls. Since he was a busy doctor, she never suspected anything out of the ordinary. "Wow, you're a busy guy!" Mauve said kiddingly, yet a little perturbed. Chianti simply brushed it off.

Aside from the phone nuisance, Chianti was entirely attentive and enthralled with Mauve. He complimented her all evening, held her hands romantically and spoke futuristically about their budding new friendship. At the end of the night, he whispered, "I can see us spending a whole lot more time together." His low tone of voice made Mauve melt like a bowl of fondue.

They started dating under the assumption that their relationship was exclusive. Mauve was proud to be Chianti's girlfriend and became known as "the new X-Ray tech that snagged the dreamy doctor". But there were whispers.

Didn't she know that Chianti loved to '*have his cake, and eat it, too*'? Some wondered.

She always made sure she looked good, wearing makeup even when she rushed into the ER while on call. They spent a lot more time together over the months to come and were known as one hot item at the hospital. Mauve felt like a few of the women turned on her. They jealously wished to be in her shoes. Since she didn't know any of the women well enough to have real close ties with them, Mauve didn't let it bother her. Haters were everywhere, but that wasn't about to ruin her time with Chianti.

That was partly why she didn't take it too seriously when one afternoon, two of the catty nurses approached her with some gossip to spill about her prized Chianti.

One of the nurses, Melinda, pulled her aside. "Listen, I don't want to be the bearer of bad news, but I think your doctor is still seeing his ex."

"That's impossible." Mauve retorted.

"Is it? Well I know it's true, because they were together last night. I am good friends with his ex, Susie. I don't know you that well, but I feel bad for you because I know he's a player," Melinda said.

"Why are you trying to start trouble between Chianti and me? You're just jealous," snapped Mauve, as she quickly walked down the corridor.

But as she left, Mauve wondered if their gossip could be true. She had been working last night and thought it was strange that she had been unable to reach Chianti on her break, even though it was late. When she left work a little early, Mauve had expected Chianti to be at her place, waiting for her. Perhaps chilling with a bag of popcorn and a glass of their favorite wine, watching the History Channel. He was not there.

When Chianti finally arrived three hours later, it was just before the time she was due to return home from work. Chianti was all dressed up and wearing a few fresh squirts of cologne. He claimed to have gone to a movie by himself while he was waiting for her to get out of work. Mauve cringed a little, still suspicious. After all, if a guy goes to catch a flick on his own, he is more apt to wear a simple t-shirt and a pair of jeans or sweatpants, not date-wear. However, Mauve didn't want to disrupt the trust between them by questioning his whereabouts. So, she dropped it.

There were other strange times when Mauve wondered about Chianti's behaviors, too. He often took great lengths to dress up just to go "run a few errands" or would go jogging for an hour and a half without breaking one bead of sweat or even ruining his clothes. Most people who exercised that long would at least be moist. The fact that he cancelled on their normal Friday night rendezvous a few evenings prior also made her wonder if the nurse was right.

Later on, Mauve confronted him. "Do you remember that night you cancelled your date with me? I have been meaning to ask you where you went that night."

Ever the smooth sailor, Chianti ponied up. Just as an expert player does, he half-told the truth, so that he could never be accused of lying. "An old friend of mine needed me. She was having relationship troubles with her boyfriend, so I had to console her and give her some advice. I used *our* strong relationship as an example," Chianti fibbed, reaching for Mauve's hand. He had determined that flattery worked with most everyone, especially women.

*Hmmm. Sounded a bit suspicious.* Mauve wondered what kind of "consoling" this supposed female friend entailed. She also noticed that Chianti always had a lot of female friends who needed "reassuring" and support. He had a very soft shoulder to cry on. It was a great strategy of women to use the broken heart approach to throw a lasso at this mustang. It didn't hurt that Chianti was good looking, either.

"Well, why didn't you call me to let me know?" Mauve asked. Chianti squirmed uncomfortably, yet was able to come up with answers in seconds.

"Oh, my cell phone died. I left the charger at home," he quickly offered.

*How convenient*, she thought.

Later that night, while Chianti was sleeping, Mauve saw his computer. Even though she knew it was wrong, Mauve sat down to surf the net. She couldn't sleep, wondering if Chianti was juggling more than just one girlfriend. Right in plain sight was a conversation he had been carrying on in a chat room with Kitty32 and SS_Cowgirl. They were somewhat flirtatious, although not entirely incriminating. Upon further digging, Mauve discovered the profile of SS_Cowgirl was his ex, Susie. She was from Texas. Kitty32 was just a random girl in another city.

Mauve slid into bed and said, "So, you're still friends with Susie?"

"Yeah, but we haven't dated in years and she has a boyfriend. We've always remained friends. Do you have a problem with that?" Chianti asked. If he had known that Mauve looked at his computer, he would have been upset. She let it go, so as not to make Chianti mad for being nosy.

Mauve lay awake staring at the ceiling and pondering what to do. She thought about her odd suspicions. The last thing she wanted to convey was insecurity, but she couldn't help but wonder if she was being played.

A few of the other *things that made her go hmmmm* over the past few months included many red flags of infidelity. For one, Chianti had a maid who came to clean his townhome at least twice a week. However, every time Mauve went over to his place, it was never really that clean. There was a lot of dust and noticeable un-cleanliness that a real maid would never leave behind. Sometimes there were dirty clothes, towels or dishes left behind, even on days the maid supposedly worked. Once she counted the dishes in the sink, and there was exactly two dirty of every setting. Two glasses, two plates, two forks and two knives. A few mornings when Mauve called Chianti, the maid was there very early. And Chianti always let Mauve off the phone very quickly on those days the maid was there.

On another occasion, Mauve went on a fun day with Chianti to Roller Coaster Valley, where they spent a wonderfully romantic day at the amusement park. Roller coasters were a noticeable theme with Chianti. What was most bizarre was that after they returned to her apartment, instead of staying and spending the night as he often did in the past, Chianti told Mauve that he had to run home to "pick up a few things." Strangely, he never came back. Mauve blew up his phone, wondering if something happened that was taking him so long and why he had insisted that she did not go with him.

The next day, Chianti told Mauve that he was so exhausted from their amazing fun day together that he had simply passed out on the couch accidentally. How convenient. By the time he woke up, it was the next day. Chianti apologized profusely. Now, Mauve wondered if Chianti had double-booked another date for that evening after their adventurous day at the amusement park. *How could someone fall asleep while packing clothes?* This wasn't the first time. Chianti used this story twice before, and just within a few months' time.

Finally, Chianti told Mauve that he had to leave town for a business trip. It wasn't the first time he had gone away by himself, as he was often asked to fly to different hospitals when needed for training interns. Other times, Chianti was asked to speak in front of crowds about a particular medical method that he developed. It was revolutionizing the health care world.

Only a couple of times, Chianti had asked Mauve to accompany him. And when she traveled without him to visit her family across the country, Chianti called her more often just to say, "I miss you so much baby, come back soon." He could reach her anytime, 24/7. Mauve always answered when he called. That was a big mistake.

So when Chianti went on another business trip, she reciprocated by calling him at 1:30 a.m. Of course, he did not answer. He returned her call the next day.

"Hi baby, is everything okay?" Chianti asked her.

"I don't know, you tell me?" Mauve replied.

"Well, I see you called last night while I was sleeping, so I just got your message," said Chianti.

"I just missed you," she said. "I wanted to hear your voice before I went to bed."

"Oh, yeah. I miss you too, hun. I was so tired, I turned in really early last night," Chianti lied.

"I see," she went along with it. "So, what's it like there?"

"Oh, you would love it. The hotel is so beautiful and it's great here. I'm having a blast. It's definitely nice to get out of town," he said.

Mauve asked, "What could be so fun about staying at a hotel if you're all alone? You are alone, aren't you?"

Realizing how it sounded, Chianti quickly recovered. "Of course, it would be much better if you were here."

As she thought about their exchange, Mauve wondered why Chianti had yet to invite her home to meet his family. After all, he had told her how close he was with his mother, stepfather and younger sister. In all of the ten months they had been dating, never once did Chianti ask her to join him whenever he went to visit them. By now, if he were truly serious about her, Mauve felt like it should be time to meet those who were special to him. She wondered if he was trying to hide her, or if his family even knew that he had a girlfriend. Mauve felt purposefully excluded from his family, especially since they all lived within the same city.

One night, Chianti left Mauve a tempting opportunity to get some answers to her questions about his secrets. Unlike most evenings when Chianti purposefully left his cell phone in his car, on this night he brought his prized phone inside and left it on the back of the toilet seat. He must have forgotten it when he took a shower. So, in the dark, Mauve carefully went through his phone. She knew it was wrong, but her hunch was more like a brick that smashed her in the head. Mauve read at least 20 or 30 racy text messages that Chianti had been carrying on all day with three separate women. She also watched a very disturbing video of Chianti involved in a ménage a trois.

Furious, Mauve woke Chianti up by shaking him, holding the incriminating video over his face. He blindly tried to focus after the abrupt awakening. "What are you doing going through my phone?" Chianti asked her, snatching the phone out of her hand.

"NO! A better question is what are YOU doing in this video? How could you cheat on me?" Mauve burst into tears.

"That video has been on there a long time. I just never erased it. Plus, it happened WAY before you and I started dating," Chianti said. He was smoother than butter on crispy rolls. He was a practiced player who could deliver instantaneous lies, even after being rudely awakened from a dead sleep.

"NO... NO... look at the date on this!" Mauve exclaimed.

"The date and time feature is messed up on my phone. You know I've been having problems with it," Chianti calmly explained.

Mauve went to work, gathering her belongings. She grabbed everything of hers from his place, including her toothbrush. Chianti followed her around the townhouse. "C'mon baby, this video was from way before you. You're the best there is!"

"This is the last lie, Chianti! We're through!" Mauve was only half dressed as she ran hastily out the door.

❖❖❖❖❖❖❖❖❖

# PROVISO

**You will be unquestionably attracted to Chianti.** And yes, Chianti will seduce you. You may even wish to have an affair with this sexy, fragrant and bountiful berry flavored gem. Chianti is certainly not boring. You will never be disappointed if you choose this wine; that is, if you leave your expectations behind and just enjoy it for what it is. Expect the unexpected and enjoy Chianti while it lasts.

Upon first impressions, there may be no easy drawbacks to determine about Chianti. Especially if all you want is to have fun. Chianti is a good wine to choose if you want to live it up with no strings attached. Just be wary of the high acidity levels. Although it gives the wine a fresh vivacity, the acidity makes drinking Chianti better as a casual wine, rather than with more serious fare.

Chianti always knows the right thing to say and has an answer or excuse for every step. The thing is – Chianti is believable – especially to those who fall under its spell. Its sweet anything's makes women melt. Speaking of anything...

Be warned that Chianti has a habit of loving and leaving. It has too much energy and unbridled spirit to be kept very long, so enjoy Chianti while it lasts. Some Chiantis take about a decade after their initial production to yield true flavor. Those that age past this 10 year cusp may be even more devious, but beware of those past their prime. Some overly aged Chiantis look good upon first appearance, and then lose their appeal. Like a chubby middle aged guy driving around in a too-small convertible Miata, too well-aged

Chianti may be too out of place for its character. Chianti should be enjoyed in its younger stages, while it is most virile.

Undoubtedly, Chianti is a respected wine. Its one often thought of as a game player in the wine industry. Who could forget Chianti's budding acting career that sprouted from a special guest appearance on *The Silence of the Lambs*?

Nearly every woman has tried Chianti and loved it, at least until she knew the outcome of its cunning disposition. Some women even try many different brands of Chianti because they love it so much. The player can come disguised in many uniforms. For those women who have experienced Chianti, it has likely invoked a feeling of tingling passion mixed with a frustration of not having it anymore. Chianti is delicious, but it won't stay in your life for very long. Even if you do try different varieties, it's best not to get too attached to Chianti.

Players are heartbreakers. Deep down, you know that Chianti is a wine destined to be shared and enjoyed by others. You can't keep Chianti all to yourself, even though its luscious ruby color and enchanting disposition is something you will adore. Chianti is just too wild spirited to be inhibited by commitment.

This wine loves the chase and chases for love; although once caught, Chianti doesn't want to be labeled with the stigma of branding with any special name. Especially the name "boyfriend."

# Sauvignon Blanc

## "THE HOMEBODY"

***Although it has a highly recognizable name and is*** *widely planted and distributed worldwide, Sauvignon Blanc has never truly been represented on the list of "spectacular" white wines of the world. People rarely save it in their wine cellars or spend a great deal of money to buy it, although the pricier bottles often fare better than the less expensive ones. That's because Sauvignon Blanc typically reaches its apex while still young. After settling in for awhile, it becomes rather dull and flat as compared with more vivacious whites like Zinfandel or Riesling.*

*In fact, the liveliness of other whites can make Sauvignon Blanc seem dreary and less memorable. It lacks passion and at times can be sour. With acidic whets in the aftertaste, it's sinisterly delicious in the beginning, but short-lived. A subtle array of grass, stone and grapefruit guava gives Sauvignon Blanc its citrusy crispness. You could say it is dry, yet refreshing.*

*Some try Sauvignon Blanc many times, giving it chance after chance to prove its worthiness of a place in their hearts. Nevertheless, it rarely changes, even from one brand to the next. It just has too many vices to ever elevate into the echelon of wines to keep forever. Once you've tasted one Sauvignon Blanc, you've basically tried them all. They all take you on a roller coaster ride, sometimes great, but on most occasions a huge let-down.*

*Often tangy and intense, Sauvignon Blanc does have its place. It enables wine drinkers to be pickier about the next types of wine to buy. It may be best to choose one that is more suited to your personality than to just hope Sauvignon Blanc will be that 'forever' something special. Some may stick with Sauvignon Blanc for quite awhile before realizing there are better options. After all, Sauvignon Blanc does have its own charming qualities, albeit diffident.*

*One who tries another type of white wine after Sauvignon Blanc and then returns to give it another go may feel differently than they did the first time. Its seeming lack of identity is confusing, with one batch being exceptionally refreshing but then the next lacking "umph".*

*That's due in part to the winemaker. You see, there are a few tricks to getting Sauvignon Blanc to be great. The timing of the harvest must be well planned. Pluck the grapes too early and the wine will be thin, acidic and bitter. Too late will leave you with a heavyset taste that can be lifeless and blasé. This nonchalant character is a little too laid-back for some who prefer an energetic wine. .*

*Of course, it's much simpler to make a mediocre Sauvignon Blanc than it would be to create an extraordinary one. Yet, its cuttings have been imported and exported worldwide. Winemakers around the world are nothing if not eternal optimists. Vintners have quickly developed a sense of style for Sauvignon Blanc that has been met with overall deception of originality.*

*Sauvignon Blanc has a very distinctive personality that is quite casual. If you want something for a backyard barbecue or with textured cheese, Sauv's chalky texture matches well. Hence, Sauvignon Blanc does have a few likeable qualities, but none so lovable that it will capture your heart or make you jump up and down with glee.*

❖❖❖❖❖❖❖❖❖

# SAUV ❣ Peach

**Peach met Sauvignon Blanc at a backyard barbecue** at the neighbor's house. He was a coworker of her friend's husband. Ever the social butterfly, Peach loved to flutter here and there to as many parties, festivals, vacations, concerts and events as possible to meet up with friends and enjoy life. Her first impression of Sauv was that he seemed relaxed, intelligent and witty. He looked a bit like Clark Kent, with a tall frame and handsome sideburns that matched his long face. He wore glasses and had a carefree persona.. Several drinks led to many, and Sauv became downright chatty.

It wasn't supposed to be a setup; although, Peach's friends seemed pleased that both of them were hitting it off. The wife snuck by the husband as he was flipping burgers on the grill and whispered, "Look honey, we're natural-born matchmakers!" The husband chuckled.

Sauv was like an encyclopedia of knowledge, which Peach rather enjoyed. He wasn't like most of the other "oglers" who simply stared at her breasts as they conversed. Sauv was rather handsome and smart.

Although he asked her out at the barbecue, she explained to him that she was about to leave for a retreat in New Mexico and that she wouldn't be back for a few weeks. "That's okay," Sauv assured her. "I'll wait. What are you going there for?"

"Well, I'm a massage therapist but I wanted to expand my horizons and teach yoga classes. So I'm going to become a certified yoga instructor," explained Peach.

"That's really neat. Maybe you can work those magic hands on my back when you return," joked Sauv.

She rolled her eyes. It was a cliché statement that everyone said whenever they learned she was a massage therapist. "Yeah, but it's going to cost you," Peach replied.

So, she committed to contact him upon her return, which she did. Peach found herself thinking about Sauv while she was gone on her trip. The old Santa Fe style monastery where t she had enrolled to attend her yoga retreat had a policy of no communicating to the outside world while you were there, except on Sundays. You got one free day per week. No laptops, smart phones, internet or anything of that nature were allowed. They really wanted to absorb the participants in Ayurvedic yoga principles to make students more in tune with the whole "mind/body" philosophy.

While there, Peach's one free day on Sundays was the only chance to catch up with family, friends, or go into town and shop. Peach liked to go sightseeing and take pictures by herself, as well as catch up on her emails and zillions of voicemails. She called Sauv one Sunday afternoon.

"Hello?" he answered.

"Hi, this is Peach. You know the girl you met at the cookout a couple of weeks ago?" she asked, wondering if he remembered.

"Of course! Are you home yet? I've been waiting for my backrub," joked Sauv.

"No, we're just on a free day," she explained.

"Well, how lucky am I? You used your one free day to call me?" Sauv asked, surprised.

"Yes, I wanted to see if you still want to get together when I return? I should be back on Thursday," she said.

"How about Friday, then?" Sauv replied. She agreed. So after she flew home, Sauv called to confirm the time and place to meet. He knew she was an adventurous type from their conversation at the BBQ, so he wanted to impress her by bringing her out of town on their first date. The nice Italian Restaurant that he took her to was about an hour away..

She had an amazing time with him. In fact, their first couple of months together was nothing short of wonderful. He brought her flowers, they went on dinner dates, and sometimes antiques shopping or strolling for shells on the beach together. Sauvignon was very smooth and persuasive, although quite dry. On those nights they weren't together, Sauvignon Blanc usually had plans with a couple of his guy friends. They liked to come to his house and hang out watching sports.

This was never really a problem, as Peach also had many friends of her own. However, Sauv had a secret that he did not reveal right away. He liked to drink. A lot. He loved to watch sports. Obsessively. He had to watch every sport there was. Baseball, football, hockey, and basketball. He loved them all. It wasn't just the watching of them, Sauv liked to drink and participate in the action from his big 48" flat screen.

As they spent more time together, Sauv rarely wanted to go anywhere with Peach because he didn't want to "miss a game," no matter how unimportant it was.

"I don't get why in baseball they need to play seven games to determine the winner. Like in football, they play one game and whoever wins, wins. Shouldn't that be good enough?" Peach asked.

"No, that's just the way it is. It's the best of seven. They play 156 games in a season." Sauv seemed annoyed.

"That's a lot of games. Think about it. That's like 156 wasted days in front of the TV. I like football better. There's more action," Peach told him.

"Yes, I know. You mentioned that before." He said, snidely.

However, Sauv took his games very seriously. He would yell and jeer at the TV as he watched the games. He wore shirts to accompany his favorite teams and knew every batting average of every player since the beginning of baseball, even from the opposing teams. He acted like a recruiter; often following along with whichever player was getting traded with what team or which rookie he thought should play for whom. He missed his calling as a scout.

Yet, when it came to his keys or his wallet, Sauv was constantly looking for them. Strange, how his memory operated. So intelligent, yet such a scatterbrain.

Peach continued to date him, though. Sauv had a dog that she absolutely adored. It was a golden retriever named Maxx. She didn't want to part with Maxx and the sunshine-colored dog was just like a kid to her, although it had been Sauv's dog prior to them becoming a couple.

However, the dog was also a frequent excuse for Sauv to want to stay close to home. Every time she suggested they "get away" for the weekend or even take a day trip to the beach or nearby state just for a change of scenery, Sauv said he didn't have anyone to watch the dog.

It wasn't true. Sauv lived only two houses away from his mother, who he was very attached to. He went there most every evening for dinner and his mother still cooked it for him. Peach thought it was nice that Sauv was so close to her, but maybe a little too close for comfort. He still clutched onto his mother's apron strings, even though he was in his early thirties. He relied on her for help with cooking, cleaning and even running errands for him. Sauv had never been married but had never cut the umbilical cord, with his Mom either.

When Sauv finally did agree to get away for a day trip with Peach, she found it quite amusing how he had to pack his bags as if they were going to be gone for a whole week.

"Why are you bringing so many t-shirts?" she asked, as she watched Sauv stuff his black Nike backpack full of clothes. "We're only going for the day!"

"You just never know what could happen," Sauv explained. It seemed he had anxiety over leaving the comfort of his home even for a daytrip. In contrast, Peach often traveled for her job. She taught yoga retreats that were often in other states, which gave her the chance to see other places and meet new people. She loved her job.

"You need to expand your horizons. There's more to life than this place!" Peach emphatically threw her hands up in the air. Sauv looked at her, crossly. She added, "I mean, how can you stand living here with socks and clothes on the floor everywhere?"

"I don't have time to clean much," he defended.

"What do you mean?" Peach scoffed.

"I mean I get home from work and I'm busy, and tired. I like to relax. What's wrong with that?" Sauv asked.

"You sell insurance. It's not like you're out digging ditches and sweating in the hot sun," she rolled her eyes. Peach was realizing more and more how different they were from one another personality-wise. There was really nothing wrong with Sauv's desire to relax, except that it clashed with Peach's naturally "go-energy", socialite character. She liked to relax occasionally, but rarely at home. Peach was more the type to relax by going to the pool for an hour and reading a book than to sit in front of the TV. In fact, she didn't even subscribe to cable and had to dust off her old TV that had silver antennas floating from the top.

Peach got her fill for adventures and travel by going places with her sister and friends. Every year they went on a Spring Break, or they'd get in the car on a spontaneous "girl trip" with no destination in mind. They'd end up in Quebec City, Providence, NYC, Las Vegas, Virginia Beach or Florida depending on where their car took them.

Another thing. Sauv was also not very creative in bed. Sometimes he drank too much and passed out before it could happen, whereas other days he had some terrible headache or another excuse. Their frequency of intercourse was only about once a month. They would often argue about this, as well. Peach had a high sex drive and wanted more physical intimacy and romance in their relationship.

"Most guys would fall over backwards to have a girl who wanted to get busy more than once a month!" She exploded one day as she found herself exasperated with Sauv's excuses.

"Well most women would appreciate a guy who doesn't charge at them every five minutes," he defended.

"I am not most women!" she replied.

"I'm not most men." Sauv said.

"That's for sure," they both said at the same time.

"And what's up with the t-shirt thing? I've never met a guy who always had to wear a t-shirt while they're getting it on with their girlfriend, anyway." She hated those t-shirts he wore, which either featured sports team themes or a 'saying' of some kind on the front. There was nothing worse than having to look at "Don't follow me, I'm lost too." Or "Bad Boys go to Sturgis," even though he didn't own a motorcycle.

Sauv shook his head. He asked, "How did we get on this topic, anyway? We were talking about going away and the next thing you know we're talking about dirty socks on the floor and other attacks on my choice of apparel."

Then, Peach laughed. He was right. This was a silly argument that was going nowhere. She was ready to brush it all off and forget about it, until Sauv said, "Besides, shouldn't you be helping me clean, anyway?"

The words stunned her. At that moment, Peach realized that Sauv wanted a girl who would take care of him. A domesticated Bessie who could cook, clean and do good deeds.

She wanted something different, too. Sauv had gone from refreshing and comfortable to dull. His lack of creativity was a letdown and he didn't even know how to fix anything. At one time, Sauv had been the Quarterback of his high school football team. This couple of years of stardom had given him a taste of what it felt like to be a sports legend, which was why he liked watching them so much. He lived the dream by watching others play, only wishing he had done something more with his life.

Sauvignon Blanc was all gale with no gusto.

❖ ❖ ❖ ❖ ❖ ❖ ❖ ❖ ❖

# PROVISO

**At first Sauvignon Blanc is bright, flavorful and** magnetic. He will shower you with attention and make you laugh. But as you keep drinking the bottle, you will eventually realize that Sauvignon Blanc loses its luster. It becomes rather flat, lifeless and sometimes bland.

Sauvignon Blanc's laid-back character is one that goes well for a moderately social setting. Yes, those backyard barbecues would count. However, don't expect this wine to attend any fancy gathering with you or escort you to an important shin-dig. It's just not that type of wine that feels comfortable in a highly social atmosphere. It would rather stay at home and chill. Relax.

Also lacking the creativity of other more vivacious whites like Riesling, Chardonnay or Zinfandel, Sauvignon Blanc usually looks and tastes the same from one version to the next. It has issues stepping away from its maker, so know that Mama probably lives somewhere nearby, if not with him.

The tart finish will be very intense. Sauvignon Blanc may even become bitter. This may be one of those wines that you can't live with, but you can't live without.

# Malbec

## "THE MUSICIAN"

***Like a fine musical instrument, Malbec absorbs you*** *in its mystery. To watch this delicious red wine bloom into its vibrant finish, the grapes must be planted early to ripen mid-season. Doing so will bring the lovely finish of violet, plum or ink colors to its warm glow. Malbec's ample tannins yield an intoxicating element that is anything but sweet. Hence, Malbec can only be taken seriously as a wine that is complex, juicy, mysterious and supple.*

*Its ancestry stems from the famed Bordeaux region of the old French plantations; however, most of the current Malbecs can be found in Southwest France, South America, Australia, Bolivia and New York (on Long Island), Washington, and California. Depending on where they are harvested, the grapes of Malbec have a savory texture.*

*It's intriguing aire is richly inviting and robust, having never been known as the subtle type. Its thin-skinned grapes are sensitive and particular; therefore, Malbec can only reach its mark through careful attendance of the vintner. If cultivated properly, Malbec can progress into a truly worthy table wine for a chilly night. It's warm and tingly blend will give you warm sensations.*

*Give Malbec a chance; however make sure to choose a good bottle. A bad batch could taste like road construction or tires, not that you'd know what any of those things taste like. Malbec is hyper-sensitive to heat, needing more sun than other red wines such as Merlot or Cabernet, who are "nice" and "always right," respectively. Malbec flourishes better in certain climates than others. Like an artist needing a perfect scene to paint, Malbec thrives only when raised with adequate sun, moisture and coaxing.*

*If you are the creative type, Malbec will appeal to you. That's because Malbec is creative in its own way. Every bottle has its own distinctive flavor. Some Malbecs have a lip-smacking taste of chocolate, blackberry jam, fig, smoke and plum. Another variation may please your palate with black raspberry, cherry, licorice, and white chocolate. Taste a third Malbec and you may note hints of pencil shavings, hazelnut, cedar, blueberries and violets. Each comprises many different hues and rotund styles that vary greatly. Therefore, each bottle of Malbec is quite unique, and individually beautiful.*

*If it could only play, Malbec would strum you a serenade. It would sing quietly from the corner of a crowded room or in the privacy of your own living room. All the while, Malbec will lull you into a state of happiness and bliss.*

*But Malbec has its own set of temperamental nuances, despite all of its worthwhile attributes. Malbec's propensity for creativity and passion are crafted only among the most structured of elements. Everything must fall into place just so for the grapes to grow, flourish and be harvested at precisely the right moment. This need for organization is a hindrance to*

*Malbec only if its yearning for sun and moisture is not met. If the summer climate is too dry or too wet, Malbec simply cannot withstand the differentiations in weather circumstances. Alas, not every Malbec grape will make the cut to become a fine bottle of wine. Some will either fall by the wayside or be shortlisted, leaving only room for the best to come alive.*

*Even wine critics cannot deny the complexity of Malbec. You may come across one who does not like a particular brand, but most wine critics appreciate at least one type of Malbec with tenacious enthusiasm. Its velvety texture, perfumed character and lively personality lives large, long after the last sip.*

❖❖❖❖❖❖❖❖❖

# MALBEC ❣ Indigo

**The whole crowd gathered around as the clock** neared the countdown to midnight. Up on the stage, Malbec pointed at his watch as he stopped the final set. “Are you ready for the New Year?” he asked the eager crowd. They cheered.

Down below stood a girl, clapping and smiling as she looked up at the stage. Malbec grabbed her hand and pulled her up on stage. She felt like the luckiest girl in the world. People wondered if she was just a random girl in the audience, or someone special, as they looked on, craning to get a glimpse of what was next.

“Here we go! Count with me, people!” yelled Malbec into the microphone. “10, 9, 8, 7, 6, 5, 4, 3, 2, 1... HAPPY

NEW YEAR!" Then he turned to the pretty girl next to him and swept her down into mid-air, planting a juicy kiss on her lips that lasted for more than a moment. Her cheeks were blushing as she wrapped her arms around his neck and hugged him.

The truth was, the two had been dating for awhile. The only way for Indigo to spend time with Malbec was to travel to his gigs with him. Like a groupie, she faithfully attended as many of his shows as possible. He was the lead singer and guitarist for his band.

Malbec was not shy. He was energetic, charismatic and noticeable, even if he was a little on the grungy side. His brief patch of facial hair was carelessly trimmed to look like a goatee, with longish dark brown hair that was barely short enough to pass for a dude. Plus, he was easily the sexiest kisser Indigo had ever locked lips with. Like his finely-tuned guitar, Malbec had mastered the art of sensitivity.

He sang to Indigo and wrote songs about her, which he read to her on the phone sometimes whenever his band played in other towns. Malbec always took a half hour out of his evening to call. Sometimes, he'd sing the songs he wrote to her on the phone...

*"Indigo, oh Indigo, I miss you so...*
*Your luscious lips and fingertips...*
*Like weaves of webs on tired beds*
*As thoughts of you dance across my mind*
*All the time*
*Oh Indigo... I miss you so..."*

She was mesmerized, especially when he made a big deal about her presence in front of an audience. After such an amazing New Year's performance, Indigo was sure it would be a year to remember. No one had ever written songs for her before! It was flattering.

As long as he could remember, Malbec never had any trouble getting girlfriends. There was something about musicians that women found irresistible. Even those who didn't have much going for them looks-wise were able to lure girls with the use of their sentimental words and musical instruments. Malbec's drummer could attest to that. The drummer's scrawny build and bold tattoos made him look malnourished. And the bass guitarist was quite the opposite, having a heavy build and potbelly that overshadowed his taut face. Yet, women flocked to them and to Malbec, just hoping to be one of the few who were chosen for a backstage pass after the show.

Secretly, Indigo worried about that fact. Musicians were notorious for getting quickly bored of the same girl. Some pursued "open" relationships, while others just cheated. Not all, but many musicians she knew had this reputation. Just as Malbec had snagged her out of a pool of pretty girls who were attending one of his shows, Indigo wondered if he would easily bypass her one day in favor of another. Yet, he constantly assured her of his devotion. His songs were flowing and his music was in demand.

After she got to know him better, Malbec invited Indigo to his house. Because he was in a band, she expected chaos or the typical bachelor pad with socks and dirty dishes lying around. It was quite the opposite. When she first stepped through Malbec's door, Indigo noticed that he was extremely clean. In fact, he was a bonafide neat freak. He needed structure to balance his crazy schedule of road shows and gigs.

"Wow, do you have a cleaning lady?" asked Indigo.

"No, why?" Malbec replied, as if offended.

"I mean... well it's just so clean. I know you're on the road a lot... so I thought..." she stammered.

Malbec interrupted. "You thought just because I'm in a band that I'm some kind of slob?"

Her cheeks turned redder than a burner plate. "No, I..."

Unexpectedly, Malbec laughed. "It's alright, I'm just joshing ya!" he joked.

*'Note to self,'* she thought. *'Offends easily.'*

As she observed his habitat, Indigo noticed Malbec's extremely nice collection of guitars, meticulously polished and strategically placed throughout his house. Each guitar had a specific stand to display that particular guitar. The two were designed to match perfectly. Of course, Malbec brought this observation to her attention. "Look Babe, this is a rare Auerswald electric guitar. He made Prince's guitars. And it's on an antique maple stand made to match the body of the guitar," he said, as he lovingly stroked the instrument with just a fingertip. Then Malbec wiped the barely noticeable print with the underside of his T-shirt. "They're made for each other, just like us."

When it came to his equipment, Malbec only bought the best. He was quite snobby about the brands and the people who were allowed to touch his precious collection. Indigo realized this as she went to reach for one of them. Malbec grabbed her wrist in mid-air, startling her. "Please, don't touch my guitars," he said firmly. "I have them positioned just so, and I am methodically trying to keep them where they belong."

A little taken aback, Indigo thought it was strange but didn't question it. In fact, she was so stunned that she didn't say a word.

However, over the next few months, Indigo started noticing other strange "OCD" tendencies from Malbec. His perfectionism was one of her biggest pet peeves. Even though she was crazy about him, Indigo found it difficult to deal with his persnickety personality.

For example, Malbec constantly created new songs to play, but he could never finish making a CD to give promoters or to sell because he was so dogmatic. Malbec always found things to critique or change about the melody, lyrics or the music itself, which was a deterrent to his success as a major industry player.

Then one day, Malbec's band suddenly broke apart when an argument between the three of them ensued. "It's the nature of the business," Malbec explained to Indigo, when she asked what had happened. "They didn't see things my way. So, they're fired!"

"But I thought you were a band? Doesn't that mean you are a team?" Indigo asked, naively. "Couldn't you just compromise?"

"NO!" he yelled, with steam coming from his ears. "I wrote the songs. They have to play them the way they were written!"

His way, as Indigo learned, was the only way. Malbec went through band members faster than he went through picks for his guitars. Whenever one of the fellows he recruited tried to suggest something that was not Malbec's idea, he shot it down. It was HIS band, not theirs. Malbec was the lead singer, therefore he was the leader. He also refused to listen to anybody else's creative suggestions.

Plus, Malbec was also an extremist. Just like his structured home and detailed positioning of his instruments, if ever he received an unfavorable comment or review in any way, he would work on that part of a song over and over and over again a hundred or thousand times to get it right. Malbec spent so much time practicing his music that it left very little time for his relationship. Indigo was his girlfriend and his possession, just as much as his fancy guitar collection. Furthermore, spending quality time together with Indigo meant asking her to follow him around to most of his shows. He wanted a number one fan. Malbec expected her to be there as much as he expected cooperation from all of the members of his band.

One day, Indigo griped about her unhappiness with Malbec's oversensitivity to one of his close friends from high school. He was a guy she had met through Malbec. "I'm sick of being second string to his band," she said. "He takes his music so seriously that he never even notices my interests."

"Yeah," the friend agreed. "He's like the music Nazi. Malbec has always been that way, even back when he was just playing in the basement at his parents' house. I used to play with him, but I decided that in order to save our friendship it was best just to quit."

"He let you do that and still maintain a friendship?" asked Indigo.

"Well, I had to tell him that I was too busy to play because of college, which was true," admitted the friend. "But in reality, it was not fun anymore and I didn't see myself going in the same direction. I just wanted to have fun, but Malbec wanted to become a big star."

Indigo thought about this for a minute and knew it was true. She, too, felt like spending time with Malbec was not as much fun as it had been in the beginning. The night club scene was getting old. She was tired of standing there alone in the crowd, clapping and waiting for Malbec to finish his sets just so she could spend twenty minutes listening him complain about a note or two that was off key. Rarely did he take any interest in Indigo's hobbies, passions, friendships or dreams.

Dating a musician was unstable, she decided. *How could Malbec ever become husband material if he played music at bars and venues four or five nights a week?* Indigo wondered. That was not the lifestyle she longed for, although sometimes Indigo did enjoy the social aspect of it and met a few cool people who had attended the shows. Overall, she found dating a musician to be a lonely alternative. Malbec was either on the road or too preoccupied with practices, gigs and marketing of the band to truly notice her. She felt like a groupie instead of a girlfriend.

Malbec longed to be famous, but because of his hypersensitivity and inability to compromise, he was only destined to be known locally. He dreamed of one day being on a big stage with hundreds of thousands of people cheering for him, but the only crowd he could draw with any frequency was a few hundred fans who thought Malbec was pretty good or who happened to be attending the establishment that night.

Even though he didn't realize it, Malbec held back his own success both in music and in relationships because of his rigid ways. He only felt comfortable playing in certain conditions, and with only certain people, and for only the right price. His terms were steadfast. Malbec liked structure.

As with many of his past relationships, eventually Indigo moved on. For her, dating a musician was a novelty that wore off. So after Indigo broke up with him, Malbec had to "face the music" on his quest for the perfect girl who could tolerate his fastidious overtones and who didn't mind tagging along to all of his shows.

At least it made for some new creative material for writing sad, sappy songs that people could relate to with their own dramas. Alas, Malbec was always just a melody away from living the dream.

❖❖❖❖❖❖❖❖❖

# PROVISO

**Although it is stylish, Malbec is not nearly as well-**known as many of the world's top-selling wines. That's because there are fewer vineyards that make Malbec. Only the pickiest ones can create something perfect enough to bottle for consumers. Yet, this is also one of its main selling points. Malbec is unique, just like every musician and every song and every lyric. The production is methodical, melodramatic and precise.

And dating a musician can be very similar to the experience of enjoying Malbec. At first it will warm your heart and please your palate. Your taste buds will be satiated with every delicious sip of this juicy, berry-like red wine. Malbec may even give you that heady feeling, like hearing a terrific song.

Just like a musician who must tirelessly play the same songs over and over to get the perfect harmony and sound, Malbec takes much effort during the crafting process. Certain conditions must be in place for it to flourish. That is something for consumers to appreciate.

However, if you are a woman who is looking for a little flexibility with less rigidness in a man, then Malbec may not be the best choice. Music will always be his first love, no matter how hard you try to please him or show your support. Even if it means sacrificing every weekend and many week nights to play out in public, the musician will do it. Sure, you may get invited. You'll be the lonely one sitting in the front, clapping all by yourself. Malbec loves playing because he loves music, not just the attention that comes with it. Yes, he loves that too.

A handful of musicians out of thousands – even millions – might "make it big" and reach national recognition, but how many others have you run across who are still standing on the city sidewalk with an overturned hat, waiting for loose change to pay the next month's rent? There is no magic recipe for stardom. The musician either has what it takes, or he is destined to be strumming, humming and tooting or hooting at the local pub well into his middle-aged eminence.

It is flattering when someone writes a song about you. It's personal and touching. Never let go of that as you drink a delicious glass of Malbec. Its creativity will dance on your palate and leave rhythms in your loins. And still, the circumstances to brew Malbec must be done perfectly in order to get that satisfying harmonious blend.

# Sangiovese

## "THE POLITICIAN"

***The richly fascinating history of Sangiovese begins*** *in central Italy, where it still thrives and enjoys wild popularity as Italy's most favored wine. Within the heart of Tuscany, its temperamental grapes have become an icon for greatness. Sangiovese is named after a Roman God of Sky and Thunder, also known as "the Blood of Jove". This classy red wine has since made its way to North America, Australia, Canada and other parts of the world where it has earned great respect and status as a sophisticated and often complex choice in wines.*

*Italian settlers first brought the grapes of Sangiovese to California in the latter part of the 19th Century. Many believe that Thomas Jefferson even made it part of his own vineyards. But the grape itself has led a peculiar life, often becoming one of the many delicious varietals used to create field blends. Therefore, it would not be so unusual to find Sangiovese that is 'put' with another similar grape to make a fine bottle of wine.*

*Chianti (the Player), or Pinot Noir (the Bad Boy), or even Merlot (the Nice Guy), and Cabernet Sauvignon (Mr. Right) are four favorites that often partner with Sangiovese, depending on the preferences of the wine-maker.*

*The Sangiovese blends appeal to a greater pool of taste buds. Therefore, you can't count on whether a glass full of this fine elective might taste like sour cherries, blackberries and plums when fully ripened. If you're lucky, it will taste more like butterscotch and vanilla, or even mocha with a spicy nip at the finish. These changing characteristics are what make Sangiovese somewhat anticipated and often surprising. And it does so with such grace and finesse!*

*Sangiovese has great genetic variability and good bloodlines, often yielding brilliance that can shine through the other types of wine with which it may be blended. The liberal views regarding Sangiovese vary as much as the grape itself, with some people preferring it as a standalone wine, while others prefer it mixed with other well-known varieties.*

*Because it has long been so popular in Italy – where it originates – Sangiovese is officially recommended in at least 53 Provinces. There is thought to be anywhere between fifteen to fifty clones of the original Sangiovese grape. Some clones mentored under the umbrella of Sangiovese include Brunello, Torgiono, Sangioveto and Montefalco. Its ability to set the standard for so many other great off-spins makes Sangiovese a natural born leader, if only it weren't so sensitive.*

*Indeed, Sangiovese is so sensitive that only one year of bad weather can wipe out an entire year's worth of great candidates. However, Sangiovese remains undeterred in its ability to rise again in popularity. It's not a matter of 'if' it is a matter of 'when'. The recovery process can take three or four years (at least). It depends on the quality of the grape and how it is handled. Exactly how fast can Sangiovese overcome the setbacks? It all depends on what level of office it is running for. Those vintners who strive for the top shelf with Sangiovese will be more vulnerable to scrutiny among wine critics.*

*Fear not, for whenever you see Sangiovese rise in popularity in another wine-bearing region of the world – from Texas to Argentina – it's a sure bet that it will flourish. This tenacious wine often reappears again with all of the greatness you would expect.*

*Because of its lightweight and acidic nature, the blending of other noble wines gives Sangiovese more structure. Considering the many outside influences that can hinder its destiny of prominence, Sangiovese always strives to improve its partnerships with other great wines. Its temperamental nature never deepens to a rich color; making it nothing more than a medium-bodied wine when not paired with the right candidate. However, when all of the right dynamics fall into place the way they should, the results can be magnificent.*

*In some wine growing regions, the cooler temperatures can result in Sangiovese not fully ripening or having higher acidity. Heavy rains can leave the thick-skinned grapes at risk of rot. Yes, they are delicate on the inside. Sangiovese can handle a beating in the public eye and still come out glowing by the next season. These fussy invariables make Sangiovese a wine that is peculiar, because in good years, its reputation can be elevated to the viticulture likeness of sainthood; whereas in poor years it can be fervently disregarded.*

*Most bottles of Sangiovese age elegantly, especially those from batches that are able to withstand the public scrutiny. Sangiovese has earned respect in the New World as one of the most aristocratic wines of Europe. It's very essence gushes with the element of surprise, and some with hidden scandal. For example, as recently as 2008 it was discovered that major winemakers were "tweaking" Sangiovese to manipulate the taste, which goes against government regulations of using only 100% authentic grapes. The scandal was heavily covered in the press, especially in Italian markets. Sadly, this was not the first time in history that a dirty little secret of a bold candidate would be revealed.*

*As a political contender in the wine industry, the grapes of Sangiovese require an extended growing season. Although the grapes bud early, they are slow to mature on the vines. They need adequate warmth and sun to fully ripen. This presents a cautious cusp of either being too diluted or not ripe enough; if the timing and weather don't cooperate.*

*Harvests reach their full peak right after the first part of autumn, typically in the last week of September. Depending on where they are located, the growing season of Sangiovese varies. Generally speaking, by the end of October Sangiovese has already soaked in as much public anticipation as it can. How ironic that its release falls upon a similar timeline as voting day! After growing its place in the wine industry all year long, Sangiovese will either finish victoriously or plummet to the bottom shelf, at least until the next campaigning efforts can begin.*

❖❖❖❖❖❖❖❖❖

# SANG ❣ Wisteria

**Although she thought better of the lunch offer given** to her by her handsome boss, Wisteria couldn't resist. After all, it was just lunch and a harmless office flirtation, nothing more. Besides, Sangiovese told her they had important matters to discuss, like his upcoming re-election strategy.

It was the power that attracted her to him. Yes, he was pretty good looking, but Wisteria knew that Sang was married. Plus, it would be difficult to get anything past the security staff that surrounded him all day. Then there were the paparazzi close by. They were always trying to get a good shot of anything out of the ordinary. Armed with long white camera lenses and pen cameras, they were hungry for something incriminating to sell to the tabloid magazines.

Yet, whenever Wisteria spent time with Sang, all of her cares and anxieties melted away. There was noticeable chemistry between them. It gave her an adrenaline rush to date someone who was ineligible, at least by public measures. Up until that first lunch date, it had been nothing more than a harmless crush. However, Wisteria felt like her daily working relationship with Sang was changing. After all, he had asked her to call him by the nickname he preferred instead of the more formal-sounding Sangiovese. She felt sparks whenever he was near. Wisteria often overheard the whispers and the warnings at work behind her back, but she did not listen, nor act responsibly.

Sang was definitely a blend of everything she liked. He had a naughty 'bad boy' side that could stand up to any topic. He had served in the military as a decorated general long before ever running for office. Therefore, Sangiovese was not afraid of danger. He was very brave when it came to fighting for what he believed in. He even took a bullet or two in the name of serving his country with pride.

But there was another side to Sang that was very tender, sweet and good. He had wholesomeness about him that the public liked. Although Wisteria had heard the rumors that Sang was a flirt and womanizer, she still couldn't resist the power that Sangiovese had with the public favored to back him.

After a delightful and provocative conversation over lunch, Sang wiped the corners of his mouth with a white linen napkin. He boldly looked into Wisteria's eyes, knowing that his entire career lay on the line, yet finding her beauty irresistible. She was a voluptuous brunette in her prime. He knew he had a way with her, yet in the back of his mind he knew it was wrong to lead her on. Wisteria played the part of the hopeful mistress effervescently.

The temptation was too great for Sangiovese. He reached across the table with a free hand, raising his glass. "Here's to this year's campaign. I want you to be part of this and to be right by my side throughout the campaign. I know we can win the re-election. People like me; especially after this week's unemployment rate went down by a whole percentage. Now that's an accomplishment, wouldn't you say?"

Wisteria blinked. "Yes, it sure is."

Then, he blurted out, "Do you want to play hooky with me this afternoon?"

Surprised, Wisteria smiled coyly. "What did you have in mind, Sang?" she asked, full well knowing what he had implied.

"I mean, we both deserve the afternoon free. We've been working ... traveling ... you deserve a break, so I'm asking you if you want one?" Sang skated around ever saying the words of his intent.

"I'll go anywhere with you," she replied. "You know I'm loyal to the team."

"That's my girl," he smiled. "We have to go somewhere discreet. Wouldn't want the public to get the wrong idea, would we?"

She agreed. "Of course not."

Sang got on the phone with his assistant. "I'll be taking the Benz back myself."

"Are you sure?" asked the man, who was on speakerphone. "Do you want me to have security accompany you?"

"That won't be needed, thank you." Sangiovese replied.

"And Miss Wisteria, do you want us to take her back to the office for you?" asked the man.

"No, I'll give her a ride." He explained.

The doorman walked the two to the car as the valet pulled up with a shiny, black Mercedes Benz S500. He opened the door for the lady. As she slid into the luxurious charcoal leather seats, Wisteria's pencil skirt slid high up her thighs, almost revealing too much.

"Woman, you're going to give me a heart attack," mumbled Sangiovese.

"Sorry," Wisteria apologized, a little embarrassed.

"Don't be!" he exclaimed. "I haven't seen that type of sensuality in a long time." Sang reached across the console and gently stroked her thigh. "Do you want to go somewhere and enjoy some peace and quiet with me?"

"I'm all for it," she cooed.

Sang shifted the Benz and sped out of the Country Club driveway. All of the valet and service people standing outside looked on, dumbfounded. Sang was a man of influence and prestige. "Radical, dude!" yelled one of the parking attendants.

Sang sped out to the countryside, often looking in the rearview mirror. *Was he checking himself out or was he looking out for the paparazzi,* Wisteria wondered. It was the latter.

"I think I got rid of most of the eyeballs back there," he said. "Now we can enjoy an afternoon of solitude." He drove to a steep cliff, overlooking a beautiful lake from a scenic drive that had been built just off the highway. They spent the afternoon there talking and making out. Sang pulled the car into the back of the lot, underneath a big oak tree to give them shade and privacy.

On that day, Wisteria Pink became a mistress. After she crossed the line with Sang, it was too late to ever take it back. Yet, she loved the secrecy and the fear of being caught. As she discovered, being the mistress of a prestigious politician had its perks.

After nearly a year and a half into his term, Wisteria had her own penthouse, right in the heart of the most sought-after neighborhood in the area. Since Sang had to spend most evenings with his wife, she had the whole penthouse to herself. She took advantage of this by having Cosmo parties with her best girlfriends. However, Wisteria was under strict orders not to talk about her relationship with Sangiovese, for fear of anyone leaking to the media. Sang made her promise not to talk.

Other perks of being the politician's mistress included whirlwind travel adventures. She got to go on a lot of the campaigning trips and spend plenty of great sessions between satin sheets of luxury. Plus, Wisteria didn't have to be with him 24 / 7, so she was free to do as she pleased. Sang had to spend time with his wife, too. Especially in front of the cameras, since it was such an important part of his campaign efforts to convey the family man to the voters.

Meanwhile, Wisteria's friends speculated on her affair. A couple of them were envious of her arrangement; however, they did not push her to admit to the scandalous secret. For now, all they knew was that Wisteria Pink had a boyfriend who traveled a lot for business and who was often overseas. She told them he was in the CIA and working undercover. To her friends, instead of calling Sang by his real name, she made up a nickname. "Mr. VIP" was the name Wisteria referenced whenever speaking about her boyfriend with friends.

The fast-paced and secretive lifestyle was fun for Sang and Wisteria for two years. But one day, the inevitable occurred. Someone caught wind of their relationship. Suddenly, Wisteria Pink and Sangiovese were always looking over their shoulders as clever paparazzi followed them separately, hoping to get a glimpse of them together. It was one particularly sly fellow who dressed as a jogger and followed Sang and Wisteria on one of their walks near the north end of Crown Park.

Wisteria had parked her red candy-colored Mustang inconspicuously at the end of the lot. At least as inconspicuous as a bright red Mustang could be, since everyone knew it was Wisteria's car. Although they had met there several times in the past without getting caught, on this day, the seemingly innocent jogger remained attentive to their every move. As steam fogged up the windows and the Mustang shook a little too obviously to be "parked" without a driver, the clever paparazzi hit the jackpot.

The next day, headlines splashed across the newspapers around the country. There was a picture of Wisteria's car and separate photographs of her with Sangiovese, individually. They read, "OUR LEADER – PANTS DOWN THE BEST CANDIDATE FOR RE-ELECTION?" And "SANGIOVESE CROWNS THE PARK WITH WISTERIAS!" and "LEADING OUR COUNTRY TO ECSTACY ... AND BEYOND!"

Underneath the captions was the telltale image taken by the spy jogger. He had captured Sang's face looking out the window of the unmistakable Mustang. His expression was one of pleasure and panic as his eyebrows raised in terror. He knew he had been caught in a very precarious position.

After that, people followed Wisteria Pink everywhere. She couldn't even go buy a coffee at Starbucks without someone glaring at her, or pointing. It was as if she wore a scarlet letter on the top of her left breast. "*That's her*! *That's the home wrecker*!" people rudely yelled.

Although Wisteria contemplated the regrets of getting involved with Sang, she thought better of it. Instead of lamenting over him, she laughed. To her, it was just another fun life experience that she would have missed. Plus, she had become a household name. When she thought about it that way, it helped Wisteria Pink to get over Sangiovese.

Sang was enjoyable and the brief encounter lasted much longer than either of them anticipated. There was only one small hang-up that she struggled with in good conscious. It was the fact that taxpayers paid for her wicked awesome penthouse. It was a place that many people dreamed of living in or even vacationing in. Yet, Wisteria had been able to get into the new place and live in it without worry of ever paying a dime in living expenses. For now, she thought it best to vacate before someone from the media brought it to the attention of the public. Now that she already had the reputation as a scandalous girl, she didn't want to make it any worse with additional revelations. The media was so snoopy these days.

Despite the sexual debacle, Sang won his re-election. In the end, it didn't come down to whether he was faithful or not to his wife. It came down to results. And Sang had plenty of success under his belt. He used his power wisely and his fun cards sparingly. People determined that Sangiovese was human and just as susceptible to temptation as any other guy. He was not so different than many of the other politicians who had their "somethings" on the side, except that he had been caught red handed.

❖❖❖❖❖❖❖❖❖

# PROVISO

**Politicians are well respected, whether people agree** with their points of view or not.

In other countries, such as Italy, France or in many throughout South America, politicians are seen as the most powerful people within a country. People rarely diss on politicians as they do in Western culture. And many of them have a mistress or two, although people rarely speak about it or even make a big deal about it. Having a mistress is even *expected* in other countries, whereas in the US and Canada it is frowned upon.

Sangiovese is a worthy candidate for election on the tables of those who can enjoy its charismatic and controversial persona. It flourishes especially in Tuscany; however, Sangiovese can be wildly popular in other wine-growing regions. The fluctuating reputation and popularity of Sangiovese makes it a trendy gossip topic, if nothing else. One year disliked, could be the next year loved.

# Champagne

## "THE CHARMER"

***What's a party without a great bottle of the fizzy*** *stuff? All around the world, Champagne is synonymous with celebration. Yet, its zesty carbonation and festive attitude are truly nothing more than sparkling wine. Does that make Champagne the ultimate imposter, posing as the world's favorite commemorative beverage, when in fact it is nothing more than a carbonated wine?*

*Maybe. Yet, who doesn't love a charming glass of Champagne? Whether you believe it is genuine or not is hardly relevant. When you're in "party" mode, just enjoy Champagne for what it is.*

*At first taste, you may find Champagne unpalatable. Then, within a moment's notice it will steal your heart, making you giggle uncontrollably. Champagne will compliment you. "My, what lovely eyes you have. Are those hazel?"*

*After your knees buckle, you will savor the sensation of Champagne. It comes in a variety of price points; however, its content is much the same from one brand to the next. Champagne will say most anything to get you to fall in love with it. "Happy New Year!" or "Here's to you!" or "May all Your Wildest Dreams Come True!" or simply, "Cheers!" It will stare at you with those sparkly little winks that start at the bottom of the glass and float their way to the top, just popping a little bit when they reach the surface.*

*This jovial wine first gained notoriety when it was used to anoint the Kings of France. As word spread throughout Europe of its vibrant spirit, Champagne became associated with power and luxury. It was a tradition that began somewhere around the eighteenth century. Even children were allowed to participate in the festivities, as Champagne often had less alcohol content than other wines.*

*However, their distinction within the wine industry changes, depending on the conditions in which the grapes are grown. Given the proper amount of sunlight, they can thrive. Even the way the vines are planted on leaning slopes that reach for the right blend of showers and sunshine plays a vital role in the flavor and quality of Champagne. The grapes must be carefully monitored, trimmed and plucked by hand and then pressed at harvest time to ensure maximum quality output. Only then will you achieve a fine version of Champagne that is suitable for most any occasion.*

*The truth is, many sparkling wines created in other parts of the world employ the same production techniques as those made in the original Province of Champagne. And although they produce very good results, they are all still just a variation of sparkling wine. Fine wine? Yes, they can be very fine and some even receive notable recognition in the marketplace. No one can deny Champagne's admirable centuries-old process.*

*The grapes of Champagne can also be found in many other wines, making for a fascinating mish-mash of tastes and aromas. For example, Chardonnay and Pinot Noir can be very beguiling when made with the grapes of Champagne. Therefore, Champagne is known for its remarkable diversity. It can taste very different from one brand to the next, or from different areas of the world.*

*Unlike many other wines that are very sweet and sipped often as a dessert beverage, Champagne is better before dinner. Some might call it an aperitif wine. Even alone, Champagne makes for a charming toast.*

*Champagne has a natural ability to liven up a whole crowd with a charismatic demeanor and witty flair. It makes an appearance at just about any special occasion, from pre-wedding Mimosas celebrated with a bride and her bridesmaids to an evening's commemorative toast.*

*Champagne just wants to be loved and adored. The only bummer is that the longer it sits out, the more it loses its fizz. The bubbles eventually go flat and by morning, whatever is left in the glass will look like nothing more than the remnants of last night's fun.*

❖❖❖❖❖❖❖❖❖

# CHAMP ❣ Hazel

**Champagne had more one-liners than a two lane** road in New Hampshire. They both seemed to go on forever and go nowhere.

For the longest time, Champagne desperately wanted a girlfriend. He never admitted this to his friends, who believed quite the opposite. They saw him as the bachelor who loved to have fun and take vacations, live frivolously, go to strip clubs or fly to Las Vegas and hit the poker room just for shits and giggles. Women rarely took him seriously after only a few dates. Champagne seemed to lose his luster.

Upon first glance, Champagne was sophisticated, lively, conversational and funny. "Bubbly," as some described him. Nicknamed "Champ", Champagne was quite intelligent and able to wow a crowd with engaging conversation, at least in certain circles. He was polite enough and always shook hands with everyone he met. People always found him to be funny and likable.

Champ also liked to use big, fancy words to impress people. Sometimes they laughed – not because of his jokes – but because Champ often took things out of context. After he contributed something that sounded "brainy-ish" enough to enhance the topic of conversation, people would sit and look at each other, bewildered by the need for deliberate gibberish.

Indeed, Champ knew a lot of people everywhere he went. He was often the life of the party. Everyone invited him to celebrate their special occasions. They found him to be eccentric, yet fun to associate with infrequently.

Despite the fact that he had come into money from a trust fund of his father's passing, Champ also had a cheap side. He would spend hundreds – sometimes thousands of dollars – on fun adventures with friends who he enjoyed partying with. They went to Key West, Disney World, and the Bahamas, strip clubs, casinos and other known "party-villes." Yet, when Champ needed something for his bachelor pad or for his own personal use, he always chose the cheapest items. Therefore, everything he touched seemed to break or malfunction within only days or even minutes of use. His possessions were as high quality as his personality.

Champagne's father had been a successful real estate investor. He owned string of hotel chains and was well-known throughout the region as a captivating and handsome gentleman. The one night stand he had with Champ's mother yielded the byproduct who was destined to follow in his footsteps, if only Champ had been motivated to do so. However, Champagne had little interest in such things. He just wanted to party, party, and party. He partied on New Year's Eve. He partied on St. Paddy's Day. He partied on Cinco de Mayo. He partied on his birthday and on everyone else's birthdays. He even partied on random Saturdays for no particular reason. For Champagne, life was a celebration.

Needless to say, Champ's father was not about to hand the reins of his corporate fortune to a son whose only mission was to attend the next holiday or birthday bash. But when he died unexpectedly of a heart attack, Champ was left with a fair share of the family fortune.

Despite his lack of drive, Champ did have other assets that some women enjoyed. Namely, his sense of humor.

Whenever he first met a girl, Champ always dressed impressively. He bought a new outfit for every new date to avoid having to iron his clothes. He was not too savvy when it came to clothing and often dried clothes that were meant to be hung or dry-cleaned, which made them shrink. As a result, Champ's entire wardrobe was a bit too snug or too short in the sleeves, which looked strange. They were often wrinkled, as well. He was a tall guy with average good looks and long limbs.

Although he didn't realize it, Champ's lack of style contributed to his inability to find a girlfriend. He had a dorky cuteness about him but for a woman, it was embarrassing to be seen with a guy that dressed like Champagne. To him, it was just part of being eccentric and thrifty. He'd rather spend money on a trip to Bermuda than to update his outdated apparel.

However, one day, Champ met a girl named Hazel who fell for his wit and money. Knowing he had a trust fund, she didn't care too much about the lack of fashion sense. Such things were insignificant to her.

They met at a party. Champagne was invited to give a short speech and toast the guest of honor. Hazel was there as the tagalong of a friend who had invited her at the last minute. The two were introduced and Champ didn't waste any time trying to "woo" her with his vocabulary.

"My friend never mentioned that she knew the most beautiful girl in the whole state!" Champ said, as they were introduced.

Blushing, she said, "Oh, thank you. That's so sweet of you to say." She was interested.

"You remind me of a stunning hibiscus flower in the backyard of my seasonal home in Miami," Champ said. He often used analogies that didn't fit well within a current conversation, just to raise eyebrows. Most likely it was for the chance to brag about something he had.

"Oh, you have a winter home there?" she asked.

"Yes, not just one. I have a few other properties here and there that I rent out. I'm just here visiting for a couple of weeks to attend this party and then I'm going to visit my family in France," he boasted.

"Oh, how nice!" Hazel's eyes grew bigger. If he was single, she knew she had hit the jackpot.

"Yes, some of them live in France. Some in Greece. Pack your bags, sweetie," Champ joked. "You can come with me!"

"I'd love to, someday," she replied, but only half kidding. In her mind, Hazel wondered if this was the man who could take her out of this place. The small town lifestyle was getting to her. Besides, he seemed well liked by the guest of honor and by the whole crowd, who clapped when Champ asked them all to raise their glasses for a toast.

Just two weeks prior to meeting her, Champ was dumped by the girl of his dreams, a smart public defender who he dated for a month. Once she had realized that Champagne was not exactly as he had portrayed himself to be when they first met, she quickly ended things. Champ bawled like a Kindergartener who forgot his lunch pail on the bus. He cried to his friends over a round of beers. "But I love her so much!" Champ exclaimed, as if they had been dating for years.

"But you only knew her for a couple of weeks!" yelled one of his buddies. "Snap out of it! Besides, having a girlfriend will only slow you down from going to Mardi Gras and football games."

"You're right," Champ admitted. Afterwards, Champ purchased a ticket to Myrtle Beach, where he planned to forget about this last girl by partying. In "Fertile Myrtle," every night was a festival! He planned to buy a new outfit just for the occasion.

Although he claimed to have a couple of businesses, no one ever saw Champ working. People wondered how he had so much money to travel and go on the town like a rock star. Most assumed it was inherited. Champ's supposed business endeavors were only a show to make it appear as though he did something worthwhile and productive. Instead, all Champ really liked to do was party, party, party. He didn't really work that much anymore because he didn't have to. It gave Champ time for personal pursuits instead.

Like Hazel. He wasn't going to let this one get away. She was the hottest girl Champ could find who would tolerate his carousing lifestyle for any length of time. Hazel fell for Champagne's bubbly personality and vibrant persona. She came from a tiny, rural community and had never been anywhere exciting. So, when Champ came along and offered to spoil her and take her on exotic vacations, Hazel was thrilled. He represented the "big life" and flaunting Hazel coveted, having been a single mother for most of her adulthood. She had never been able to afford such things – or have the time for – vacations. Now that her kid was nearly full-grown, it was finally Hazel's turn to see the world. And Champ was just the man to show it to her.

Champ was nothing, if not vainglorious. He spoke to her in foreign languages that he learned using software, although he told her he had learned them from immersion in foreign cultures. "Tu est très belle, mon Chérie!" Champ said, kissing the back of her hand with his lips.

"I don't know what that means, but it sounds sexy!" replied Hazel, smiling.

"It means that you are the most beautiful woman in the whole world, my darling," Champ replied.

"Does it really?" she asked, suspiciously.

"Well, yes ... give or take a few words," he answered, with a wink.

Champ also told her that he had lived in France, Scotland, South Africa and Australia. Only the former was true. In reality, Champ had been ousted by his family at a young age. He was too irresponsible to participate in the family business and was also a reminder to them of their father's indiscretion with Champ's mother. So, at the influential age of eight, Champ was sent to live with his great aunt in a mobile home park in Pennsylvania. At first, he balked at the idea, not having flourished in that region in the past. This time, Champ took up sports and made it all the way to the state finals. But his team lost the championship game, which Champ never truly got over and carried with him for his entire life. He saw himself as a superstar athlete and continued blowing his own horn about his position as a leading quarterback of the Mighty Marks for his entire adulthood.

Champ's great aunt was a nice lady, but she was firm. She raised Champagne with strong hands and valuable lessons. She made him study, study, study. She transitioned him from being an overproduced anomaly to a man of character. But throughout his teens, the only whirlwind adventures Champagne ever had were in his imagination. He was content enough wearing his K-Mart clothes and eating Oodles of Noodles, which was what his great aunt could afford. To Champ, noodles were just as luxurious as calamari, at least before he knew any differently.

Even though he spent many of his years growing up with a relative who was on a fixed income, Champ often snubbed those who were less fortunate than he was. The inheritance money turned him into a baller.

When he met Hazel, Champ treated her royally with extravagant dinner dates and trips out of town. By then, he had his trust fund to spend. However, after only a couple of months, the charade expired. After Champ knew he "had" her, then he broke out his gigantic T-Shirt collection, most of which had unusually offensive sayings on the front. He wore his obscene T-shirts with cheap cargo shorts and flip flops. Even though Champ could afford to dress nicely, he chose not to. There was no need to impress Hazel anymore. And that's when his bubbly personality began to lose its fizz.

Suddenly Champagne's wayward sophistication and elegance diminished, as class turned to crass. Yet, Hazel stayed with him, hoping for that glimpse of charm to return again. Plus, she already told everyone in the world how madly in love she was with Champ, so it was too late to dump him. Hazel hoped the enchanting man she had met would magically reappear. She stuck to Champ like cling wrap to a bowl of leftovers, the kind often left sitting in the refrigerator too long before it gets tossed into the garbage. Champ found Hazel's clinginess a nuisance, yet he kept her around for fear of loneliness. Plus, he also introduced her to his family as the love of his life.

After they dated for six months or so, Champ's friends noticed a dramatic change in his behavior. Some no longer recognized him anymore. He stopped hanging out with his best friends' altogether and instead just got some new best friends to party with. The old longtime friends were discarded like newspapers sent to the recycling bin, in exchange for friends who only liked Champagne for his convincing exterior. It didn't seem to faze him in the least bit; even though many pointed out that he didn't seem all that happy anymore. '*Had Champagne been this way all along*,' they wondered? Or was it the influence of love that had changed him?

Meanwhile, Hazel suffocated him. She smothered him with mushiness and gushiness and wouldn't leave his side. Whenever he wanted to go out and party, Champ had to bring her along. It was like carrying a purse, which most guys simply don't do.

Some speculated that if Champ did not have the inheritance money to court her or bring her on vacations around the world, she probably would not have stayed with him. Hazel was the naive girl who thought she had found the somewhat handsome Prince. He was able to give her the lifestyle she had never experienced, yet had always longed for. To her, Champ was a dream come true.

In reality, Champ was nothing more than a playboy. Fun, carefree and charismatic. He was the life of the party. To some, it seemed as if he had a bottomless bank account, but that was not the case. Eventually, the inheritance money ran out. Deep down, that was something he worried about; although he never let on to those who knew him.

Even when the well ran dry, Champ was resilient. He was popular and well liked by many, especially those who wanted to be part of the action. Champ was always surrounded by action. He was durable and always found a way to come out on top. And whenever he lost friends who had been by his side throughout his ups and downs, he simply replaced them with new friends. Champagne was never alone for long. The friends, the stuff, the material things, the trips, and even the girls came and went just as easily as another New Year's Eve. New friends, new stuff, different trips and different girls.

❖❖❖❖❖❖❖❖❖

# PROVISO

**Nearly every woman has come across a charmer.** He's the guy that starts out with a bang and gives you lots of goose bumps, compliments, affection, attention and plenty of warm fuzzies. Champagne's naturally bubbly and zesty personality is sure to liven up any room. Just remember that Champagne loses its fizz quickly. It is only meant to be enjoyed as a celebratory beverage, not as a wine that you fall in love with.

As far as being "great," Champagne is not much better than a fruit bowl centerpiece that stays on the table for a year or two. The apples and oranges look shiny and enticing at first; almost good enough to eat. But after you wipe the dust off and take a bite out of one, you'll soon realize it's only meant to be used for decorative purposes.

Oh yes, Champagne is somewhat an imposter, although fun to be around. He's a smooth talker and will say anything to get you to like him or buy what he is selling, which is usually for his own best interests. Champagne especially likes the rookie wine drinkers who have yet to find better options. His dashing smile and sparkling persona will entice even those who rarely drink wine. After all, who doesn't love to partake in a celebration?

There is a reason that Champagne is the world's favorite wine used for toasts and parties. Even the cork is fun to open, coming off with a loud "POP!" and making a spectacular entrance. However, this sparkling party wine is best imbibed only on special occasions. For that reason, Champagne is perfect. Champagne is also a delightful companion as a standalone dessert beverage. But rarely is Champagne one that is chosen as a day-to-day wine.

In fact, it's probably best to enjoy it with an attitude of short-lived expectations. Champagne is a happy drink with plenty of effervescence. It's got a lot of surprising openers that will make you smile. Just be prepared for the day when the carbonation evaporates. Save this wine only for special occasions. It's probably best not to get more involved after the celebration ends.

# Tempranillo

## "THE DREAMER"

***This dreamy wine is amorphous, not belonging to*** *any category except that of its own. Tempranillo has numerous outstanding qualities and any one of them is fame-worthy. It longs to be as successful as the more known red wines like Merlot, Cabernet, Chianti or Pinot Noir. Yet people don't realize the excellence of Tempranillo, at least for now. However, Tempranillo will keep trying to make stardom, no matter how many attempts it takes. It dreams of being famous.*

*Early ripening propensity for Tempranillo grapes means they only need a brief growing season before harvesting. They bud late, yet ripen sooner than other red wines; thereby earning the name "Tempranillo," which literally translates to "little early one." The grape's vigorously thick skins are best cultivated within a climate of hot days and cool nights. Tempranillo won't take NO for an answer in its desire to be discovered and adored.*

*Loose references indicate the existence of Tempranillo wines from centuries ago, when it was first documented within the lyrics of a thirteenth century poet from a southern province of Spain. Its indigenous cultivation of predominantly Spanish descent is also prevalent in today's versions.*

*The grapes of this Spanish wine were introduced to other countries of North and South America during the seventeenth century by the Spanish Conquistadors. Fittingly, these famous explorers could be defined as the ultimate dreamers. As they set out on their adventure to find new trade routes, one can only wonder what the Spanish warriors were dreaming to find in unchartered lands.*

*In Spain, Tempranillo is known as the noble grape to this day, where it savors in its celebrity status. Like a bull-fighter, Tempranillo is a quiet warrior that is well-respected and recognizable on a national level. Its rise of popularity in other countries is quite modest, considering the undeniable sophistication this wine does possess. Countries like Portugal, Chile, Argentina, America, South Africa, Australia and others have caught on to its optimistic traits and refreshing determination.*

*Tempranillo has long been an ambitious wine that is well traveled and cultivated throughout the world; at least in its present form. It first appeared in California's Central Valley in the early 1900's, disguised with a stage name of Valdepeñas. Tempranillo received only a modest reception; partly because of the inconvenient interruption of production during the Prohibition era. The hot, dry California climate was also unfavorable to the grapes' productivity.*

*Because of numerous bewildering aliases, few wine connoisseurs are aware of its Spanish heritage. In addition to Valdepeñas, Tempranillo has been called Aragonêz, Cencibel, Extremadura, Tinta and a few other names – none of which roll off the tongue as profoundly as the real thing. The truth is, this type of wine can be blended well with many other red table wines of capricious merit.*

*One of the notable drawbacks of the grapes compared to other reds is their lower alcohol content and acidity. Therefore, Tempranillo fruit must often share the spotlight by merging with other wines. Less frequently, Tempranillo is bottled solo, often sharing up to a 90% blend with other tasteful wines like Merlot, Carignan, Grenache, Monastrell or Cabernet Sauvignon. Its union with other great reds only serves to make Tempranillo brighter and more remarkable, mainly because of low sugar content.*

*Overall, Tempranillo remains highly underrated and under-discovered, considering its extensive bookmark within the wine industry. You never know, this red wine could be the next big thing – or it could be just another pipedream lost to a more popular choice. The Italian cousin of Sangiovese comes to mind.*

*Look closely and you will undoubtedly see a twinkle in the glass of any Tempranillo red wine mix, much like a twinkle in the eyes of any explorer, entrepreneur, inventor, singer, or untainted child; right before they become a household name. For some, it takes longer than others to achieve greatness.*

*There has long been a misconception of Tempranillo's resemblance to Pinot Noir. That is because of its aroma-filled hints of leather, cherries, spice and tobacco, combined with the blue-black hue of the grape. Although it has been genetically disproven to have any relativity to Pinot Noir whatsoever, Tempranillo shares an apathetic disinterest for anything that hinders its continual pursuit of growth. Therefore, the wine is particularly known for having sensitivity issues within changing conditions. Some thrive here while others thrive there, without rhyme or reason.*

*It seems as though Tempranillo has been impatiently waiting for an appropriate introduction to the world. No less than a red carpet arrival of the highest accolades should suffice. However, because of its infrequent bottling as a solitary varietal, the grand induction date of Tempranillo has yet to be determined. Nevertheless, the dreamer within each bottle continues to inspire taste buds.*

*To those fortunate enough to enjoy Tempranillo, they will be rewarded with lingering elements of berry, vanilla, plum, herb, dried cherries and black currant. Hints of earthy dust and black olives are barely legible amid the gorgeous ruby red shade of a poured glass. This is a red wine that longs to attend any fancy event, not as a mere spectator but as a starring attraction. After all, every dreamer longs to be discovered.*

❖❖❖❖❖❖❖❖❖

# NILLO ❣ Jade

**Even as a young boy, Tempranillo just knew he** would be famous. He was raised in a small town, with a population of little significance. It was boring there in the middle of nowhere, so little "Nillo" spent much of his time bossing around his younger brother and playing games of gladiators, cops, or any super hero. Of course, he was the winner of every battle. Nillo used his imagination in order to keep occupied. Books were also his best friend and Nillo read every chance he could, giving his mind a chance to escape the boredom of his surroundings.

Even while at school, Nillo's imagination took him far away from his daily surroundings. He often lay in the tall grass of a nearby field, staring at the clouds and daydreaming for hours. He studied the shapes of dragons and horses; or baseballs and boobies. All of the things boys liked. Nillo was especially intrigued by pirates and explorers; like the Spanish Conquistadors. *"I want to go on an expedition!"* he secretly wished. So, one day he ran away.

The next night, Nillo returned to his angry mother. Of course, he had nowhere else to go after the sun went down except to his aunt's house; about five miles away. Once Nillo realized how cold the evening woods were, and how scary the crackling noises that were coming from every direction after the sun went down, he crawled home with his tail between his legs. "It's not safe for a seven-year-old!" cussed his Mom. "What were you thinking?"

All throughout his youth, Nillo had a lot of endeavors that were short-lived as fleeting entrepreneurial marvels. There was a squirrel removal business, a library that charged neighbors to rent books, a detective agency called the Junk Yard Dog Patrol (although they never officially solved any crimes), and a sports card bartering service. Nillo really hit the jackpot when he found his uncle's VHS porn collection. He charged his buddies a rental fee and borrowed only a few movies at a time so that his uncle wouldn't notice them missing. But the business folded after only a month, when Nillo's uncle must have noticed something out of place and hid all of the movies in a different place.

Nillo even tried to raise money by setting up a road block at the end of his street. Any neighbors who wanted to pass through had to pay a toll. Unfortunately, the stint ended when Mr. Fenderson tried to pass. "Nillo! Go home. I shall not pay to drive down my own street," yelled the cross man.

Nevertheless, Tempranillo's unsettled spirit continued throughout his teens. He constantly brainstormed different ways to get out and see the world. It was not that his home life was so bad; rather an overpowering allure to see all there was to see.

Throughout high school, Nillo was a good athlete, although not always the best student. It was not for his lack of brilliance, but for other distractions that made his grades suffer; namely girls. Between studying, playing sports and girlfriend(s), Nillo had very little time for much else.

An athletic scholarship to an out-of-state college came his way after a stunning year as a point guard on the basketball team. "*We think you have what it takes";* the scout said, showing Nillo the glossy brochures of the university.

Mostly though, he continued to scheme and daydream. Tempranillo jotted ideas on the edges of paper towels and frayed notebooks. He looked up patents for many of his ideas, although he could find no way for any of them to come to fruition.

The last year of college, he decided that his new burning desire was to be an actor. He enrolled in every class thespian-related. Tempranillo even grew his hair long to look like his favorite actor, Johnny Depp. After a year, he looked more like Jesus than Johnny. Nonetheless, upon graduation Tempranillo set out for California; the land of eternal dreamers.

Once in Cali, Tempranillo adjusted very well. It was his first time alone out in the big world. Until his acting career blossomed, Tempranillo took on silly jobs at local places. He was a bartender, valet, golf caddy and barber's assistant. He never held jobs very long because in his mind, they were only temporary on his path to fame and fortune.

There was even a brief three week spell of homelessness, as Tempranillo struggled to make ends meet. The minor setback did not deter him in any way as he kept dreaming of his big break, which he knew would happen any day. He slept in his car or popped in at friend's houses for a night here and there until his big debut.

One day, it finally happened. Tempranillo landed a tiny role on a TV commercial advertising fishing lures. On the set, he met a budding actress named Jade. She was a perky fitness model and quite the dreamer, in her own way. She was impressed by his lavish plans and aspirations. One thing she noticed, however, was that Nillo never had a plan. He flew by the seat of his pants in every situation.

"Someday, I'm going to open a huge training facility for elite athletes to come from all over the country and train," Nillo said to dazzle her.

"Oh, that's a great idea," Jade said, enthusiastically. She didn't realize the many hundreds of 'big ideas' that Nillo had dabbled in throughout his life, most of which never came to fruition.

"Maybe I can help you. I know a business investor you could meet with." Jade wanted him to succeed and make his dreams finally come true. She arranged an appointment.

As he sat before the gray-haired man in the silver suit, Nillo babbled on about all of the people he knew. "One of my buddies is a linebacker for the 49ers," Nillo bragged to the serious investor. "He said he would tell all of the NFL players to train at my center. It's going to have a huge track field and stadium for fans to come by and watch. Basketball players, baseball players and football players will come. Only the most elite," he told him.

"Do you have a business or marketing plan?" asked the investor?

"Ummm, yeah, in my head!" Nillo said, proudly.

"No, you need something on paper," the man replied, trying not to laugh.

So Nillo went back to the drawing board.

"How did it go?" asked Jade after the interview.

"He's down with it! We'll be breaking ground next spring!" Nillo replied. And he truly thought the interview went well, in his imagination. "I just have to get him a business plan."

Honestly, Nillo had never gone about anything with a plan. All of his endeavors throughout his entire life had been done haphazardly and spontaneously. But he believed they would all come true, if it weren't for the fact he constantly changed his mind about what the next big idea would be. Nillo lacked focus, although he had plenty of emphasis.

One day while he was with Jade, they ran into one of his supposed friends. He was an outfielder for the Oakland A's. "Hey, there's my man! I know him. We partied together back in college." He pointed.

"Oh really?" Jade asked. "Well, why don't you go say hi?"

"I would, but I'm late for an appointment," he fibbed. He was always trying to impress people with who he knew, when in fact he mostly knew them from television. The stars rarely remembered him, although sometimes when given the opportunity he would approach them and pretend they were old friends from back in the day.

After spring rolled into summer, Jade wondered what had happened to the training facility. "Hey, I thought you guys were breaking ground for your new center for athletes?" she asked one day.

"Oh, well it got stalled. It seems the surveyors are dragging their feet on getting the land ready," Nillo told her.

*Hmmmm...* Jade was beginning to wonder if her boyfriend was just a clam hoping to become an oyster. Meanwhile, her own career was sprouting. She appeared on the cover of Oxygen Magazine and won several fitness competitions on a national level. People were calling her from top TV stations to ask for advice and she became highly sought-after as a fitness trainer.

Nillo was proud to be there for her. It gave him a chance to rub elbows with more influential athletes. He always told them about his imaginary fitness center. "When Jade and I get this place going, you guys can all come and train!" he invited the bodybuilders and fitness models to the center that had not even been written down on paper, as of yet. Now he was including her in the dream, as if to piggyback on her rising fame.

However, Nillo didn't have a lot of time to spend with Jade because he was often working. He worked from morning until night on his ideas, inventions and plans. She was beginning to get frustrated with their relationship, realizing that after three years together, Nillo had not accomplished much more than he had when they met. Although Jade admired his ambition, Nillo seemed to be all dream with no scheme.

After many days spent dreaming of great wealth, travel, having four children and houses in several states, Jade got tired of never seeing him since he spent so much time working. So, she found a nice way to break up with him. However, not with a clear escape. She got pregnant right before the breakup. Tempranillo offered to stick around. Jade didn't seem interested.

More years went by; as Tempranillo drifted in and out of business ventures, pyramid schemes, network marketing, lost opportunities and close calls to stardom. He was stuck in California if he wanted to see his son. He wasn't a terrible father, because inside he was still a kid himself at heart. He picked the young boy up every other weekend and every Wednesday night for dinner and a movie, assuming funds were on hand that week. He kept dreaming as he had his whole life, that one day he would achieve "his big break!"

Aside from the long-lived dream of becoming a Hollywood actor, Tempranillo developed a patent idea that intrigued the interest of an influential friend. An offer was made, but Tempranillo's stubbornness over the particulars of the contract caused the deal to fail. He would not budge. For a solid decade, he kept trying over and over with the same plan, yielding the same results. Now approaching mid-life stage, Tempranillo was not much further ahead than he had ever been. Although it was always his dream to have the perfect wife and mother of his children, he was still unmarried and struggling by his 40th birthday. Yet the stoic dreamer was still unwavering in his belief of the imminent fame and fortune he so deserved.

Finally, a chance tennis match with a well-known business icon gave Nillo the break he needed to mention his "big idea". The man was more than intrigued and offered him a huge advance. Now approaching a ripe age, Nillo was finally mature enough to rise to the occasion. His persistence paid off and his big dreams finally came true after hundreds of rejections and many failed relationships along the way.

Not long thereafter, Tempranillo went to watch his now teenage son at a high school football game. While there, he initiated a conversation with a striking blonde. Turns out, her father was a famous producer of family sitcoms. "You look a lot like Johnny Depp", she said.

❖❖❖❖❖❖❖❖❖

# PROVISO

**Tempranillo ripens well and eventually reaches its** peak after many years of being undiscovered and underappreciated. Because of its difficulty in reaching full potential as a respected varietal, Tempranillo can either be consumed right away or saved for later. This delicious wine could sweep you off your feet, if only he wasn't flying by the seat of his pants. This man doesn't have a plan. And even if he does, those plans may change. Yet it's hard not to love him or respect him because he's just so darn upbeat.

Sometimes maturity and good luck happen faster for one dreamer than for another. He may even be rejected many times throughout his life until one day someone realizes how wonderful he is. After a well-made bottle of Tempranillo ripens perfectly, things can fall into place and the flavor develops masterfully. This Spanish wine is ardently worthwhile. Even though variants of Tempranillo have been around for centuries, it is still considered somewhat rare among other more popular wines of the world. At least for now.

Once he finally achieves fame – whenever that may be – the dreamer may eventually be ready to settle down. But that could be awhile. You may have many fun nights together, lying around thinking of all of the exotic places you'd like to see together. He may fondly include you in his plans for wealth and stardom. In reality, he has been dreaming of these big plans for much of his life, perhaps even since childhood. There is nothing you can do to compete for his conquest, even if you have all of the qualities in a woman that he so desires.

He could inspire you to achieve your own dreams. He could even make you realize that having dreams is what life is all about, no matter how many times he fails or pushes the limits of his own capabilities.

Tempranillo is a perseverant wine, indeed. Its gaining popularity could even be the next big thing. Try it, and you will see how delicious it is. It is optimistic, enthusiastic, 'fruit-abulous' and dreams of getting noticed. Without dreams, many great things would not be accomplished. For some wines, it just takes longer than others to be recognized for greatness.

One has to respect a dreamer, for inside there is just a perfect wine that is waiting to be discovered and turned into something great. The best way to deal with a man like this is to quietly encourage him, rather than to rain on his big plans. No matter how unrealistic they may seem to you, his dreams are just on the cusp of happening any day within his soul. His big debut could be tomorrow, next month, next year or near the end of his shelf life.

# Muscadet

## "THE YUPPIE"

*I**t seems like Muscadet would be an expensive wine** because of its persistent, fresh and quirky attitude. It dresses sophisticated enough and plays the part of an affluent alternative; although in most situations, it may be dry and overextended.*

*Muscadet is the angel cake of white wines, with a pure blend of lemon hues intermingled mysteriously amid paraffin. Some might taste a hint of sea salt, laced ever-so-slightly among citrusy grapefruit or mineral tannins. You'll find it to be popular along the Atlantic Ocean, as an invited guest to a seafood dinner or as an appetizer with oysters.*

*The grapes of Muscadet offer little flavor, as a result of the "Sur Lie" process that is used to create the wine. The hearty skins of the grapes add texture to the wine throughout the autumn fermentation, making Muscadet appear fresh, but with a sparkling carbonation.*

*Muscadet grapes are harvested from a vigorous soil, giving it an intense acidity with acute mineral notes that flicker mildly through the grapes' principally drab flavors. Honestly, there are too many bottles of Muscadet in existence to compete with other largely-favored white wines. Overproduction has been a problem in recent years, bearing immense quantity, rather than quality of the finished product.*

*Be prepared for a nervy, tart attitude. Muscadet can be both brilliant and lively, despite its background of bearing little flavor. It's the Ivy League of wines with pristine white shoes that are too cute to set foot in the mud. Muscadet feels most at home near the seagulls of an oceanside retreat.*

*Muscadet is an excellent choice for an afternoon game of polo, a fitting choice for brunch, or as an aphrodisiac after a rigorous game of tennis. It has a rich flair with twinkles of honeysuckle, ripe peaches, chalk and flour. Although not the most athletic of wines, Muscadet can appear lean and taut; almost bony at the finish.*

*In Europe, Muscadet can be found at most any intimate café. For that reason, it could be deemed quaint, yet with the charming curiosity of skepticism. It tries to impress people with luxurious qualities. Even if you wanted to pay more, it is simply impossible to find an expensive bottle of Muscadet. The truly exceptional bottles of Muscadet can be difficult to locate, although not impossible. There are those old-fashioned vintners who still hand-select the grapes of each batch of Muscadet. These winemakers pride themselves on better grape selections as opposed to imbalanced machine winemaking techniques.*

*Overall, Muscadet is plentiful enough, but has yet to gain the respect of more popular white wines. Muscadet is witty and captivating, but not fascinating enough to hold interest for any long period of time. You'll want to drink this one soon after it is opened and be sure not to hang on to it for too long because it will lose its tart freshness and can become rather dull after the cork is popped. Only then will you find Muscadet to be a refreshing choice among the many other popular wines available.*

❖❖❖❖❖❖❖❖❖

# MUSCADET ❣ Apricot

**He pulled up to the night club wearing his dopest** outfit. A pink prep shirt with an alligator on the front pocket; khaki Dockers; freshly-shined loafers; and slicked-back hair just long enough in the back to be feathered. Muscadet was ready for a night out on the town. He was hoping to get lucky with a few ladies. Or at least one, if nothing more than for bragging rights at the next frat party. Muscadet knew that he would be the coolest dude there because his Dad was the richest man in Sanfolk County, having made his wealth by acquiring the largest string of convenience store franchises in the whole state.

Muscadet rolled through town in his gleaming silver Volvo, which was freshly washed and waxed by thorough auto detailers the day before. He had a couple hundred bucks in his Ralph Lauren wallet, just waiting for the first pretty girl who made eye contact. Those devious girls often tricked him into spending more than he wanted to, with their coy flirtations and kind thank-you's, even after wasting $50 bucks on shots. They sometimes left him standing at the bar after they shared drinks, usually to go dance with the first bad-boy type of guy that walked in off the street. Muscadet couldn't understand why girls liked those tattooed mongrels. Bad boys were his main rival. How dare those muscle-heads come along and snatch up the prime ladies?

On this night, Muscadet's strategy was to sit at the edge of the bar, scoping the scene like a Cheetah searching for the weakest gazelle. Bingo! He cast his sights upon two lovelies at the middle of the bar. They were flirting with the bartender, who was buff and tough with a tight black tank top. Muscadet beckoned. "Hey Mister, I want you to send those two ladies a drink. Whatever they're having tonight. On me."

They giggled and waved. It would soon be time to make his move. Muscadet wasn't sure which one was digging him the most... the one on the left, or the right? Maybe both. He waited. About midway through the drinks, the girls stood up and made a beeline for the ladies room. '*Why do girls always go to the bathroom together?*' Muscadet wondered. '*What exactly do they do in there?*'

Fortunately, one of them stopped to talk to him on the way by. "Thank you for the drinks, honey," said the brunette with the big teeth.

Muscadet squinted. '*Oh well... I could put a bag over her head. She does have a curvy figure,*' he murmured as she passed. He had been hoping for her friend, the strawberry blonde. She had a cuter face and big jugglies. Muscadet liked the jugglies.

After the ladies reseated themselves at the bar, Muscadet made his way over to their seats. Both turned an ear back to hear which corny cliché he would use. "Excuse me, you dropped something over there when you came back from the restroom," Muscadet said, pointing at the floor.

"I'm not falling for that," laughed the strawberry blonde.

"No, really. Look!" Muscadet said. She bought it, and turned to look.

"My jaw!" Muscadet finished his greeting with his classic punch line. Both girls smiled at each other. Neither seemed as amused as he had hoped. They politely laughed. At least he was still standing there without getting slapped or spilled with a drink.

"So, would both of you lovely ladies like to dance? I just love this song by Snoop Dog," said Muscadet, trying his best to sound cool.

Bugs Bunny brunette snickered. "Snoop Dog? This is L.L. Cool J."

Just then, Muscadet spotted a woman on the dance floor who appeared to be dancing by herself. She was standing on the outskirts of a pack of girls. One of the girls was wearing a fake white veil. His eyes lit up. Bachelorette party! "I gotta go," Muscadet excused himself from the two snobby chicks at the bar, since he was getting nowhere. They weren't that attractive anyway. He knew that bachelorette party girls would be hot and bothered. '*They probably just left the Chippendales show*,' he thought out loud.

The Cheetah had found a gazelle; the lonely girl dancing by herself. She looked to be having fun. Muscadet snuck up behind her, strutting like a peacock. It was best to be sneaky, for fear of rejection. It was more like stalking. He began dancing right behind her, without even letting her see what he looked like. Muscadet liked to use that approach. This strategy had worked for him several times, although occasionally he was met with an angry girl or two who swung around to slap him. Or there were those who simply walked off the dance floor to get away. It was a hit or miss system.

Eventually, the girl turned around. "I'm going outside to get some air," she said.

"I'll buy you a drink, honey. What'll you have?" asked Muscadet.

"Um. Sure. I'll have a vodka and cran. With rocks." She touched the front of his shirt. "Thanks!" she yelled over the music, before darting off the scene.

Muscadet fought through the crowd at the bar. The place had filled up. He waved a big bill at the bartender. By the time he finally got service, he turned around with a drink in each hand to see the inevitable. The girl he had just bought the drink for had come back in and was already dancing with some bad boy type. She was laughing and staring into his eyes, completely oblivious to Muscadet staring at her by the edge of the dance floor. Unfortunately, there was nothing he could do. The bad boy guy was well-built and muscular. If Muscadet went up to her, he was surely looking for an ass-whooping. Rather than trying to compete, he held both drinks, trying to get her attention by glaring at her.

Drats. She did not look up from her intensely smitten smile. Muscadet had already been forgotten and replaced by the tough guy with the tattoos. '*Why do women like those darn bad boy types, anyway?*' Muscadet walked away after a ten minute stare down. She had hardly paid him a glance.

Muscadet glanced at his Tommy Hilfiger watch. Time was ticking and so far he had chosen the wrong targets. He had already blown it with the strawberry blonde and Bugs Bunny. And now the lonely dancing girl had already become enraptured by the bad boy muscle-head guy. All within the short amount of time it took him to buy drinks. And where was the bachelorette party? It looked like those girls were long gone. Muscadet should have pursued them, as it was his first inclination.

Frustrated, Muscadet walked back to the other side of the club near the couches. He sat down for a minute, sipping the extra vodka and cran that was meant to be an elixir for the lovestruck dancing girl. *'I just don't get it,'* he shook his head. *'I'm a good-looking Harvard kid with gobs of money. Maybe I should pretend to be one of those tough guys.'*

As he was sitting on the pleather sofa, Muscadet looked up to see a skinny girl with fake boobs. She was highly intoxicated. "I just broke out of prison," he blurted out, while trying his best to make the little bumps on his biceps look bigger.

The skinny girl immediately clapped her hand over her mouth and said, "I don't feel so good." Muscadet had just enough time to slide down, hoping she wouldn't barf all over the sofa. She looked at him and said, "You're a very funny guy. That's the funniest thing I've heard all night. What kinds of prisons accept Mr. Rogers?"

"Mr. Rogers?" Muscadet emphatically shook his head back and forth in a peculiar manner. "I just got out for .... for ... robbing a bank and stuff."

"Oh s-s-seriously. You should be a comedian," laughed the skinny girl. "They would have their way with you in prison. You're a pretty boy."

"I'll have you know I am very tough, indeed!" that was enough small talk for Muscadet. It was now 1:30 and he had only a half an hour before the bar closed. It was time to cut to the chase. "So, you want to go listen to some music or something?" he asked the drunken prospect.

"No." she said, still laughing and wobbling.

Muscadet stood up. There was no time to waste acting desperate with this one. She seemed a little over the cusp of potential illness anyway. Out of the crowd of leftover women who were still dancing, he figured the horny ones would be easy to spot, especially those girls who had been left behind by some of their friends who had hooked up.

He scanned the crowd again. Muscadet spotted another ripe lead. She was a voluptuous girl with crazy hair, who was wearing long strands of beads. She was kind of hippie-ish. As a bonus, the girl was so wasted it looked like she would run into the wall at any given moment. Muscadet studied her patterns, like a mathematician studying a formula. Bounce, bounce, trip. Bounce, bounce, trip. She stumbled every couple of steps. '*Perfect.*' He thought. '*This one's easy. I could get her without slipping a roofie in her drink.*'

On her next trip (after the bounce, bounce), Muscadet grabbed the girl's waist and held her up. "Whoa there, cutie. Don't be falling for me just yet. We just met."

She looked up at him. "Yer my hee-ro," she slurred as her eyes looked off at the disco ball spinning from the ceiling.

"C'mon. Let me make sure you get home safely," said Muscadet. "You seem to have lost your friends. Who did you come here with?"

Crazy hair girl replied, "I dunno. A buncha people." She struggled to remember.

"What's your name?" he asked.

"Apricot. Like the color, not the fruit," she replied.

He rolled his eyes. *Great, another fruitcake.* "It's okay," Muscadet assured her. "I'll get you home."

"But I don't know you. Maybeeeeee you jusss escaped from prissson," she sloshed.

"Hmmm... you know me too well already," Muscadet said, charmingly. "Not unless prison is at Harvard. I'm majoring in nuclear radiology engineering."

"Wowie! So yer a smart fucker, ain'tchya?" Apricot giggled.

"C'mon. It's not nice to swear." Muscadet grabbed her hand. She stumbled along the cobblestone side streets, clinging tightly to his arm. Muscadet placed his arm territorially around her waist, not letting her go. "This one's mine," he pointed when they arrived at his car.

Apricot tried to whistle. "Wow. It'ssss some bad whips you got. What kinda car is it?"

"A Volvo S40 sedan. It's a luxury car," Muscadet bragged.

"Jazz so spatial 'bout it?" she barely made sense, trying her best to stand on her 4" pumps. Apricot was severely intoxicated, to the point where it was borderline whether or not Muscadet even wanted to bother with her. It was too late. He had offered. "Where to?"

"Where are we?" she asked.

He answered, "Club Hypnotic. Downtown."

She stared at the sky through the sunroof. "It'sss 321 Northwessst Boulevard. Or is it Northeassst? Wade-a minute," Apricot was confused. "Na na na. Isss Northwessst. Always go with your firssst in-sync. Izz my philosssaffee."

Muscadet drove, annoyed by her apparent drunkenness. He reached in to touch her knee. "Donchew go tryin' anything funny," she scolded. He reached up higher as they sped up the street. Muscadet figured if he could just get her past the outskirts of the lights, Apricot would fall for his seductive strategies.

"C'mon honey. We've been having fun together all night," he wooed.

"Pull over! Pull over!" Apricot choked back, as they drove to the edge of suburbia. "I think I hafta be sick."

Muscadet rolled his eyes as she stuck her head out the door next to a ditch. Another lost evening. After her disgustingly torturous retribution from a whole evening's worth of drinking, Muscadet dropped Apricot off outside her door but thought better of inviting himself in. In fact, he practically shoved her out of the Volvo.

Apricot stumbled out of the car, blowing Muscadet a kiss. "Thunks a myyllion. What wuz yer name? Nexx time I'll try to remurmer yer name."

He sighed, as he drove home defeated. His stereo played the "Sounds of Silence" with the legendary melancholy hum of Simon & Garfunkel. Muscadet sung along.

*Hello darkness, my old friend*
*I've come to talk with you again ...*

~ © *Paul Simon, 1964*

Knowing another lonely evening back at his folks' house was the only thing in store; Muscadet sped down the road, enjoying the turbo power of his prized Volvo. '*Oh well, there's always Friday night.*'

❖❖❖❖❖❖❖❖❖

# PROVISO

**Although dry, Muscadet is still fascinating and** sometimes even witty. The Yuppie entertains women; if not for the laughs he will entice, than by the stories they will tell. He is matter-of-factly suggestive, and sometimes too smart to be clever. However, Muscadet's shallow upbringing offers little creativity, making it corny on the top sip.

Often illiterate when it comes to women, Muscadet is refreshingly naïve and best sipped when it is first released. Most Muscadets have lived a cushy lifestyle with butlers and valet parking. Women may sense a man of little depth. On occasion, you may find those who have put themselves through an Ivy League school, rather than through a trust fund. Perhaps it could be compared to those Muscadets which are handmade by winemakers, rather than by wine-making machines. To some extent, people and grapes often turn out as good as they are raised.

Muscadet has to work hard to entertain a woman's fancy. It's because he is not as noticeable as some of the more aggressive wines. Fewer people come across Muscadet than they do a nice Merlot, Chardonnay or Zinfandel. These are the "alpha" wines that fly off the store shelves much faster than Muscadet or Beaujolais.

Muscadet would have a better chance by exposing more depth. A woman likes to be strummed like a beautiful harp, rather than shaken up like an electric guitar. That is where Muscadet errs. It tries too hard to be noticed, which makes it seem silly. Just saying "Muscadet" is enough to bring up the giggles. Come to think of it, Yuppie is quite a giggly-licious word, too.

Quite honestly, most women are looking for more creativity in a wine than Muscadet can bring. Women are soulful creatures. They are drawn to confidence and charisma. While noble, going to Yale or Harvard is not the only thing needed to impress them. Sometimes even the finest wineries – the Ivy Leagues of wineries – will put out very similar products, which is something more consumers are becoming aware of.

Muscadet can be a fun wine, for sure. Yet it's extremely difficult to find a bottle that's not cliché. Don't let that stop you from trying it to determine if you will like it. Muscadets vary depending on how the grapes were raised and if they have gone through the process of fermentation to finished product properly. Just beware of the lack of differentiation between brands.

When you do happen upon a great Muscadet, its freshness will be like a slap in the face. It's surprising citrus will bring a sparkle to your eye. You might even wonder how you got so lucky as to find the sexiest Yuppie of the whole batch!

At first glance, Muscadet looks expensive. It does have a classy-looking elegance that looks polished and neat. Occasionally, you'll even get a cute one. Certain bottles of Muscadet can be very dashing. Overall, Muscadet is definitely worth a try, especially if you find one that is not too tart and incompatible with your taste buds.

# Port Wine

## "THE SUGAR DADDY"

***With its sophisticated taste and well aged maturity,*** *one of the richest of the sweet wines on the market is undoubtedly Port Wine. Yet the fact that it's so sweet makes Port Wine a choice only to be enjoyed on special occasions, perhaps with dessert or as an aperitif instead of as a main course. Port prefers to be surrounded by fine company rather than by itself. Port Wine is a social butterfly.*

*Like a fine pair of Italian stilettos, Port has an elegance that extends beyond its initial appearance, leaving a lasting impression that is difficult for anyone to look past. Its higher alcohol content, as compared to many of the world's other wines, is only one of the many selling points of Port. Unlike many of its sweet competitors, Port has an added element of distilled grape spirits that fortifies the strength of the alcohol content. By halting the fermentation, Port Wine maintains the lingering sugar content prior to its conversion to alcohol. Therefore, even small sips of this delicious wine will give its drinker a warm, tingling feeling all over. It's a buzzy, heady type of sweetness and intensity that is saturated in a history of wealth.*

*Known as being more of a dessert wine, this entirely rich, heavy and intense red is very appealing, indeed. One of its unique characteristics is the distinctive process of making such a fine wine. Having aged perfectly in wooden barrels that allow the wine to breathe, fortify and develop its fervent richness for many years, Port Wine comes out on top as one of the most exciting, yet often overlooked of all exotic wines. Vintage Port is especially delightful and can be enjoyed at any fancy party in which it would be acceptable to court luxury.*

*Top chefs at the classiest of five star restaurants will gladly reach for a bottle of Port Wine to cook with. Its candy-like sugar bearing will bring a smile to the face of any well-to-do patron, especially those of whom have a taste for the finer things. With a heritage dating back to the mid 1700s, Port Wine was once significantly scarce. Coming from the highly protected wine region in Portugal, Port was often stored in vats at the bottom of caves and cellars after aging for many years in wooden barrels. This maturity process is still a part of Port's rich winemaking tradition. Because of its prolonged aging requirements, Port Wine is able to soak up a lot of wisdom and knowledge. Vintage Ports must be bottled within two years. And the very best can age 50 years or more.*

*Although there are hundreds of grape varieties that are sanctioned for its production, Port Wine uses less than a handful of grapes for its introduction. Vintage Ports are the best and most expensive. They must be made from grapes of single vintage and only from the best "declared" or superior vintages. The difficulty in growing grapes for Port Wine is one of the reasons for its affluence. As a general rule of thumb, a Port producer won't make a traditional vintage Port in undeclared years. However, they will make other types of Port. The small yields make it highly sought after, yet undervalued in certain circles.*

*The brilliant success of Port Wine comes from having a well-managed reputation. Consuming Port too early will make its taste unpleasant because of the high tannin content during its youthful stages. The gradual improvement in taste comes from the softening of its tannins as it matures. Coming from vineyards designated especially for Port, the grapes are easily characterized as dense and small. This makes for long lasting flavors that will remain intact and get better with time.*

*Port Wine is not to be guzzled. It is not to be wasted. In fact, Port Wine is meant to be drunk meaningfully. A special colorless, yet narrow glass is reserved for Port so that it can be filled halfway, leaving the remainder of the glass free for swirling and breathing. This releases the vibrant bouquet of smells and highlights the colors that have been quietly developing during the prolonged process of fermentation.*

*But there are many styles or variations of Port Wine. There are those who have matured in sealed glass jars, others who have matured in freshly cut wooden barrels and some lucky enough to have done both. You have smooth Port Wines and the viscous kinds, some that are sweet and doting and those who are intense and dominating. All are dignified. Its classy flair is quite anticipated, however not always appreciated until after it is consumed. Yes, once that bottle dries up and becomes empty, it is a sad day without Port Wine in your life.*

*Few wines can compare to the expectations of Port Wine's type of consumer. They are the type who yearns for luxury and who demand richness. Ports can be very pricey because of the strict qualifications that must be met and the intense fortification process. Tangible traits are the most influential when it comes to pricing Port Wines.*

*It is recommended that all novice Port drinkers begin their love affair with Port's full-bodied nature by trying a ruby or tawny version to become familiar with the complexities. These lighter variations will elicit sparkly feelings that will spoil you in a way that makes you crave more.*

❖❖❖❖❖❖❖❖❖

# PORT ❣ Ruby

**Sauntering down the aisle of the first class section** of the Boeing 767, Ruby couldn't help but to swish her hips as she walked past the distinguished gentleman in the second row. With his salt and pepper hair and square-set jaw, he certainly looked chiseled and dapper in his expensive suit. "Hmmm... this could be an interesting flight," she thought. Ruby sat down and turned to wink at him. Coyly, he peeked out from under his rectangular glasses and sent a flirtatious smirk in return.

He bit. After the flight took off, the man extended his hand across the aisle. "Excuse me; I just wanted to tell you that you look very stunning today. I hope that doesn't offend you." He paused. "Of course I don't know what you look like any other day, but today you do look exquisite."

"Thanks," said Ruby, gently shaking his hand in return.

He shivered, slightly. "Your touch gave me goose bumps. The name's Port. Port Wine," he said.

"Ruby," she replied, shaking her strawberry colored mane and leaning back in her recliner. Yeah, she was a diva. And she knew it.

Throughout the flight, the two flirted merrily and exchanged details. Ruby was 26 years younger than Port, working as a successful administrator for one of the country's leading pharmaceutical companies. Port was a self-made entrepreneur. In fact, he was on a flight for business, on his way to attend a big trade show in Chicago after launching his male hair growth invention into a national enterprise. The two were, in fact, headed towards the same trade show, except Ruby's job was to man a corporate booth, while Port's was to spy on the competition by posing as an attendee.

"Let me take you out to dinner, Ruby," Port said assumingly. "If you're not doing anything later."

"Sure, I'm staying at the Renaissance just above the convention center where the tradeshow is to be held. I'll meet you in the lobby after I freshen up. Say, 8:30?" Ruby agreed. Why not let a handsome gentleman buy her dinner? It would beat take out, hands down.

So as the two departed the airport, Port agreed to meet Ruby at the Renaissance. He was staying in a friend's penthouse nearby. Ruby went back to her room and showered, put on her makeup and quickly ran a straightening iron through her beautiful mane of hair.

When she walked down the stairs to the lobby, Port was standing at the bar, sipping a rich-looking wine. "Aperitif?" he asked as Ruby slid up beside him.

"Why yes, I think I just might like one of those. Wine makes me giddy," Ruby giggled.

"Perfect. And by the way, you look amazing. That dress is very becoming," he smiled.

"Becoming what?" Ruby asked, with a puzzled look.

"You've never heard of becoming? It's like ... another word for flattering," Port explained.

"Hmmmm, that's pretty old school" she mumbled.

The two chatted and laughed and he wined her and dined her all evening. Ruby played the role well and laughed at all of his jokes, placing her hands ever so flirtatiously on his sleeve as he spoke.

"Tomorrow I would love to take you shopping," Port offered.

With a twinkle in her eye, Ruby said, "Oh you don't have to do that!"

"It would be my pleasure," he said sternly. "Please, I really want to take you shopping if you'll let me. No strings attached."

For a moment, she thought about it. No man had ever offered to take her shopping. Ruby liked the thought of having a few new things to add to her wardrobe. "Why not?" she reasoned. Silently, she told herself how much she deserved it after all of the BS she had put up with in past relationships with younger men. Now, it was her time to be spoiled.

So the next day, Ruby showed up wearing her nicest sweater dress with a fashionable belt she had acquired from her roommate's closet back at their apartment in Ft. Lauderdale.

"This will be fun," said Port, upon seeing her come through the elevator. His eyes grew bigger than snow cones. Ruby smiled sweetly, kissing him on the cheek.

They spent the entire day at the mall, visiting stores like Victoria's Secret, Saks Fifth Avenue, Bloomingdales and

Macy's. In her head, Ruby estimated that Port had spent about $1,500 on the purchases they made. There were a couple of things he had bought for himself, as well. Namely, a new bottle of Montale Aoud Blossom Cologne, which Ruby told Port would drive her wild, and a pair of Balenciaga sunglasses that made him look ten years younger. At least, that was what she told him.

They ate lunch together and Port grabbed Ruby's hands, lovingly. "I want you to be my Sugar Baby," he said frankly.

Nearly spitting out her drink, she said loudly, "You're what?"

"My Sugar Baby. I will spoil you and make you happy. In return it will make me happy and I will enjoy your companionship whenever I'm in town," he explained.

"Well, how often do you visit South Florida?" Ruby asked.

"I have three main corporations that I manage across the country. One in Miami, another in San Francisco and a third in New York," he told her.

"I'm going to have to think about this," Ruby muttered, with her head down. "I really like you and feel a spark with you, but I'm not sure how I feel about being with someone who is gone all the time. Plus, I'm not ready to settle down yet."

"You don't have to. When I'm in town, you will be all mine. But after I'm gone, the choice is yours," Port said reassuringly. "I'll even put you up in a nice condo so that you won't have to worry about working so hard and trying to pay your rent. We'll have fun together, you and I."

And so it was to be, that the following week Ruby agreed to become Port Wine's Sugar Baby. Port hired a limo to go pick her up from work and bring her to him. He blindfolded her with a blue satin eye mask and drove with her for what seemed like a half an hour. "Don't worry, my dear. This is going to be the surprise of your life."

She opened her eyes to a wealthy-looking townhome, with Spanish revival décor both inside and out. Yellow and fuchsia hibiscus flowers graced the doorway, making her breathtaking walk up the stucco stoop one that tempted all of her senses.

"What do you think?" he inquired, staring into her eyes with lust. "Would you like to live here and see me on a regular basis?"

How could Ruby possibly say no? After living in a run-down apartment on the West side of I-95 – with a sloppy roommate who had a dog that often pooped on the carpet – living in this gorgeous townhome all to herself sounded like a dream.

Port was the perfect gentleman. He was handsome, sophisticated and fun. He was often part of the socialite scene and attended swanky gatherings at Country Clubs where other rich folks gathered. Ruby would have been in heaven living the lifestyle, had it not been for the fact that he was gone most of the time. Yet, Port continued to assure her that change was in the works, right after their business affairs were taken care of.

Silently, Ruby wondered if this man was just stringing her along. *Perhaps he had Sugar Babies in other cities?* She wondered. But the benefits outweighed the cons. Port was fun and loved spoiling her. And Ruby loved to be spoiled. Soon she was outfitted with the best of the best. He bought her hair extensions, jewelry, shoes, designer purses and clothes, and even a small Chihuahua named "Blinky" that she could put in her purse.

He also offered to buy her breast implants. It seemed like everyone was getting them. However, Ruby was already quite endowed with big "C's" so she declined, thinking that somewhere down the line she may want to have a kid or two when she was older. Ruby knew that if she did, it could adversely affect her breast size. Plus, she heard from a few other girls at the fitness club that it hurt for months afterward. She was much too spleeny to go through any self-inflicted pain, even if it were for a great cause like fake titties.

After dating Port for nearly a year, Ruby was smooth, sexy and spoiled. Her hair had never looked better. She was able to hire a personal fitness trainer and spend her days getting manicures and facials. She met other women and became part of their clique of spoiled wives and mistresses of rich men. It was true: money could make you look like a supermodel. One thing that Ruby noticed, however, was that many of the women were not happy. They had everything money could buy, yet constantly talked about how miserable they were. Some of their whining was over the most inconsequential and trivial of things.

"The other day, Hans messed up my bangs and cut them too short!" griped one of the rich bimbos.

"Oh, you think that's bad, well the other day I came home to find my teenage son getting it on with his high school girlfriend in my house!" exclaimed the other one.

All of the women hushed in silence and looked at her.

One of them piped up and said, "I have both of you beaten. I got a parking ticket the other day for leaving my golf cart too close to the handicap zone at the beach. I mean, don't they have better things to do than give out parking tickets for golf carts?" she whined. "I didn't even realize those counted as real vehicles."

"Well, they are bigger than your average skateboard!" said Ruby, trying to fit in by being funny. But the women just looked at her as if she had three heads.

All of these women were boring and simple-minded. Birds of a feather flock together. If Ruby wanted to be with Port, she had to play the role of socialite and hang out with these little squawkers. She was his Barbie Doll and he was Ken, except a little older and more distinguished with his salt and pepper hair.

Even though he tried his best, Port was not available to spend much time with Ruby, especially during the week. He was either working or on a business trip. So, Port was really more of a dessert date for her. His lack of emotional and physical presence made Ruby lonely, so she sought out the companionship of other males when not with Port.

Ruby also found Port to be very controlling, both in his business and personal affairs. She often heard him on the phone, dealing with clients or employees who dared to defy his concepts. "*How bossy*," she thought out loud, just under her breath.

Yet Ruby had come to love their arrangement in other ways. Because of his lack of availability, she was able to live in a luxurious home for free and still have plenty of time to do the things that made her happy. Like going to the tanning salon, the hair salon, the nail salon, the spa or the mall. Plus, she could work out with a personal trainer, both at the gym and at home. Ruby realized how lucky she was to have the best of both worlds.

But after a year of living the lifestyle of luxury, Ruby realized how shallow she had become. She couldn't remember the last time she had read a book or worked for anything. Her ambitions and aspirations had drifted away, like the mist after a hot rainstorm. Ruby's relationships had no depth or meaning. They were just as phony as the plastic on a mannequin at the lingerie store. Or as superficial as some of the women she hung out with.

Other women envied her, but deep down inside, Ruby did not feel truly good about herself. Her beauty was bought, along with her body and soul. Remaining bonded to the Sugar Daddy was like being a call girl, except with a fancier name: "Sugar Baby". Ruby secretly wished for a break so that she could find and fall in love with her "Mr. Right" and start a family. Port Wine already had kids who were almost adults, so he had no desire to have more. In fact, he had undergone the knife to ensure that no accidents could ever happen. Surely that would have been difficult to explain to his adult kids that his twenty-something girlfriend had gotten herself knocked up.

Finally, Ruby had to look in the mirror and be truthful with herself. She had enjoyed the company of Port Wine and all his sweetness and spoiling, but alas, all good desserts eventually do end... even after the cherry on top has been plucked and eaten. She had to find some way to end it before things went any further, and before she lost the chance to do something meaningful with her life. It was never her intent to keep Port Wine for the long term. Really, all Ruby had wanted was to have fun and be spoiled. She had never tried dating a man like Port and it was wonderful.

Port had brought out the gluttony in her and she was ashamed. As she looked around, Ruby realized that she could have all of these luxuries even without a man to buy them for her. All she had to do was come up with a successful idea of her own. Now that she had a lot of influential connections, Ruby was confident that it could be done.

And so it was, on that day, that the Sugar Baby told the girl who stared back at her from the mirror to "Get Real."

With that, Ruby packed up everything she could fit into the Lexus SUV that Port had given her on their one year anniversary. She thought about returning it to him but kept it instead, deciding that she deserved it. "*All's well that ends well,*" Ruby happily chanted. With that, she hit the road. Her new destination was success.

❖❖❖❖❖❖❖❖❖

# PROVISO

**A wine as rich and sweet and wonderful as Port** Wine will be memorable to drink. By the world's standards, you have made it. Men who represent a fine Port can have most any woman they want, just by tempting her with the lure of shopping and a fancy vocabulary. Women will fawn all over this luxurious red wine, no matter what it looks like or how old it is. In fact, the vintage Ports are even more sought after than the young ones. Age does not matter for the Sugar Daddy. He can buy companionship if he has the cash to do so, which he does.

Many guys envy the Sugar Daddy in a way. It seems unfair that this vintage wine can sweep up some of the young ladies just because they have 20 or so years of sophistication and wealth under their belts. For some women, Port Wine is a better choice than younger wines that spoil too soon.

Port Wine is luxurious, as is the Sugar Daddy. Women may love the lifestyle he represents even more so than the wine itself. Unfortunately, the grapes of Port Wine may get stomped on a time or two because of the age difference. He may find his woman in the arms of another tempting red – such as Pinot Noir, Shiraz or Chianti. Port Wine is just not a wine to drink frequently or for the long term. Its super sweetness is better as a dessert.

Women who have tried dating a Sugar Daddy know of the benefits. He is worldly and urbane. He spoils you and treats you like a lady. He gives you things you could never afford for yourself or that you would never expect any younger wines to be able to buy. Plus, Port Wine screams "great taste." It will enhance beauty. It will make you feel good about yourself. It may even lift your self-esteem with compliments and chivalrous acts. The younger wines simply don't have that kind of wisdom yet. Plus there's just too many of 'em. Port Wine is outnumbered by its sheer scarcity. Most wines this age are long gone, having been drunk well before their vintage release.

Some people may stare if you order Port Wine. Some will gossip and whisper. They may wonder what a younger woman is doing with a glass of such a sweet older wine. But Port Wine will not budge, at least for a while. As long as it remains rich and sweet. As long as everyone is happy with the arrangement and knows what it's all about, then there's no harm in trying it. Everyone has a different definition of happiness.

Enjoy it while it lasts. The Sugar Daddy is probably not a forever thing. It's an enjoyable relationship, at least for now. The feeling of being spoiled is something unforgettable and will set the bar high for other wines. Port Wine is classy, well-to-do and will leave you buzzed in a daze of its decadence. Its sophisticated richness is undeniably delicious and will give you a feeling of longing. Drink up! Everyone deserves a glass of this ultra fabulous wine at least once in a lifetime!

# Chablis

## "THE WORKAHOLIC"

***In many parts of the world, Chablis is a desirable type*** *of wine. That is, if it is an authentic Chablis. The table jug wines that have cleverly made their way to convenience stores, supermarkets and on the tabletops of less picky wine drinkers are hardly considered the same Chablis as that of its origin in the northernmost wine district of French Burgundy territory. Those overly fruity, corner market blends are not something to give the host of the party. It's like giving the equivalent of a fruitcake.*

*However, authentic Chablis is dry, crisp and earthy on the palate. The grapes have endured many wars, epidemics and hardships on their way to what is currently sold as Chablis. Some say the vines were first planted by the Romans. Then during the Dark Ages, monks put forth great efforts to develop a respectable wine for monastery communions. For a long time, Chablis remained in the dark until a few centuries later when it was reintroduced on the country slopes of England to the marketplaces in Paris and Belgium. However, the Little Ice Age, French Revolution and Prussian invasions ravaged the vineyards of these territories. Once again, Chablis was shunned to the dark and all but forgotten until the nineteenth century.*

*Before Chablis could fully recover from several eras of war and turmoil, the industry was met with even more hurdles when a phylloxera epidemic and two World Wars ruined all the crops. It wasn't until the second half of the 20th Century that Chablis bounced back to become a successful wine. Once it finally rebounded, sales of Chablis surged in the 1970s through the 1990s. It became a wine industry anomaly as people clamored to know this bright and prosperous wine.*

*Known for its pale, yet brilliant colors and refreshing point-of-view, Chablis displays distinctive characteristics of sophistication and slightly acidic tones. Its personality can be lively, except in the jug table versions. However, Chablis is more concerned with success than good taste.*

*Chablis wines are actually made from the grapes of Chardonnay. Therefore, it has many of the same characteristics as the "Friend with Benefits.", except that Chablis is often too busy working at marketing itself than to be concerned with intimacy. It longs for admiration, although never gaining the same respect as other more favorable wines. Frost can wipe out an entire crop. Indeed, sketchy temperature fluctuations can put Chablis out of business for an entire season. If that happens, then competing Chablis vineyards from other wine regions of the world will prevail. Alas, that is the effect of today's competitive global marketplace.*

*Moreover, Chablis must overcome hard winters and sultry summers. Spring frosts are not the only endangerment to this fluctuating variety. The careful process of planting and cultivating Chablis must be done with care, making it more costly when compared to other more "easygoing" types of wines. New technologies have been effective in salvaging Chablis' place within the wine industry. Techniques like spraying the grapes with water to avoid freezing have helped to improve their likeliness for success. A lot of producers are in favor of fermenting in stainless steel barrels, as opposed to oak barrels. Those wine makers operate more traditionally than some of today's new fangled wine-making 'mad scientists'.*

*Described as crisp, dry and steely with an aroma of minerals, slate or wet rocks, Chablis delivers a rich texture with bland tones of almond, green apple and butter. Its pale yellow façade matures into something like bitter peach pits. Chablis is forward on the palate with a simple body, although rather short on taste. The star-bright clarity ages well and mellows as it becomes more mature, deepening its golden color.*

*As a food wine, Chablis is a fascinating choice. By itself, not so much. Its personality is all business with a plain first impression and cleansing character that can be quite complicated. Chablis takes more work and effort to earn a spot at the table, but in certain circles it does very well.*

*Some wine experts believe Chablis is one of the most authentic expressions of the Chardonnay grape because of its simplicity in the winemaking process. There are four known types of Chablis, each having their own level of distinction.*

*Going up the scale, Chablis gets more rounded, brilliant and complex. Lesser known vineyards often borrow the name of Chablis from a group of reputable vineyards; therefore you must do your homework to determine authenticity of the quality. Just as with any type of enterprise, there will always be knock-offs that are never quite as good as the originals.*

*Knowing the four categories may lead to better luck in finding Chablis wines that have both character and substance.*

- ***Petit Chablis:*** *A lower end jug wine that many wine snobs find despicable. Although some like it, most Petit Chablis are not worthy of sharing the authentic and great Chablis namesake. You might call this the blue collar of the entire Chablis enterprise.*

- ***Chablis:*** *An acidic and slightly innocuous village wine that varies depending on the climate, soil and craftsmanship of the vintner. Its mineral base can be likened to seashells, which are very delicate and fresh. These popular white collar table wines get the job done.*

- ***Premier Cru:*** *Since there are only forty variations of Premier Crus, these complex Chablis wines are rather expensive, ranging between $20 - $100 (depending on the year of production). It can be likened to upper management or entrepreneurial pursuits.*

- ***Grand Crus:*** *These intense Chablis are grown only within a selective group of seven vineyards. They have optimum grounds of sunny hillsides and fertile soil. Although very expensive, Grand Cru Chablis is the most revered and age-worthy of all Chablis in production. These are like well-established corporate masterminds or millionaires.*

❖ ❖ ❖ ❖ ❖ ❖ ❖ ❖ ❖

# CHABLIS ❣ Fern

**Even as a young boy, Chablis was taught the values** of a hard work. His parents owned a big potato farm and Chablis was required to labor on the family farm from sunup to sundown. He was assigned numerous responsibilities, from milking cows, shoveling manure and plucking eggs from the family chickens; to picking peaches and apples from the family orchard or turning the soil to plant the annual harvest. Chablis was no stranger to working hard for his survival.

What he did not learn was how to express his feelings. That was something people only displayed on drama series ... like *Dallas* or *Knot's Landing*. Instead, Chablis stuffed his emotions deep inside and learned to bury them under piles of work. It was better that way, since there was always work to be done; it kept his mind focused on what he had to do. Therefore, Chablis developed a stoic demeanor that was more difficult to crack than a safe at the Federal Reserve.

From an age that he could barely remember, Chablis satisfied the requirements of his family by working six long days a week. His brain was always thinking of ways to break out of the manual labor rut. Chablis often dreamed of becoming a policeman, lawyer or an inventor. In his mind, he was constantly solving cases or dreaming of new ideas that could make things easier for people. Chablis was driven to become rich and successful – despite the grim outlook. Considering his need to drop out of school by the eighth grade to work on the farm full time, his family's expectations did not make it feasible. However, this did not faze Chablis in his pursuit of a serendipitous journey.

Even through early adulthood, Chablis constantly thought of new concepts, day and night. Whether he was asleep or awake, his mind was moving faster than a laser across the moon. Yet, how could he break free from the circle of expectations? If one simple frost or mysterious weather pattern wiped out the entire crop, the family farm would have struggled for an entire season. He wished for a day when his family would no longer have to rely on the farm to sustain them financially. So, Chablis enlisted in the Army . He knew that after he fulfilled his four years in the army, he would be able to enroll in college and secure a future for his family. Once he made the decision to do it, Chablis was more determined than ever to succeed.

After making it through bootcamp, Chablis was assigned to Fort Bliss in El Paso, Texas. As an eager new rookie, Chablis was anxious to do something great and was excited to finally see something in the world besides the small town atmosphere of the farm where he was raised.

Not long after arriving in Texas, Chablis went out with some of his new friends to a billiard hall called the Texan Topshots. There was a cute brunette there with curly locks and a sweet Southern accent. Back in his hometown, there were not many girls that Chablis had been interested in dating. Not that he had ever had any time in between work and going to school, which occupied most of his days and weekends.

Their eyes met across the pool table as he bent down to take a shot. Just then he spotted cleavage, and lots of it. “Better not sink that ball in the wrong pocket,” the girl smiled.

“And what if I did?” Chablis asked.

“Well it just might get ya in a heap o’ hot water,” she jived.

"With who?" Chablis looked around for a bouncer.

"Don't underestimate a Texan lady," she said. "I could wrestle you down just fine if I had to."

"Now, that I would like to see," Chablis dared. "As a matter of fact, I just might let you do it."

After a night's worth of flirting, Chablis went back to the girl's apartment in a nearby neighborhood. She had it decorated interestingly enough, with a bunch of random things thrown together. There were knick knacks, western-style pots, cowgirl boots, exercise equipment and a lava lamp sitting next to a vintage lamp from the early twentieth century.

Fern was working as a hairdresser, but also studying to be a nurse. Chablis had never been able to date girls much back home because of working so many hours on the farm. There was also a lack of any real prospects in the village he had grown up in. So just as any guy his age would do, when the first pretty girl came along who showed interest, Chablis seized the opportunity. They began dating.

The dark haired beauty was fun, although she lacked the depth that Chablis longed for. Fern was quite simple and wholesomely good-hearted, which was worth even more than intelligence to some guys. Her domestic skills were noticed and appreciated, since Chablis often had to work long hours. His cute Texan girlfriend loved to cook him dinner and had a sweet romantic side. But after seven months of dating her, Chablis was suddenly called upon to go overseas to fight in the Gulf War. He didn't want to break up with Fern because he really liked her, even though he didn't really have a chance to experience any other real relationships.

So, Chablis asked Fern to marry him. They had to do it hastily, for he was scheduled to ship out within three weeks. Talking about feelings wasn't something Chablis was good at, since his family had always been too busy working. Hence, his proposal was carried out somewhat simply. While lying in his bed staring at the ceiling for what seemed like hours, Chablis gently shook Fern's arm to wake her.

Startled, she looked at Chablis, wondering if something was wrong. "I have something on my mind," he said. "I'm going to be gone for a long time, and I really want you to be here for me when I get back. So ... do you wanna get married ... or something?"

"That's the strangest marriage proposal I've ever heard," Fern whispered, still half asleep.

"Do you need me to get down on my knee?" he asked.

"Not necessarily," she giggled.

"Oh, I have this ..." said Chablis, handing Fern a small velvet box.

Inside was a small, yet sufficiently- sized diamond. "It's more of a promise ring for now, until I get some more money," Chablis offered .

"Sure, honey ... I'll marry yoooou," she smiled sweetly, wiping a tear from the left corner of her eye. Fern's accent was still adorable, even in the middle of the night. After the proposal, they made love and then shared a big bowl of Chunky Chocolate Chip ice cream.

Instead of all the usual fuss of a big wedding, they agreed to get married by the Justice of the Peace. Fern promised her family they would have a bigger wedding on their one year anniversary to make up for it. Her parents were concerned about her rush to tie the knot , even though they liked Chablis and thought him to be a good guy.

What Fern hadn't considered was how lonely it would be to get married to someone who was never home. She loved Chablis, but while he was gone overseas, she was extremely forlorn. So Fern made friends with some of the other women at the military base. They all bonded because they could all relate to the heartache of having their husbands away for too long. Besides, it was only for a year or so and then Chablis would be home for good so they could be together.

At least, that was how she justified it. When he finally did come home for a visit, Fern got pregnant. By the time he went back to his platoon overseas, she was already three months along. There was a chance he may not be home for the birth of their newborn, a baby girl. Chablis spoke to Fern on the phone as often as he could, but it was not the same as being there for support throughout her pregnancy.

Fern's fears came true when she delivered early. Chablis had tried to arrange a return visit around the same time as his wife's due date; however, she delivered two weeks early. Nevertheless, Chablis was able to come back to meet his baby girl and hold her for a few days before returning back to his assignment.

On the bright side, Fern was less lonely since she had a baby to focus her attention, but their marital differences spanned greater whenever they talked on the phone. All Fern talked about was baby stuff. The baby did this today; the baby did that today. It rolled, it pooped, it giggled, it ate green beans. Chablis was not good at talking about his feelings, but he felt so far removed from baby talk. His world was filled with covert missions and stressful work assignments, like dodging IED's that were hidden in the ground by enemy forces. Talking about baby poop was not high on his agenda, so he often drowned out Fern's stories with cordial "Uh-huh's" whenever they spoke. Chablis had never really gotten to know his wife, even while they dated. She was just a girl he really liked. His first love.

Finally, after a year and ten months serving overseas, Chablis was sent home and relieved of his obligations. He was able to continue working for the Army if he chose to do so. Chablis could also get a free education, which he planned to take advantage of. So, he took a job in a security position and was promised a great shift of three days on and four days off. Since he shared a car with his wife, Fern drove him to work on those days he went to work.

The schedule promised was not what Chablis received. Instead of three on and four off, Chablis worked five day stretches with two days off and a couple of hours here and there in the evenings. His wife picked him up late in the evening and then had to bring him back to work sometimes by the very next morning, leaving very little time to spend with his family.

"Seems like even though you're home from war, you're still not home," Fern commented one day as she dropped her husband off at work.

"Well there's not much I can do, I don't set the schedule," Chablis replied, defensively.

"I know sweetie," Fern tried to be understanding. "Me and the baby just miss ya, that's all."

Chablis kissed her goodbye. "It's just temporary 'till things get straightened out," he assured her. It bothered Fern more than it bothered Chablis. After all, he was used to working long hours on the family farm and while he had served his time overseas.

Even though she was unhappy, she hung in there, knowing that soon Chablis would be able to get out of the Army soon. However, his burning desire to work carried through to all of his jobs thereafter. They even picked up and moved to the East Coast, where jobs were rumored to be more plentiful. Fern had never strayed too far from Texas, so for her it was a big move.

Not long after moving, Fern picked up a new hobby. Infomercials. She loved watching them and buying things on them. It was a great way to pass the time, since Chablis was never there. She had always battled with a shopping compulsion, but now that they had a little extra money coming in, Fern was able to watch the programs and make purchases.

Yet, Chablis hardly noticed. Within their first five years of marriage, Chablis was a Jack-of-all-trades and worked day and night. He worked as a vacation specialist (which was a glorified sales position), a boat waxer, and a security guard for a gated community, a landscaper, a roofer, and as a casino surveillance agent for a racetrack that was in a town 45 minutes away. Within all of these job titles, the common denominator was a lot of long hours and many excuses.

Whenever somebody quit, Chablis took the extra shift. Or if the boss needed Chablis to stay longer, he did it to earn the extra overtime pay. Or if there was quick cash to be paid under the table from someone who asked him to do a job on the side, he did it eagerly. Or if there was a special client coming into town, he needed a couple of weeks to prepare for it. There was always a reason for Chablis to stay late and work longer. Always.

On top of that, he was trying to earn a degree and took morning classes on Mondays, Wednesdays and Thursdays. Meanwhile, in her desperate attempts to fill the void of emptiness of a husband who was never there, Fern kept shopping. He made extra money and she spent it. He was never home to spend it anyways and was always too busy to take a vacation. On those rare occasions when Chablis planned to get away with his family, there was always something that came up.

In a way, maybe Fern shopped just to spite him, or for attention. Maybe she did it to fill the void. Either way, both of their behaviors caused a lack of intimacy and fulfillment in their marriage. Yet, they hung in there for the sake of their daughter.

One day, while searching for his old work boots, Chablis discovered a closet full of things that had boxes stacked to the ceiling. Some said, "As Seen on TV" and there were others that had never been unwrapped from the packaging. He made his way down the stairs of their home, where Fern was preparing scrambled eggs and bacon.

"Honey, what are all the boxes in the upstairs closet?" Chablis asked his wife.

"Oh, those are just some great deals I couldn't live without," she replied.

"From where?" he gulped.

"Ya know, on those TV programs!" Fern said, now fearing her husband's reaction.

"I'm busting my butt to get us ahead and you're spending all our money?" Chablis questioned.

"Not all," she murmured. "Just a few things here and there."

He walked in the den where the roll-top desk revealed a stack of bills and credit card statements. "You're a shop-a-holic!" he yelled.

"Well you're a work-a-holic!" she retorted. "You're missing your daughter's growing up. You should've seen how broken hearted she was the other day when you missed her beauty pageant after she reminded you for the last two months."

"I didn't forget. I had to work. I had to work so that you can buy Snuggies and Ab Rockets and George Foreman grills." After he said it, Chablis clammed up. He didn't talk about his feelings. Instead, he stormed off and called a co-worker to come pick him up.

The simple fact of the matter was that Chablis *had* to work. It was in his blood as much as plasma. It was the way he was raised and the way he would continue to be. For Chablis, downtime was a waste of time. He was afraid that if he stopped working too long then everything would fall apart. In reality, by working too much, he was in danger of his fear coming true. Without his wife and daughter, all Chablis would have left was a job. But he didn't think about it that way. Instead, he was driven to keep working harder and longer.

Over time, Chablis and Fern grew accustomed to each other's bad habits. He missed many of his little girl's school functions, although he often promised to attend. There were piano recitals, school plays, field hockey games and other extracurricular activities that many of the other proud parents came to. But Chablis always had to work. His daughter always looked around the theatre or the stadium, hoping to see her father's face or hear his hands clapping to reward her for a job well done.

After eventually earning a degree in his "spare time," Chablis became a private investigator. This profession was a lifelong dream he had always wished to fulfill, along with becoming a police officer or a lawyer. The PI job was a cross between the two and came with a lot of perks, like a flexible schedule. Chablis was able to schedule some of his assignments around his family. For awhile, he did just that.

However, over time Chablis once again overloaded his schedule and could not say no to any new clients.

Meanwhile, Fern absorbed herself in her own hobbies and interests. She started a business on eBay so instead of just shopping, she became a merchant. Fern spent many hours in front of the computer. She sold denim jeans and jumpers from yard sales for dirt cheap prices and even sold some of her closet full of infomercial purchases from the last decade. In a way, Fern's hobbies were her own way of filling the void of having a transparent husband. It also empowered her to spend more on shopping since she felt like she was earning her own money.

Anytime they needed money, all Chablis had to do was take on a few assignments under the table. They rarely struggled for anything and were never late on any mortgage payments, car loans or any other debts. They even had a little extra money for a small boat, although they rarely had any time to use it.

After awhile, Fern just accepted her husband's huge workload and long hours. She realized that he would never change, so instead of lamenting, she chose some positive outlets to fulfill her loneliness. Fern had a good circle of friends who frequently got together for social functions and community fundraisers for the kids. She attended all of her daughter's activities. It was a shame that Chablis' daughter never got to know her father very well because he was so busy and managed to avoid many of her childhood milestones.

The way he perceived it, having a father who was rarely there was better than some kids who don't have one at all. Everyone adjusted.

❖❖❖❖❖❖❖❖❖

# PROVISO

**So, Chablis is not going to set your love life on fire,** like other wines may do. It isn't a wine known as "passionate" by wine lovers anywhere. It is a worker wine that works mostly towards approval. And it does so just to be noticed. It strives for success, yet continues to remain somewhat indistinctive among the many better choices out there.

As a provider, Chablis will give you nourishment. It takes care of your basic needs. Thirst. Conversation. That's about the extent of it.

On the bright side, Chablis is respectable. It is among thousands of wines that experience the same dilemma of balance and ambiguity. There are simply not enough hours in the day and Chablis has more on his plate than he can possibly handle. Whether he is part of a big, major winery or made by a solo entrepreneur – such as one who pounds out the grapes by hand in a small, private kitchen – Chablis has many varied responsibilities. Yet, people rarely notice Chablis' attempt to be good.

Working too much is not something Chablis set out to do; however, he knows that if he wants to get promoted from the lowly pool of supermarket jug wines to something greater, he must change his image. Therefore, he is driven to do just that. Succeed. Come to think of it, have there ever been any commercials on mainstream TV for Chablis?

We'll have to look into that. None are coming to mind. Maybe one day Chablis will step up its marketing and succeed to become one of the greatest wines known to man. Yet, at what cost to his family and social life? Workaholics often miss those special family milestones and rarely are there to help with raising the children.

Could Chablis' fierce drive be rooted from having a difficult childhood? If you remember, Chablis vineyards have endured the Little Ice Age, French Revolution and Prussian invasions. That's enough to make anyone search for a way to escape.

Business owners and entrepreneurs often have a propensity to become workaholics as they become obsessed with the need to get their business off the ground, then to make it grow, thrive and become successful. They need to manage their company and the demands to achieve are great. For an entrepreneur, it's either sink or swim. Even after the workaholic achieves the desired result they seek, it will never be enough. They will always be driven to do more, achieve more and taste that ultimate feeling of success, which is what they set out to do.

Is a workaholic worth dating?

Well, is Chablis worth drinking?

# Beaujolais

## "THE BON-BON"

***Known as the life of the party, Beaujolais is a*** *charming, fun and fruity concoction that is satiated with flavor and zestfulness. Wineries recommend drinking young Beaujolais within only a few weeks of its release, which falls faithfully each calendar year on the third Thursday in November. It's well-advertised and heavily commercialized production is just that – a production. Most Beaujolais is made of machine harvested grapes that are barely ripe enough to be plucked, and confectioner's sugar is sometimes added to intensify the sweetness of the wine.*

*Of course, only the snooty wine followers might know this, so to the average wine drinker it might taste just fine. Beaujolais is especially appropriate for those Americans who love to celebrate Thanksgiving with a fresh bottle. But what would the Pilgrims think of this commercialized imposter of* fine wine? Many a glutton will be attracted to the splashy advertising used to sell this festive holiday vino.

Made of leftover grapes from all of the better, high-profile wines, Beaujolais does not age well and remains immature. Gamay from other wines, such as Chardonnay, Pinot Noir and Aligote make up the distinct flavors of citrus, with a hint of banana and ripe, delicious wild berry. The berries are fresh, with a delightful palatability that excludes the bitter tannins of richer wines. These energetic ingredients will dance in your mouth. Hmmm... and is there a hint of cranberries in there, too?

Indeed, Beaujolais is inexpensive, but can be well worth the investment as arm candy at the next social gathering. It's pretty bottle and trendy dressings will disguise its simplicity with an overcoat of perfection. You might say that Beaujolais advertises itself very well. A marketing genius must have invented such a spacey, yet loveable wine. The trick was to decorate the bottle of Beaujolais with colorful designs for unsuspecting trend-seekers who are drawn to the least important elements of its worth.

Unlike many red wine competitors, Beaujolais must be served chilled. The coolness feels good to your taste buds with a refreshing bite that will permit consumption and rapid intoxication. It could be the ultimate companion for days of high school tail-gating parties, as a replacement to wine coolers. And Beaujolais is definitely fun for any holiday that falls within late autumn to early spring. Christmas, Hanukkah, New Year's Eve, Valentine's Day... (Hiccup)... President's Day... Memorial Day... (Hiccup)... uh oh! Too late. Running out of holidays. Right before summer kicks in, the wine is just about to expire. So, drink up and enjoy by mid-spring, at the latest.

*Beaujolais could be described as approachable, yet hard to hold on to for any long period of time. Yet, one will appreciate the refreshing sweetness and lightweight proportions while it lasts. Some may deem its simplicity as unacceptable. However, upon tasting, Beaujolais has a way of working its way into your heart. After all, how could one not appreciate the youthful ripeness of Beaujolais, so lip-smackingly full of positive energy? The wine projects refreshing character that is difficult to define. It has underlying greatness that just wants to graduate to the next level and explore the real world, if only it could last long enough to do so.*

*Because it is made with very little tannins, Beaujolais can be scorned as immature, yet able to maintain fascination with remarkable finesse. Drinkers may feel a sensation of transitory refreshment, with an unmistakable hue of novelty that is both racy and ever-ripe. Beaujolais is a pleasure to drink; yet embarrassing to introduce to your influential friends.*

*Overall, Beaujolais is harmless and will leave a nice taste in your mouth. Zesty Beaujolais does have undiscovered strength, much like a young soldier willing to fight for his worthy cause.*

*For those who are new to red wine or those who only drink it on occasion, Beaujolais is more than a pleasant choice. It complements light appetizers and is thoughtful as a romantic companion for a picnic in the park. It could also be a nice gesture for a weekend rendezvous. And who knows? For some, it may become a favorite.*

❖❖❖❖❖❖❖❖❖

# BEAU ❣ Razzmic Berry

**His stupidity was almost forgivable, like an** innocent puppy who chews shoes. How could you blame the puppy for not knowing any better? It hasn't learned right from wrong yet, and it's not smart enough to learn new tricks.

Beaujolais had a job and a car when he met Razzmic Berry. That is *had*; past tense. He thought her to be quite the catch, indeed. Razzmic Berry was almost exactly eight years older; a woman who had her shit together. As called by friends, Razz was '*Miss Independent*'; a beautiful chic with her own career and house. Beaujolais figured he could probably get ahead in stature by choosing an older, already established woman. Coming from nothing that would truly be something.

At first, Beaujolais' boyish charm and innocent adorability was alluring and fun. Razzmic was a bridesmaid in a wedding when they met. It was late autumn, just before the holidays and Beau (as everyone called him) had been hired as the musical entertainer – the DJ and emcee of the day. His angelic voice when he sang was a charming turn-on for Razz, so much so that his invitation to a post-party following the reception was a welcome distraction from the day's events. Beau's shy first kiss was such a buzz that they became inseparable for the next few weeks. Their relationship became all about lust; although, Razz grew to care for him deeply by the end of his term.

Beau was lively, spunky and always smelled delicious, despite his need for a new wardrobe and for a few grown-up things. He was austerely uneducated and had strange manners, which Razz found to be a combination between funny and embarrassing. Simplicity was a disappointing trait. Some of the questions Beau asked were so ridiculous she often wondered if he was even for real. Questions like; "*Who's that guy on the front of the dollar bill, is he someone important?*" and "*Does Canada border Washington D.C.?*" or "*Is the Pope really Catholic or is that just a saying?*" Beau even wondered who puts the erasers on pencils and if that guy liked his job. Often, their conversations went something like this:

"Where is Europe? Is that country next to Venezuela?"

"Are you even kidding me?" Razz replied in an amused tone. "Europe isn't a country, it's a continent."

"Isn't that the same thing? " Beau asked, in all seriousness.

"Did you even go to school?" she questioned.

"Yeah, I just don't remember. I guess I wasn't paying attention." Beau giggled like a 12-year old.

"Then why would you care now?" Razz answered snidely. "Venezuela is in South America." The novelty of Beau was wearing off.

Yes, Razz was a Cougar. Or at least that's what people called it. She had tried dating older men in the past but found them to be boring. And too quick in bed. Razz loved the energy of younger men; although, she wished that she could find one that had a bit more brainpower.

Even though it went against her better judgment, dating Beau was fun at first. Razz attended many of his DJ gigs, which took place on off-nights. However, things took a different turn when Razz made the mistake of letting Beau move into her gorgeous house because he complained of a dilemma with his roommate. What she didn't realize was that all of his complaints were true, except backwards. Beau said that his roommate didn't pay rent on time. She later learned it was Beau, not his roommate, who was not punctual with payments.

After only one day, numerous red flags manifested as ugly gasps of doubt. It turned out that Beau had horrible credit, with debtors following him with nasty phone calls. Excuses salvaged the situation, with new lies compounded by doting on her to win her good graces. His intention was to resurrect Razzmic's faith in his worthiness as a valid boyfriend.

"You need to get a job, since you just moved here and gave up your job. Didn't you expect to contribute to this relationship?" Razz asked with worried hyperventilation. "How did you become so irresponsible? And where is the car you had a few weeks ago?"

Beau peeked around her, half-listening as he clicked away on the Xbox. "Oh, I sold that car because it wouldn't start. Turns out the guy that bought it said I just needed some belt that would've cost $50. I guess I should have had a mechanic look at it first but I thought the whole car was shot. Ooops!"

Razz huffed and slammed the door.

It took several weeks of laziness and threats for Beau to finally get a job. It was not of the highest aspirations. He worked at a local warehouse, packing toiletry imports to Caribbean vendors. She drove him to work every day, like a soccer mom taking her son to school.

After only a couple of weeks, Beau called one day from work to be picked up early. He claimed to have a sprained ankle. "How could you have sprained your ankle just standing there? It wasn't sprained this morning. You're going to get yourself fired," Razz said.

"You don't believe me? Look! It's swollen." He showed her.

*Great*, she thought. *He's a hypochondriac.*

"It looks like a bug bite to me," Razz said, as she rolled her eyes.

Within a few days, the warehouse fired Beau because he was within the probationary period of 90 days. In his mind, he already thought of an impending lawsuit for a workman's comp case. Beau complained often, of any small headache, toothache, insomnia, anxiety, sniffles or belly-button lint disorder. His chronic complaining drained Razz.

Meanwhile, she worked over sixty hours a week to manage the bills. Razz often came home after a long day only to find Beau sitting on the couch laughing hysterically while watching South Park. "Is that all you've done all day? Watch cartoons?" she asked, in her most disgusted tone of voice.

After complaining one day with co-workers about the lazy guy she had attracted into her life, one of her friends offered to help. "My husband is the manager of Home Depot. Just tell him to come in tomorrow and he will hire him. I'm doing this for you," Razzmic's friend said.

With a glimmer of hope, Razz excitedly reported back to Beaujolais. "Guess what, I got you a job today!" The discussion didn't bode well with Beau.

"I will not work at that place. There is not ONE bone in my body that wants to work there. It's not my life's aspiration!" Beau exclaimed, adamantly. "I refuse!"

After an argument she couldn't win, Razz wondered, *what have I gotten myself into? I need to get rid of this guy.* He was perfectly content waiting for her at home, playing video games and watching cartoons or goofing off. Of course, he did have his music shows, which brought in very little cash once or twice a week.

Beau sensed the need to get a job to appease her. So after the fight, every time they went to a store together, he conversed with the help. Beau spoke to the cashiers, customers or anyone who would listen. It would often take half an hour to buy a bottle of water at a convenience store. He loved talking about nonsense with the employees. It made it seem as though he was job hunting.

One day, Razz and Beau went to the bakery at Costco's. He stared at the lady baking cakes. Then he said, "That looks like a fun job. How much do you make an hour?"

The baker stared back at Beau with a blank look. "No hablo Engoláis," she replied in Spanish.

Razz kicked Beau inconspicuously. "What on earth are you doing?" she whispered loudly. "Not only is it rude to ask people how much they make, you don't even know how to cook. Why do you have to be so embarrassing?" Razz hung her head in shamed exasperation. She was a classy girl and Beau proved to be otherwise. It was a disappointment, yet not a surprise.

"What? You wanted me to get a job. I'm sure they train you here." Beau said, not understanding her frustration.

"So, let me get this straight. You'd rather bake cupcakes all day than work at Home Depot, where real men work. Real men who like tools and building and hammers and drills and stuff like that," Razz tried to reason.

It was futile. Beau was a metro man. He was tall and pretty, with handsome sideburns and freshly pressed shirts, which he took pride in ironing himself. He had eyes that were bluer than a Caribbean inlet and naturally straight teeth that were like the smile on a Ken doll. And then there was that other asset he had. But all of these physical attributes were not worth the lack of contribution and intellectual incompatibility.

Alas, Beau was nothing more than arm candy. Like bon-bons. They were deliciously eye-appealing, but if you ate too many then they made you sick.

Right then, Razzmic Berry decided it was time for him to move on. The problem was that Beaujolais really had nowhere else to go. She felt sorry for him. It was her own fault, she surmised. Razz had allowed laziness and codependency in their relationship. It created a big problem. Now she had to think of a way to fix it.

Beau's mother lived in rural Vermont. Maybe she could send Beau up there somehow. Problem was... he had burned so many bridges with his family that none were so receptive to taking him in. Razz didn't want to kick him out with nowhere to go. That would seem heartless. So she thought of another strategy to make him leave.

She would intentionally set out to piss Beau off, hoping he would leave on his own accord. Razz made his life difficult. She made Beau take the bus when he needed to go anywhere. She went out with her friends after work, often staying out until the wee hours of the morning. She partied and went to dance clubs or hung out at friends' houses until very late. Plus, Razz never answered the phone when Beau called. Instead, she let him wonder where she was. One night, she came home at 4:30 a.m. Beau was sitting crossly, in the dark, on the couch. Like Dad used to do in her teenage era.

"Where have you been?" Beau raised his voice. "I've been worried sick. I can't take this behavior anymore. I'm moving out."

"Okay. Well, goodnight!" she replied cheerily and deviously. Razz left him sitting irritably on the sofa with his arms crossed and a rotten wrinkle between his brows.

"You don't even care?" asked Beau. "Some girlfriend you are."

"Don't even go there," she smiled, unimpressed by his sudden burst of aggravation. Razz went to bed. Of course, Beau still did not leave. It had been an idle threat. Another couple of months went by.

The strategy had failed. Instead, Beau tried impressing her again by having a candle-lit dinner prepared as Razz came home from another long day at work. "I made you a gourmet dinner, sweetie," Beau offered sincerely. "I missed you a lot. We need to get back to the old us. When we were so happy."

"What did you make?" she inquired.

"Tuna Helper!" Beau proudly announced.

*'Some gourmet,'* she quietly mused internally.

Then, Beau took her out to dinner one weekend. He told her to dress up because it was to be someplace very nice. Razz silently wondered where he had found the money to take her out, not having worked at a real job for quite some time. "Where are you taking me?" she bit her tongue, knowing she deserved allowing him to pay for something.

"Longhorn Steakhouse looks pretty fancy on the commercial, let's go there." Beaujolais decided.

*Fancy, hardly...* she thought. "But I don't like steak," Razz scrunched her nose.

"Well they have other stuff there. Like chicken," said Beau.

"Fine." She didn't want to spoil the treat by being too bitchy.

As they sat down to dine, Beau said; "Wow! This place is very elegant."

Razz almost choked on the ice cubes in her water. "You think Longhorn Steakhouse is elegant? Before I met you I had a date who took me to Le Palace de Soleil. The meal cost him about $300+ dollars by the time we had wine, appetizers, a main course and dessert. Longhorn is just a family restaurant, dear."

Beau appeared offended. Then Razz said, "How did you get the money to take me out? I mean, I do appreciate it and all but I'm just curious. Since you're not working."

"I won $500 on a scratch ticket." Beau replied, with a delighted smile.

Hmmm. That explained the shopping bag of used lottery tickets she had found in the car. She suspected Beau had a gambling addiction.

Finally, one day a friend of Razzmic Berry came to visit. Don announced he was going on an RV adventure across country with two of his golfing buddies. Her eyes lit up. "Will you be traveling up north?" Razz asked, with a sneaky glimmer in her eyes.

"Well, yes but I haven't officially made my itinerary public knowledge," said Don. "Why do you ask?"

"Will you take Beau with you? I just can't afford to take care of him anymore. He won't work and doesn't contribute. It causes a huge strain. He just watches cartoons every day and plays video games like a thirteen-year-old. I think he gambles." Razz spilled the beans about her immature boyfriend.

"Sure, he can go with us." said Don, feeling pity for his friend.

Although she was nervous about everything going smoothly, Razz was glad to finally be able to move on again. She waited until the day Beau was to depart. Beaujolais went to bed early, resting comfortably with his satin sleep mask over his eyes. Razz stood over him, thinking how peaceful and content he had become in her cozy home and bed. *He thinks he's going to live here forever and have this Princess take care of him*, she pondered. *He's in for a big awakening. Time to live in the real world, Beaujolais.* Razz went to work, silently packing all of his belongings, which wasn't much. Then she went through his phone and found the number for his mother. She dialed.

"Hello?" answered a tired voice on the other end.

"Hello," replied Razz. "I'm sorry to call you so late."

"It's okay dear. Is everything alright?" she said.

Razz replied, "No, I'm afraid to say that it's not working out with your son. I'm afraid there's just too much of a difference. He'll be arriving there by the end of the week with my friends in an RV."

"Oh? Well, I'm not sure if I have room here," explained Beau's mother. It seemed she wasn't crazy about the idea. "What happened? Last time I talked to him he said everything was great between you two. That was just a few days ago. He said you went to a fancy dinner together, like the time he went to the prom a few years back," she recalled.

"Nothing happened. Everything is fine," Razz responded, imagining Beau's perception of the matter would be much different than hers. "It's just that his time here has reached its limit. He would be better suited for a girl more like he is."

"Very well, then." Beau's mother sighed heavily through the phone. "I'll be expecting him."

After they hung up, Razz got busy packing his few belongings in a tidy stash. She put most of it on the RV, with the help of her friends who were leaving the next day. She was nervous about how Beau would react. Then, Razz crawled quietly into bed, so as not to disturb the sleeping beauty in his precious satin mask.

The next day, they got up at the same time. Although Razz was not normally a morning person, on this morning she nearly sprung out of bed. "Guess what honey? I have a big surprise for you! You're going to get a chance to see your Mom."

Razz clapped enthusiastically. She was about to be relieved of an encumbrance. "I know you haven't seen your family for a while. You know my buddy Don? Well he's driving the RV across country and his first stop is going to be close to your mother's house. Don said you could go with him... isn't that great news?"

Beau seemed puzzled. He opened the closet. "Where's my stuff?"

"Oh that? I already packed it for you. You were sleeping so peacefully in your satin sleep mask that I didn't want to wake you. I called your mom. Last night. She said she can't wait to see you and she misses you a lot," Razz fibbed.

Right on cue, Don rapped on the door a couple of times. "All Aboard!" he said, peeking in. "Is everyone ready to go?"

"Let me make you all a big breakfast for your great journey!" Razz cheerily pulled out the pots and pans. Beau still said nothing and appeared to be confused.

After scrambled eggs and bacon, the boys prepared to head out. "I'll leave you two to say goodbye," Don said, excusing himself.

Razz gave Beau a sincere hug and held him tight. Tears rolled down her cheeks. “I’ll miss you,” she said, much like a mom telling her son as he went off to summer camp for the first time. Beau didn’t say much back. He stepped on the RV and glanced back. He stared out the window as the RV slowly rolled down the street.

❖❖❖❖❖❖❖❖❖

# PROVISO

**Sure, Beaujolais is cute, just like a puppy. But** don’t adopt this one. His Mom will help you plan your wedding and will be thrilled to pass him off to you. This wine comes with an expiration date. It doesn’t mature well, so don’t even attempt to buy a bottle for the wine cellar, at least for drinking. In fact, it’s better not to even let Beaujolais *ever* see where you live because he just might want to move in. Wine cellar or not, your digs are probably way better than the place he has been living in for the past few months.

Beaujolais is pretty to look at and fun for a short time. It is especially a great wine for the holidays, while it is still fresh. Any other time of year will not thrill you for the long term. It finally expires by mid-Spring when the fruitiness placates, so let it go long before that.

If you’re new to wine drinking, Beaujolais is very good. Especially if you have been drinking the same old wines for the last ten or twenty years. Beaujolais will bring that fun, deliciously sinful feeling of lust that you may have forgotten ever existed. Just like the younger man, Beaujolais is playful and fun. Divorcees are sure to love it.

Because it's made up of various grape remnants of much better wines, Beaujolais never fully matures. That's probably why it can be bought quite inexpensively. No matter how sweet or charming Beaujolais may be, just call him a cab the next day and send him on his way. Beaujolais is sure to please you when it is fresh and ripe, but could be looking for the life of luxury at your expense. Unless you want to be a Sugar Mama, just savor it for a brief spell.

Besides, these days it's quite trendy to be a Cougar, without the strings attached. Older woman don't usually stay with a younger man very long unless he brings something more to the table than his undoubtedly striking features and boyish charm. Initially, it will be fun. There will be plenty of tireless romance, sex and laughter.

Beaujolais is a winning wine if you follow the directions and only drink it between the time of its release and before the expiration. For Beaujolais, an older woman is a conquest. For her, it is equally beneficial.

The Cougar is confident, poised and already established in her career. She's not with a man because she needs him, rather, purely, for her own fun. Isn't that what men have been doing all along? Just ask Port Wine, especially one that has been around for decades.

Honestly, who needs something serious when you can have this vibrant and festive wine just in time for New Year's Eve and other winter celebrations? Beaujolais' spirited carbonation and jovial essence is as much fun as a child's birthday party – with balloons, corny hats and trick candles. It's very presence is a present.

Beaujolais is rapidly making a name for itself, overcoming the joke of its hasty entrance and short-lived existence in refrigerators around the world. Most of the time, Beaujolais is harmless enough. Both people will experience goodness in the relationship, although very rarely do these types of affairs last all that long. Like the Beaujolais wine, after a few months it will go sour.

# Cabernet

## "MR. RIGHT"

***Like it, love it, fall in love and keep it forever.*** *Cabernet Sauvignon has all of the qualities you crave making it the world's favorite and most popular wine. In fact, this amazing vino is grown in nearly every major wine producing country on the planet, spanning a wide spectrum of climates and growing seasons.*

*Part of the reason for its popularity is because it blends so well with other types of grapes, making it truly one of the most versatile wines available. It is different to everyone; therefore, no two bottles are exactly alike except those within a certain batch of one particular vintner. You can literally bring Cabernet along to any occasion. It is also one of the most dependable candidates for aging, thereby having a reputation as one of the greatest for anyone who desires a wine with stamina. As it ages, the distinctive tannic edges smooth out and soften considerably, blooming into a fine blend of charismatic flavors.*

*Some wine growers purposefully grow and harvest Cabernet grapes to create wines designed to improve over the long term. The grapes ripen later than other types. Their harsh tannins soften, while the underlying taste has a chance to intensify and develop into a rich, fulfilling flavor. Whether young or old, Cabernet is a classic and beloved best friend, if not the love of your life in wine choices. It is well known that Cabernet tastes better and better as time goes on, whereas many other varieties must be experienced right away. If you plan on buying a wine with the intent of preserving it for the long term, Cabernet is a smart choice.*

*In many ways, Cabernet reflects the personality and desires of its maker, while presenting a lustful familiarity that is typical of its character. You might experience notes of violets, leather, cedar, cherry, tobacco or cigar along with Cabernet's signature black currant smell. These appeals both to first-timers - and to those who fall in love with Cabernet for many years to come - if not forever. Its appetizing allure and often higher alcohol content will give you a lip-licking, heady buzz.*

*The delicious berries of Cabernet are thick-skinned and spherical, making them less prone to spoilage or rotting; such as that of more finicky grapes. They can withstand many different climates and weather conditions, from autumn rains to hot, sunny days, and perhaps even a frost or two. Cabernet ripens in the mid-to-late season, making it better to harvest than other types of grapes that must be plucked during certain times of the year.*

*Another aspect of Cabernet that makes it seemingly the perfect wine is the wide range of price points. You may find an inexpensive bottle that is very, very good, while others may be rich from aging and thereby more expensive. From the top shelf to the bottom, there is rarely a bad bottle of Cabernet to be found. Of course, this determination is made by the individual drinker, of which there is no "right or wrong" way to decide. Ease of acquiring and expression has made Cabernet highly marketable. Some may see Cabernet grapes as pioneers because of their explorative qualities in blends with other varieties.*

*Indeed, people are passionate about Cabernet, and rightly so. It has often been the brunt of jealousy by other wine varieties, in part because it is so perfect and difficult to find fault with. Some say it is the most noble of wines, having strong tannins that age well in barrels and in the cellars of wine collectors. Whether you experience a young or an aged Cabernet, it is undeniably delightful. So much so that you may reach for it time and time again, and again.*

*Unlike many region specific wine varieties, Cabernet is cultivated in almost every wine producing area of the world. That is because of the ease of producing, storing, harvesting and making. The grapes are hardy, strong and sentimental. From the gorgeous valleys of Canada to the charming hillsides of France, Spain, Italy and other parts of Europe, you will find Cabernet. It can also be found in nearly every country in South America and North America, as well as South Africa, Lebanon, Australia, New Zealand and Israel. It would probably be easier to list the countries that do not make Cabernet, rather than trying to list all of those who do. Cabernet is everywhere, hence it means something different to everyone.*

*Although indisputably one of the most famous wines worldwide, Cabernet's popularity is due in part to its availability. When choosing one to fall in love with, it is important to find out early whether it was meant for drinking early or for saving and stowing away for later. It may take years or even decades for certain Cabernets to fully mature, while others do so not long after production. Those who are impatient and want to find a perfect young Cabernet will rarely be disappointed. However, those willing to wait until Cabernet reaches its peak will be impressed by how wonderful and worth the wait it is.*

❖❖❖❖❖❖❖❖❖

# CAB ❣ Magenta

***"Should I go out or go home?"*** **Magenta wondered,** as she finished her photo shoot. Home was over two hours away, so it was tempting just to call her friends and stay with one of them in town, rather than making the arduous drive back to her rural community up north.

She decided to go out. Magenta changed her outfit into a sexy black and silver polka dot shirt that showed off a bit of cleavage, along with a cute pair of capris. And of course, her signature three inch pumps, which Magenta wouldn't be caught dead going without. With the intent of meeting her friends, she went to their pre-designated hot spot, a night club in the heart of town.

As she clickity-clacked up the cobblestone streets, Magenta looked forward to a night of fun after working all day. Little did she know exactly how the evening would transpire, but, of course, anticipation was always the best part.

It seemed like her friends took forever to meet her. Magenta didn't want to look desperate standing on the sidelines of the dance floor, just waiting for some stranger to approach, so, she found some cool chicks to dance with, keeping a roving eye out for the arrival of her friends.

Meanwhile, an average looking guy came out to the dance floor and made his move. Not wanting to hurt his feelings, Magenta smiled and danced with him awhile until he offered to buy her a drink. "Sure!" she said eagerly, not wanting to seem rude. "I'll just wait for you outside; it's really hot in here." The sweat rolled down her neck.

Many people were coming and going as Magenta stepped out on the street. A handsome blonde-haired guy, who was muscular, yet with a friendly face, was standing by the lamppost on the corner, finishing a cigarette. He was just about to go inside.

"Excuse me, do you have the time?" she asked.

"Sure. It's time we met," he said, stretching out his hand with a flirtatious smile. "I'm Cab?"

"Magenta," she offered hesitantly. Often she gave a fake name to those she didn't want to see again. But this guy was cute, and interesting. He had a couple of tattoos and nice eyes. He was better looking and more talkative than the guy inside; the one who was probably still standing in line to buy her drink.

Magenta talked to Cab in the street for a minute or two. Then she said, "Don't let me hold you up," in case he was in a hurry to go in.

"Hey, maybe you'd like to dance with me inside?" he asked. Cab was interested. Turns out, they had a few things in common already. For one, she lived in the very state that he had grown up, and within the same community. They both had horses as a child and could relate to the care of them.

They both loved the same type of music and had a fondness for muscle cars. He was a chef, and she needed one. Her domestic skills were not so prevalent.

Cab thought Magenta was pretty hot too, from her blonde hair to her cute spotted high-heeled shoes. (*Oh yes*, he noticed the shoes!)

"Sure!" she replied. Magenta looped her arm through his, as they strolled back inside. Her friends were all but forgotten, as well as the guy she had been dancing with before. Out of the corner of her eye, Magenta saw him standing there holding two drinks, just staring at her. He was clearly offended. "*Oh well, at least he'll have plenty to quench his thirst*," she thought, as she danced with Cab. Besides, Magenta was there to have fun, not to hook up with anyone. And Cab was definitely more fun.

As she had learned about him throughout the night, Cab shared many more things in common with Magenta. She lived in California, where he had been born and raised in Sonoma Valley. Although she was just visiting for the weekend as a photojournalist, Cab also lived elsewhere and was just in town for the night visiting some friends. What luck to run into each other! It was a strange coincidence that they both ended up in this city that neither one of them lived in, nor were from.

They had physical attributes in common, too. They both had blonde hair and blue eyes. And socially, they both loved wine. Even family-wise, both Magenta and Cab had parents who had stayed married for exactly 38 years, making them close to the same age.

Magenta might have liked to see him again; if it were not for the fact that Cab lived so far away. She was scheduled to drive back home the following Monday morning. It was a shame, she mused. Cab was the type of guy she may go out with a few times to see if there was any chemistry.

Nevertheless, as the night wore on and they talked, danced and laughed, Magenta gave Cab her phone number anyway. She never genuinely expected to hear from him again, since the distance between them was too great.

Although she hadn't spent much time with them, Magenta sought out her friends after saying goodbye to Cab. With a silly grin on her face, she found them in a corner. They were huddled over one of the girls who had participated in the festivities a little too much, and feeling rather sick, she was keeled over on a loveseat in the dark. As Magenta approached, she got there just in time to see her friend yakking into a pail. At that point, she was so grossed out that she grabbed the sleeve of one of her friends and asked, "Are you ready to go? I am."

Magenta stayed overnight at her friend's house and she told him about her chance meeting with the newfound stranger, Cab. "I met this cute guy tonight," she said giddily.

"Oh, is that why we didn't see that much of you tonight?" her friend kiddingly supposed.

"Well, we met outside and I had this other guy on the hook, but I sorta ditched him to go dance with the blonde guy."Magenta explained, smiling.

"Naughty, you!" squealed her friend.

"The thing is, he lives far away so I'm not counting on ever hearing from him again." Sighed Magenta.

"Did you give him your number?" she asked.

"Yes. But even if he called, then what? I don't want a long distance thing. And I have options," Magenta said, with a wink.

Yet surprisingly, Cab called Magenta the very next afternoon. They talked on the phone for a half hour or so.

"I was surprised to hear from you again," she said.

"Why?" he asked. "I asked for your number, so you must have known I would like to call you sometime?"

That made perfect sense. "Well, it's just that we live so far away," she responded. "I mean, we don't have a chance to even go on a date together."

"That doesn't mean I won't ever see you again," replied Cab.

So, Magenta drove home and never gave their chance meeting much more of a thought. She thought Cab was nice, but he just lived too far away. Magenta pushed the fun evening to the back of her mind and simply continued on with life as usual. Her life as a photojournalist was nothing, if not interesting. Magenta loved her job and the chances it gave her to make people smile for a living. She had enough personality to brighten up a room, just with her smile alone.

However, Cab called Magenta again, at least once a week. They talked sometimes for an hour or so and also exchanged emails and messages on MySpace. She looked forward to their calls and found Cab to be fun and out-of-the-ordinary. They shared stories and adventures from their childhoods. Both grew up with farm-style atmospheres, with cats and dogs. They both loved the beach and bodysurfing. There was much in common between them, especially the laughter and sharing of values.

Magenta found herself wondering more about Cab. He was versatile, like a mixture of many great wines blended well together. They became good friends through their phone conversations. Although they never really talked about the distance or the fact that they were too far away to see if there was something more between them, it was something they both pondered. As the frequency of their conversations increased, so did their connection. Cab and Magenta often exchanged cute text messages and pictures of themselves throughout the day.

After a few months went by, Cabernet told her about a job offer he received to move to Southern California. He was offered a chance to work as a world-class chef at Disneyland in Anaheim. It was about six hours south of where she lived, near Napa Valley. Although it was still far away, at least it was in the same state.

Magenta didn't say anymore about it, figuring if things were meant to be then they would simply work out. Meanwhile, Cab accepted the offer and moved. He knew a friend in the neighboring city of Long Beach, which was about an hour commute to and from his new position at Disneyland.

Even though they now lived in the same state, Magenta was unable to get away from her job long enough to pay him a visit. She was booked every weekend with photography gigs during the week, for at least the next two months. After more time went by and they had still not gone out on even one date together, Cab finally asked Magenta, "So am I ever going to see you again, or are we just going to keep talking on the phone forever?"

After that, her curiosity got the better of her. Magenta rearranged her schedule for the following weekend and decided to make the drive down to meet him in person. Nervously, she wondered what it would be like to see Cab again after so many months had passed. *Would he still look the same? Was he as good looking as she had remembered?* After all, it was dark at the night club when they had met. People can appear differently in the daylight.

The whole drive there, Magenta nervously wondered if she was doing the right thing. However, she figured she had nothing to lose. If Cab turned out to be as good as she hoped he would be, than she would stay. If not, she would turn around and drive home. Simple as that. There were other guys vying for Magenta's attention, so she knew there were other options available. However, the fact that she had invested so much time in getting to know Cab on the phone made her feel a special connection with him. It felt like they were already lifelong friends who knew many deep secrets about one another.

Meanwhile, Cab wondered many of the same things about Magenta, too. *Would she still look the same? Was she as good looking as she had remembered?* In her pictures on Facebook, Magenta was gorgeous, but what if in person she was not? It was like a blind date, in a way.

Before she turned on the street where they agreed to meet, Magenta pulled over at a rest area to freshen up her hair and makeup. She cared about looking good for their first encounter. She rolled into the driveway, hoping she had made the right decision to come.

Cabernet was already waiting there, standing next to his car. He was wearing a white shirt and nice pair of slacks, looking confident and sexy. He was just as handsome as she remembered. And Magenta, just as beautiful as he had dreamed.

They exchanged a long embrace and nervous smiles. "Finally!" said Cabernet. "I was beginning to wonder if I would ever see you again!"

Magenta shyly smiled. "So, what do you want to do?"

"I'm taking you to a party at one of my friend's house. He lives about an hour from here," offered Cab. "Is that something you would like to do?"

"Sure, that sounds good," she remarked. Even though Magenta was sick of driving, she didn't want to spoil the night. "Let's take my car. I'll drive," she said. That way, if for some unforeseen reason Cab turned into a creep, at least she would have her car and be able to get away.

"Cool, I made us some songs for the trip there. It's my own music that I made," he said.

"Awesome!" Magenta popped the card into the MP3 player and they listened to it as they drove off. "Wow, this is really catchy!" she remarked, after hearing a song or two.

To Magenta, that he could produce his own music was another fascinating aspect of Cab that she really liked. She loved music and dancing, and Cab's was just her style. In fact, they got so wrapped up in jamming in the car that somehow they both missed the turn to go to the party.

After driving forty-five minutes off course, Cab realized they were lost. "I'm so sorry; I don't know how I missed the turn. I think I was looking at your lovely legs," he admitted.

She melted. Cab was smooth. They both laughed about it and turned back, eventually getting to the party late. Cab seemed genuinely happy to show Magenta off to his friends. She was nice and cordial to them. All night, she sat on Cab's lap in the kitchen as they partied and hung out with his friends. It was a small gathering with just a lot of laughing and socializing.

For a few minutes, Magenta snuck away. She sat on a swing on the front porch of the house, watching the stars sparkle next to a full moon. Cab came along, searching for her. "Everything okay?" he asked when he saw Magenta sitting alone.

"Everything is great," she smiled. "I'm glad I came." He leaned in and gave Magenta a meaningful kiss, one that lingered in her head forever. It was dynamite. Cab was a great kisser.

"So, do you want to go back now?" he asked. But Magenta wondered where she would stay. Knowing she would ask, Cab added, "Don't worry, I'll sleep on the couch."

"Okay," she agreed. They left, after thanking the host.

However, once they got back to Cab's house, there was no way they could keep their hands off each other. After getting to know each other so well for so many months on the phone, the connection was already there. They barely came up for air; although, they did leave the house once to get breakfast at a cute Mom and Pop-style waffle house. They fed each other strawberry filled crepes and sipped cappuccinos with whipped cream. They spent an amazing weekend together.

It was the beginning of their blooming relationship. Without making it official, Magenta and Cab became inseparable. At least as much as they could be, considering the many hours they lived apart. They planned to get together every other weekend. Sometimes Cab drove up to Napa to see her, while other times Magenta was the one to do the driving. Whenever they hung out, they had a blast going to the beach, concerts, out to dinner and museums and playing bedroom sports.

They fell in love.

Finally, after about six months of dating and ten months after they had originally met, Cab came to see her one last time. "I have to make a choice. My job is seasonal, so I'm going to have to go back home. Unless..."

Magenta looked at him, knowing what he was about to say.

"...Or maybe I could come up here to Napa and make the next step with you. I could get a job near here."

It was the weekend of her birthday. The news caught Magenta off guard. She hadn't lived with anyone in over 10 years, so she was unsure about if it was the right time to make the next step. Inside, Magenta wondered if Cab could be "*the one?*" It felt like maybe he could be.

"Let me think about it over the weekend," she said. "Don't take it the wrong way; I just haven't made that big of a commitment in a long time."

He nodded. As always, they had a great time throughout the weekend. The more she thought about it, the more Magenta wondered that if she let Cab move back to his hometown if their relationship would regress. Maybe they would break up altogether. But long distances could put a strain on any great relationship. She didn't want that.

Cab put his coat on and gathered his things at the end of the weekend, as if to leave. He hugged and kissed her tight. "Do you really want me to leave?" he asked.

"No, of course not. I'm just not sure about living together yet," she admitted.

"You have nothing to worry about. I'm crazy about you. You are the girl of my dreams," said Cab. "I can get a job around here and if for some reason it doesn't work out, well I can just go back to Sully. Take a chance on us!"

"Okay, I will try it," she caved in.

It was a brave decision. After they moved in together, the two became joined at the hip. They went surfing together, they made friends together, they traveled together, they visited their families together and both were very happy. Cabernet loved cooking her dinner every night, which Magenta thoroughly enjoyed.

Cab was the love of her life. Magenta was his soulmate, confidant and best friend. Eventually, they bought their own home and started a family. They had three sons, which kept them very busy. Magenta went from trendsetter to babysitter; although, she was happy to be part of a family.

Their chance meeting in that small city was just the beginning of a lifetime of passion, love and understanding.

❖❖❖❖❖❖❖❖❖

# PROVISO

**Sometimes, it pays to try a different type of wine.** The thing about Cabernet that makes it so darn wonderful is that it's different to everybody. It can be a blend of other types of wine, or it can be great as a standalone variety.

To one woman, the right glass of Cabernet could be impossible to find. But don't give up; if you're looking for "*the one,*" it will reveal itself when the time is right.

Because it matures well, Cabernet can get better as it ages, just like any long-term relationship. Sometimes "Mr. Right" takes awhile to develop. Hardly anyone dislikes Cabernet, although there may always be an exception. It is the most sought-after of the red wine family.

Yes, Cabernet might just be the perfect wine. It grows in nearly every wine-bearing region around the globe, and no two shall be alike, just as no two men are the same. Therefore, to one who likes Merlot and to another who likes Pinot Noir, perhaps a blend of these with Cabernet will be most ideal. You might spot a bottle of Cabernet with Shiraz, Merlot or Tempranillo. Hence, its versatility is part of what makes it so distinctive and so different to every drinker. Cabernet exudes romance, yet is just as enjoyable with a casual box of pizza as it is with a fancy lamb dinner at an uptown restaurant.

There are many price points in Cabernets. You can find young Cabernets that don't cost much but still have a great flavor. Then there are the older bottles that can be quite pricey. Yet, whether you drink it young or after many years of safekeeping, Cabernet is most always great. At least it's something you can live with and always count on forever.

# Merlot

## "THE NICE GUY"

***Merlot is the most decent and respectable of wines.** It ripens primitively, perhaps raised by Mama's loving hands. The classic version originates from along the Bordeaux territory of France, typically yielding a soft, juicy and medium-bodied texture that is "fruit-abulous."*

*Now grown throughout the world, Merlot's kind disposition encompasses an extensive reach of rich soils from different climates, while still maintaining a high level of competence. Although it is most forgiving of moist soil, Merlot's thin-skinned grapes take a lot to maintain. Winemakers coddle to the grapes rather than risking damage or a bruised ego. Merlot is a wine to keep coming back for, or to never leave in the first place.*

*Typically, Merlot contains more sugar than other red wines. The sweet complexity provides a fruity and synergized relationship when mixed with other varieties. So, you may find a Merlot-Shiraz combination or Merlot-Cabernet Sauvignon, for example.*

*More confectionary power equates to lower bitterness, gentler tannins and a tender texture. Unlike heavier and more serious wines, Merlot provides premature accessibility and a faster period of maturing into something magnificent. You could keep it safely in the wine cellar for a year or two; five or ten and come out with a really nice taste. Other popular reds may take longer to reach full maturity. The only drawback of Merlot's sugar surplus is the potentially greater impression of fruitiness.*

*The thin skin of Merlot grapes are susceptible to hurt because of their vulnerability to spring frost, making them less resistant to rot. However, Merlot ripens sooner and is less likely to be affected by wet rains or precipitation. Its sensitivity only enhances Merlot's good taste and fine character. The grapes still have time to heal and ripen before frigid weather sets in.*

*Neighboring red wines like Cabernet and Malbec display characteristics of greater depth than Merlot, which could be good or bad depending on your individual taste buds. Some like sweet, while others prefer a deeper and longer lasting taste. Merlot is certainly softer and more sensitive.*

*Nevertheless, Merlot continues to be widely popular among drinkers. It is the "old standby" and the loyal friend. It is sometimes passed up and then remembered after a bad experience with more tart and demanding wines, such as Chianti or Pinot Noir.*

*In the end, that's what makes Merlot such a global favorite. It can adapt to most any situation; although sometimes, its amiability will be unappreciated. Merlot is supportive under most circumstances. It's a safe choice with most any meal and rises to any occasion with class. It is always a welcome asset in social circles.*

*Once discovered, Merlot is a wine to cherish and to enjoy. The pleasant, yet delightful plum-flavor of Merlot's natural sugars offers a cheerful delicacy. Be careful not to take this wine for granted, as Merlot will always be there as a faithful choice and palatable companion.*

❖❖❖❖❖❖❖❖❖

# MERLOT ❣ Red

**Merlot was French. Well, technically he was** Canadian–French. He was the perfect gentleman in every way, making it difficult to find fault with any of his characteristics. He opened doors for women and was polite to the very core. His French accent was adorable. Merlot rarely used foul language or disrespected anyone, especially females. His mother raised him to become a fine young man, one that any woman would be lucky to meet. He was the epitome of a nice guy.

There was a boyish way about him, but with all of the maturity of a grown man. Unfortunately, he kept meeting women who did not appreciate these qualities. Merlot was drawn to the types who walked all over him. He was sensitive and had been burned a time or two by girls who used him for everything from free dinners to new jewelry; or even just for temporary companionship while on the rebound from another bad boy type who hurt them. Merlot had spent many evenings consoling women, even those who were not his girlfriends. Chicks leaned on him for advice and friendship whenever things went awry with a player, a charmer or an estranged husband. Merlot was "the friend" and offered support, along with an extra soft shoulder to cry on.

He wasn't sure why women were attracted to those types of guys in the first place. It didn't make sense. Merlot knew there were other nice guys out there, too, like him. But women never wanted them except when there was nothing else more exciting to try, like Shiraz or Malbec. Patiently, he waited for the right girl to come along. Merlot knew that his "Mrs. Right" was out there somewhere. She was his soulmate, and he was on a quest to find her. Merlot wanted a "happily ever after" story.

One of the problems he had in attracting the right type of girl was that Merlot was rather introverted. He was a jeweler at a reputable diamond store in town, so he was more often "behind the scenes" than the other associates who worked there. His co-workers were mostly female. They were social butterflies who manned the sales floor. The female customers were not good candidates, either, because most of them were women who were shopping for engagement rings, wedding bands or anniversary gifts from their boyfriends and husbands.

All of the sales girls who worked with Merlot loved him. He always listened to their tales of woe in relationships and offered his "guy perspective" point of view that many of the ladies wanted to hear. But Merlot was less assertive than some of the other types of guys they spoke of. Merlot was just "nice" and sometimes overlooked by the single women who came into the store.

One day the jewelry store was short staffed, so they called in some extra associates from another store to cover the missing shifts. A voluptuous redhead was among the three new people who were scheduled to work there for a few days until the store was able to hire new staff. Merlot noticed her, especially her eyes. They were intensely blue, like his. He knew he didn't want to miss his chance to get to know her. But instead of approaching her himself, Merlot put one of his co-workers up to it. Shadow was a good friend of Merlot and someone he could confide in.

"Do you know how long that new girl has been with the company?" he asked.

"Who? You mean Red? She is just filling in today and tomorrow until we hire some new trainees. Then she's going back to her home store," said Shadow. "Why, do you like her?"

"I'm interested," Merlot admitted. "But I'm sure a girl like that is probably taken. I won't get my hopes up, but why don't you see what you can see?"

"Yeah, she's taken with you. She asked about you, too! Already! She beat you to it, that's why I came over here to talk to you," said Shadow. "Do you want me to play matchmaker for you?"

"Feel her out. Find out more," Merlot said, optimistically.

So a few hours later, Shadow returned to Merlot's jeweler's bench. He was deeply engrossed in sizing a ring. Shadow nearly startled him as she approached his station. "Knock, knock!" she said, not wanting to scare the busy jeweler.

He jumped a little and repositioned his jeweler's goggles to the top of his head. Shadow said, "So I got the skinny on the new girl and she's single. She just got out of a five-year thing, I guess."

"Great, another rebound girl who's still in love with her ex," said Merlot, rolling his eyes. "That's just what I need is another heartbreak."

"No, she seems to be over him. They've been apart for a good six months. I'd say she's a prime candidate for a first date!" Shadow encouraged.

By the end of the day, Merlot felt more comfortable approaching her. "I don't think we've had a proper introduction," he said to Red, wiping his soot-covered hand and stretching it out to her in friendship. "I'm Merlot."

"Merlot, huh? Well that's an unusual name. I like it!" Red said, catching the intensity of his eyes as they connected.

"Shadow tells me you're only in town for a couple of days, but if you're not working tomorrow night I have tickets to a comedy show," Merlot offered.

"Is that the one with Sinbad and Chris Kattan? Man, I've wanted to see them!" Red said, cupping her hand over her mouth in unbridled enthusiasm.

"So, where should I pick you up?" Merlot asked.

"The company put me up at the Marriott with the other two," Red said, pointing to her two traveling coworkers. "I'll come down to the lobby and meet you. What time does it start?"

Merlot said, "It's at 8:00 but we could have a drink or two if you want. It'd be better to go sooner to get a good seat."

"My shift ends at 5:00 tomorrow. Give me an hour or so to get ready. You know, this can be a dirty job," she said, pointing at Merlot's ash-colored welding apron.

"How about 6:30 then; that should give you a little extra time?" asked Merlot.

"Oh, that sounds great. I can't wait to see Sinbad!" Red smiled. She flipped her beautiful mane casually to one side.

The next night when Merlot showed up at her hotel, he was noticeably polished. He had gelled hair and strong, sweet cologne that blended well with the smell of his leather jacket.

Red was seated at the bar in the back of the hotel lobby. She had been there for ten minutes and already knocked back two glasses of wine. Not wanting to spoil the fun, Merlot sat down next to her. "Well hello there, Merlot." She reached out her hand. "I'm Red. Pleased to meet you. Do you want a glass, too? It will loosen you up for all the laughter. Sinbad is a pretty funny dude," she joked.

"I'd better not have too much," Merlot smiled. "I have to get us there in one piece. But I'll have a couple of sips, at least."After having half a glass, he gave the rest to his date before escorting her back to his pickup truck. It was a silver Toyota Tacoma with a king cab and running boards. Merlot opened the door for her, which was something she wasn't used to. Red's ex certainly never opened any doors for her. Then again, he never did much of anything nice.

They had a great time at the comedy show and laughed a lot. There was definitely chemistry between them, especially on Merlot's part. He couldn't take his eyes off her nor stop doting on her. Throughout the night he flattered Red with compliments and kind words. He flagged the waiter over to attend to her every need and was the perfect gentleman.

Red found Merlot's mannerisms to be a sharp contrast in what she was accustomed to. She had finally dumped a "Player" after five years of on-again, off-again turmoil. It was the perfect time for a laid-back, friendly and sweet guy to come along, if for nothing more than to show her that all men were mean or manipulative. Honestly, she might have been quite content with Merlot for a long time, had things not gone so drastically out of control after the first three months of dating.

Oh yes, that first three months was intensely high and got serious quickly. Red was the girl of Merlot's dreams, so he went way overboard to keep her happy with excessive indulgence, constantly running errands for her, bringing her flowers, fixing things for her around her apartment, helping to repair her car and even cooking for her a few times. She loved the treatment. Merlot was getting better and better as time went on.

From everything she could see; Red had hit the jackpot in her choice this time. Merlot was responsible, faithful and fun to be with. He took her on a couple of fun trips to meet his family. One weekend she met his mother, who only spoke Canadian– French. Although Red could understand her, she could barely talk fast enough to keep up. Merlot thought this was funny, but deep down; he was smitten that finally he had brought home a girl who could at least communicate with his dear mom, whom he adored.

Another weekend, Merlot took her to Pennsylvania to meet his sister and her husband. While there, they journeyed through the Amish Country and visited the Hershey Chocolate Factory. Merlot's family liked Red a lot. There was speculation that she could be "*the one*" that Merlot had been looking for.

As they followed a horse and buggy through the scenic hills of Lancaster County, Merlot said, "Wouldn't it be nice if life was simple like it is for these guys? When a guy and girl just rode together in their horse and buggy and didn't need anything more to be happy?"

"You're quite an old fashioned guy, aren't you?" she replied.

"I wouldn't say old fashioned, I would say *nostalgic*," Merlot answered.

"I can tell," said Red. "You still call dating each other *courting*. I find that to be entertaining."

Merlot said, "Well that's what I'm doing, isn't it? I'm courting you? We're committed to each other and you are the girl of my dreams."

"How did you get to be so sweet?" asked Red.

"I had a great mom who raised me right," explained Merlot. In truth, he was growing very fond of Red and had a strong desire to get married and have a family soon.

But introducing him to all of her family so soon only made Red feel overwhelmed. She hadn't decided yet if there was a hitch to all of the goodness of Merlot. She wasn't ready to settle down yet, having just gotten out of a five year relationship that still left her hurting inside. At the same time, she didn't want to give up Merlot and cared for him a great deal. He was just so.... unexpectedly... NICE.

After leaving his sister's house, Merlot and Red finally got into their first argument on the way home. She was the passenger and Merlot was driving. He had been behind the wheel for the last eight hours. Red brushed her boyfriend's arm and gently asked, "Why don't you let me drive for a while? You must be getting tired. I'm fine to drive. I had a little catnap earlier when we passed through New York."

"No, I'm fine. I got this," he said, firmly.

"Do you not trust me to drive your truck?" asked Red.

"It's not that. The man should drive and the woman should relax," Merlot said adamantly.

"OH! IS *THAT* HOW IT IS?" she raised her voice, defensively. "Aren't you chivalrous?"

"You're my woman and my job is to take care of you," Merlot snapped.

"OH, now you're really pushing your luck," she warned. "And by the way! You missed the exit. That was the way we were supposed to go!" Red pointed out the window to her right as they passed the turn for the extension.

"Great, just great," said Merlot. "Just leave the driving to me, will you?"

"OH, now it's MY fault we missed the turn?" she drawled with long sarcasm. "You're unbelievable." Then she crossed her arms and stared out the window for the longest time. Even when Merlot tried to reach for her hand across her lap a couple of hours later, Red snatched it away. "Don't. Don't touch me."

"How long will you be mad?" asked Merlot. "I just want to know how much longer you will torture me with your indifference."

"For as long as I feel like it!" she yelled.

"Awww... it's our first fight," Merlot smiled. "How cute. I love you babe."

Merlot wanted to be with Red every waking second, however sometimes she liked to have her own space. She missed her friends and they all thought she dropped off the face of the earth. One of her best friends, who often hung out with Red on the weekends, left her a message on her answering machine. "Just because you got a boyfriend doesn't mean you have to drop all of your besties!"

After she heard the message, Red felt a suffocating wave wash over her. She called back. "You're right. I'm sorry to all of you. I have been spending too much time with my man and never see my friends anymore. It's time for a girl's night. He'll just have to deal with it if he wants to be with me," Red announced.

That weekend, Red told Merlot she was going out. "Oh, that will be fun, where are we going?"

She said, "NO, you don't understand. I am going out with my friends *without* you."

"Why? You don't want to be with me?" he asked, perplexed.

"I haven't spent any time with them in a long while. You understand, don't you?" she kissed Merlot on the cheek. He clearly wasn't digging the notion of spending a night away from each other.

On the night Red went out with her girlfriends, Merlot called at least ten times. Of course, she did not answer and was beyond the point of annoyed. It was alarming and confusing. Merlot was being clingy. When she finally did return his call at about 2:00 a.m., he was really upset. "Is this how it's going to be when we're married?"

Red was breathless on the end of the phone. They had never talked of marriage yet. They had only been dating for like three months and everything was happening so fast. She had already met Merlot's family and spent nearly every minute with him, apart from work. And now he was having a conniption that she went out. Doubt set in like an elevator ride that stops in mid-air, just as you're about to reach the highest floor of the building.

Everything had been great, and now here she was, not knowing what to do. Merlot was so nice and now things took an unexpected turn. Merlot was shopping for a wife, but trying way too hard. Instead of pulling his girlfriend closer, he pushed her away. He sensed it, too. The silence between them grew thicker as both wondered what to do.

"Get some sleep," said Red. "Because that's what I'm going to do."

Merlot didn't sleep all night, tossing and turning as he contemplated what was happening. '*Women always say they want a nice guy, but once they get one they don't want it anymore*,' he mused. He knew he had to take drastic action to turn things around. Red wasn't taking their relationship seriously.

The next afternoon, he showed up to Red's house with a gift. She opened a box and inside was a beautiful bracelet. On the inside it was inscribed. *"Dreams do come true – Merlot."* It had the month and day and year of their first date next to it.

"Wow, this is beautiful. Thank you," she beamed. "It's really gorgeous."

"I made it myself," Merlot added. "Except the engraving."

"What's the occasion?" Red asked.

"Every day is a special occasion with you," he said with sincerity. Merlot was sweet, even if he was a little over the top in his efforts to please. "I was thinking... let's get back to the way we were. I think we just hit a little bump in the road. But I want to be with you forever."

Red didn't return the words, but instead said, "You're so sweet. That's really kind to say."

"I think we should go away next weekend and have a special trip together, would you like that?" he asked.

She thought for a moment. They had just gone to Pennsylvania and she was happy to just chill. However, she didn't want to spoil the moment by being bitchy. "Sure. Where will we go?"

"You leave that up to me," said Merlot.

All week, Merlot planned the perfect getaway. He knew it was time to propose. Red was his dream girl and he didn't want to lose her or risk any other guys snatching her up. Even though they had only been dating a few months, he wanted to secure his prize.

Unfortunately, he wasn't sure how to come up with the money for an engagement ring. He could make the band for it himself, but he needed cash to buy the diamond. The only thing he had of value was an extensive baseball card collection. Merlot had been saving them his whole life. His grandfather and father had given him a few really good cards as gifts. One was a 1939 Ted Williams rookie card worth at least $7,000. A few others were in the low thousand range and still hundreds more were worth hundreds of dollars. If he was going to sell one, Merlot was going to sell them all. Not only would he have enough for Red's engagement ring, he would be able to pay for their wedding and perhaps even have a small down payment for a house, too. Merlot was ready to part with them, even though he loved his cards and took great pride in their upkeep.

Merlot called some collectors and one in particular who had approached him in years past, offering to buy out his entire collection. The guy came over and gave Merlot a very sizable double-digit cashier's check and left with a whole Subaru full of baseball cards.

That weekend, Merlot gathered everything they would need for a romantic weekend together in the back of his truck. Red was ready when he picked her up, looking sensational in an orange sundress and new Zappos sandals. "Where are we going?" she asked, as Merlot opened the passenger door for her.

"I thought it would be fun to go camping and be one with nature," Merlot said. "I booked a weekend for us in the White Mountains."

Red's face was less enthusiastic than he hoped. "Oh, I'm not really into camping that much. Three days without a hot shower is more than I can bear. And the strange sounds at night make me toss and turn."

Merlot stepped on the gas, making his truck swerve. "There's not much I can do to make you happy, is there?"

Not wanting to piss him off, Red suggested, "How about we just be spontaneous and end up wherever we end up?"

They drove to Boston. Merlot found a hotel in the historical district. It was a charming eighteenth century building with iron bars on the window and fancy scrollwork from a bygone era. After being in the car for four hours, Merlot wanted to take a shower. "After I get out of the shower, we'll go sightseeing."

"Okay honey." Red agreed.

After the shower stopped, Merlot came out of the bathroom with just a small square covering him. "Man, they really make the towels small here, don't they?" he commented.

"I think that's a bath mat," Red said, snickering. "The towels are on the shelf."

Merlot laughed. "Oops! It looks just like a towel!"

The two set out for the city. There were lots of romantic spots in Boston. They walked to Copley Square, the Museum of Fine Arts, and down the cobblestone streets for lunch. Even though Merlot would have preferred camping, he was willing to do most anything to make Red happy.

They hit a pub on the Back Bay. Merlot knew how much she loved red wine. He ordered a couple of bottles. Red gulped down glass after glass, getting quite a buzz. The wine was getting to her. A slow song came on. "Would you like to dance?" asked Merlot.

"Sure!" screamed Red. She was intoxicated and felt sassy.

As they danced, Merlot chose an opportune moment to make his move. Just as '*Lady in Red*' came on – and the couple were dancing ‘cheek to cheek’ – Merlot whispered in her ear. “There’s nobody here. It’s just you and me. It’s where I want to be...”

She liked it. Merlot got down on one knee as the song neared its final chorus. He pulled out a black velvet box with a gold ribbon from his front pocket. “Red, you are the girl of my dreams. You’re my soul mate. Will you marry me?”

Shocked, she slapped her palms to her cheeks as her jaw dropped in sheer astonishment. “Well... this is really a.... surprise.” She said quietly.

“I sold all of my cards. Even Ted Williams,” Merlot proudly announced. “There’s enough left for the wedding, and I’ll even buy you a house. Marry me.”

Red looked at the ring. It caught the light of the disco ball that was swirling above their heads. She was mesmerized, entranced by its beauty. The diamond was at least two carats. She resisted the urge to slip it on her finger immediately. Merlot had gone all out this time.

“I made it myself! What do you think?” he asked, starting to get nervous by Red’s lack of acceptance.

“I think the ring is stunning. It really is,” she said, pulling Merlot up from his knees. “Any woman would be lucky to have this ring. But... I don’t deserve it.”

“Oh, yes you do! Baby, you deserve everything. I will give you the whole world and can’t wait to marry you,” said Merlot as he tried to slip the ring on her left hand. She pulled it back, but not without admiring it on her hand.

“I’m crazy about you!” Merlot added.

Red said, “I really like you and we have fun together. You treat me like a princess.”

“You are... you’re *my* princess,” said Merlot.

“I’m... just not ready. We’ve only been together for a few months. It’s just too soon.” She tried to use gentle words.

Merlot debated. "But when you know it's right, you just know. I am 100% sure you are the right one for me."

"That could be true, someday..." she struggled to explain and wished he hadn't ruined what they had by rushing. She wanted things to take their course naturally, without being too rushed. She loved Merlot, but was afraid by his over eagerness to wed.

The next day when she woke up, the prior evening was one big blur. Red had drunk too much, that was for sure. She looked at the note next to her on the nightstand. It read, "*Goodbye. I will always love you. Here is some money for you to get home. --- M.*" There were two Ben Franklins lying next to the note.

Scratching her head, it came to her. She vaguely recalled what happened, but one thing was most certain. Red had a pounding hangover.

❖❖❖❖❖❖❖❖❖

# PROVISO

**Merlot is always nice and always there for you. It is** readily available and predictably good. However, Merlot's thin-skinned sensitivity is tough to deal with. It might be best to save Merlot for later. He is definitely a "Keeper" but needs to stay in the wine cellar until fully mature. Someday you will appreciate how nice Merlot is and how well he treats you. He'll always there as a friend you can lean on and a lover that will bend over backwards to please.

For heaven's sake, just don't rush into anything with Merlot until you've had a chance to try other great reds.

Shiraz, Chianti, or Malbec will have you flipping for their rapid entry and quick finish. Merlot is safe, but perhaps you need to experience samples of other wines before you decide to settle down with just one favorite.

One good thing about Merlot is its versatility, blending well with other varieties. So to some, Merlot might be the "Nice Guy" who turns into Cabernet Sauvignon. To another, a blend of Pinot Noir / Merlot can be one woman's "bad boy" who turned into a "nice guy" for someone else. And Merlot also mixes well with certain white wines. You can find Zinfandel / Merlot combos that are a humorous blend of goodness with a zesty side and fruity finish.

Few other wines will ever treat you as good as Merlot. It will give you a great buzz like the peak of a roller coaster just before it screams down a ninety degree incline with its ups and downs of insecurities. Merlot will always be fun and spoil you.

Find a nice glass of Merlot. One glass a day is actually good for your heart. He is polite, respectful, goes with everything, tags along anywhere you want to go and is appropriate for most any occasion. He often picks up the tab, too. You could say that being with Merlot is like being with a best friend, except with many other benefits. You will enjoy his company and not get tired of the flavor.

When you're ready, Merlot will treat you just fine. You will always feel special, cared for and like the princess you know you are. When you want to be pleasured, Merlot is one of the best in wine electives. Make sure the bottle you choose is from the Top Shelf and that it has had proper time to mature. Otherwise it may be a short-lived burst of intoxication followed by a throbbing headache the next day.

# Chardonnay

## "FRIEND WITH BENEFITS"

***Chardonnay is a classic dessert wine, which makes it*** *perfect to drink after a great meal. Truthfully, what's not to like? Versatile Chardonnay is there when you need it. It is one of the most beloved white wines, made with a 'low maintenance' grape that adapts well and is plentiful enough to be found most anywhere worldwide. Chardonnay looks good in public and is just as comfortable schmoozing with the socialites at an art gallery as it is on a camping trip; of course chilled in an ice cooler.*

*It is a wine for all ages, from the lively college student to the middle aged recent divorcee. The affability is nearly unanimous. Everyone likes – and many people love – Chardonnay. It carries many facades, from very affordable to gaspingly expensive. Chardonnay makes a notable replacement when other wines disappoint. Its sugary and refreshing disposition will always put a smile on your face. You may not find Chardonnay to be the love of your life, but it will always have a special place in your heart.*

*You could say it is one of the most popular whites, although less "in your face" than other bold wines like Zinfandel or Moscato. Nearly everyone has at least tried a glass of Chardonnay, while many others have had more than their fair share. It remains one of the most popular white wines around the world, from the charming vineyards of France and Italy to the sunny branches of California; to the mixed terrain of New Zealand and Australia; or the exotic landscape of South Africa; or even the dramatic hillsides of Chile and Argentina. It has been around between 700 to 1700 years; yet, no one can be certain just how long. There is more Chardonnay worldwide than Shiraz, Cabernet Sauvignon and many of the most popular wines. That is in part because it can be easily adapted to suit various climates.*

*Chardonnay is convenient. It can be found in any wine store, supermarket, or convenience store, but the best ones will be on the top shelf. Fancier versions will make A-list appearances at wine tastings or office parties. Because there is an expected comfort level when ordering Chardonnay, it is often a hassle-free and stress-free selection. You can safely order a glass without the performance anxiety of other complicated wines. Its physical and emotional attributes will make any undesirable notes fade into the background because of its familiarity and likeability.*

*Due to the innate differences between the many abundant sources and styles of Chardonnay, one brand may bear very little resemblance to another. Nearly everyone has their own personal favorite, making it one of the most versatile wines with as many different personalities as there are people.*

*Because of its flexibility, Chardonnay can be vinified in*

*a multitude of ways – extremely dry or sweet; neutral, medium or full bodied; barrel oak or no oak aging; cold fermented or in barrels; sparkling; strong or subtle. Cool climate Chardonnays has completely different characteristics than the fruity, fresh tropical wines from the rich new regions. It is easy to cultivate and has a reputation for the ability to adjust to numerous conditions.*

*Chardonnay ages well, making it an exceptional choice for storage. It can be opened and then saved for a later date; directly from the back door of the refrigerator. Certain people take Chardonnay out of the ice chest without a cork and drink it as if it were no big deal, much like popping off a bottle cap from a frothy bottle of beer. And if you're out of cooking wine, Chardonnay can fill in quite nicely. You can leave it out overnight without worry of it spoiling.*

*Even the taste can vary from one bottle to the next. Because it is harvested in so many countries, the tastes can be altered to suit many palates. Chardonnay blends the best flavors and aromas together, with common hints of citrusy oranges, lemons, limes, peaches, and tropical wisps of mango, guava, kiwi, banana or pineapple. Lest we not forget the floral or seasoned versions; as well as those with a buttery, hazelnut or creamy twinge of sweet coconut, toast, wood, mint or vanilla.*

*A drawback of Chardonnay is associated with its overproduction as an industrial wine. The vines are low producing and susceptible to countless vices. They can be awkward, unstable and easily oxidized. Furthermore, the grapes are inconsistent. Some are big and some are small.*

*Looks-wise, Chardonnay runs the gamut between average clarity to sparklingly handsome. Mostly, it is a perennially reliable white wine that focuses more on quality over quantity. Its dependability outweighs any understated varietal characteristics. For that reason, Chardonnay is likely to remain a wildly popular selection, at least as the quiet secret of many people who are lucky enough to experience this exquisite choice.*

*However, the common denominators between the many variations of Chardonnay make it not one to fall in love with. For one, Chardonnay is a highly recognizable product. Therefore, it is in high demand. You can bet that just as much as you crave Chardonnay, there will be other consumers who want it, too. They may even want the same bottle as you.*

❖❖❖❖❖❖❖❖❖

# DONNAY ❣ Olive

**As Chardonnay drove up to his townhome complex** at about 8 p.m., he noticed a moving truck at the neighbor's house next door. He took off his chef hat and lingered in the driver's seat of his car for a few minutes, hoping to get a glimpse of whoever the new neighbor would be. The place was vacant for a few months and he had been content with the quiet. There was no one to knock on the door and complain when he jammed his Linkin Park on the surround sound, like the last people who had lived there. Peace was something he looked forward to after an evening of demanding customers and waitresses and restaurant managers at the busy waterfront hotspot. Chardonnay was the head chef, therefore the one with the most responsibility except for the manager.

Not seeing anyone, he went into his house and flicked on the lights. Chardonnay couldn't wait to get out of his hot Egyptian cotton chef's jacket. Even though the material was supposed to be sweat-resistant, the fabric was no match for the hot oven in the kitchen. He stripped down to just a pair of boxer shorts and plopped down on the couch to chill for the evening and clear his mind.

A knock on the door stirred his quiet evening. Chardonnay didn't really want to pick his tired self off the sofa, but he looked through the peephole and saw a girl standing there. "Excuse me, I don't mean to bother you. Do you have a Bungee strap?"

"Uh..." Chardonnay felt a little awkward as he stood there in his Looney Tunes boxers. "I think so. Hang on a sec." He didn't invite her in because he didn't want her to see the few things he would have tidied up, had he known there might be an unexpected guest.

Damn, he couldn't find it. He came back to the door a minute later. "You know, I think I have one in the garage somewhere but..."

"It's okay," she smiled. "You don't have to go down there tonight; I just thought I'd ask. I'm your new neighbor." She extended a hand for him to shake. "Name's Olive."

"Oh, great," Chardonnay said, somewhat distracted. "Yeah I'm Donnay. Well it's short for Chardonnay. But yeah... you can just call me Donnay." He winked.

"Got it! Well, I've got people helping me move, so I gotta go," she spun around and walked back to her new house. Olive was plain, but cute. She had a kooky-edgy style that was distinguishable. Her hair was up in a sloppy Bohemian updo and her entire forearm was filled with jingly bracelets. Olive was decidedly brilliant, yet sometimes an airhead when it came to remembering little details. For example, she could remember her telephone number from when she was eight-years-old, her driver's license number and even a long product number from the back of a cell phone after reading it only once or twice. Yet, she could barely remember where she put her keys after setting them down only minutes prior. She was not his type, but Chardonnay thought she seemed nice.

Besides, he was recently divorced. Chardonnay was really intelligent too; although, he rarely came across any people who understood him. He was a deep thinker, yet punchy and worldly. He could jump in on any topic and have something to contribute, with much wisdom.

He was not interested in dating anyone seriously, so he spent much of his free time searching for women to date on Match.com. Chardonnay found the women on there to be fun enough for going out with a few times, and some also kept him company on a lonely night or two for an occasionally rendezvous. But whenever things got too serious or if a lady liked him too much, Chardonnay immediately backed away. He was notoriously a "love 'em and leave 'em" type of guy, at least for the last year.

His ex-wife was a head trip, to say the least. Chardonnay didn't know what he was thinking in marrying that girl. Theirs was a relationship that started off with a lot of great sex, but not much else. However, she had entrapped him by getting herself pregnant. Now he had a son, which he was proud of but disappointed that he didn't have his child with a sane person.

The divorce had been dragging on and on for two years now. Chardonnay's ex was constantly changing the parameters of the paperwork. They had a house together, which she wanted to keep. Then she stopped making payments on it, which screwed up his credit. Their son was a beautiful kid with light brown hair and bright blue eyes, just like his daddy. He wished he could see his son more, but between his crazy work schedule at the restaurant and having to deal with the divorce, Chardonnay was pretty busy. He had a few nights off each week, which he sometimes used for dating girls he met online. But that was also in part because his ex-wife was a lunatic and often used the child to manipulate him. She didn't let him see the boy except when she needed a babysitter so that she could go out with her girlfriends.

Meanwhile, Olive was also dealing with her own drama. She had an on-again and off-again boyfriend who was tough to deal with. So she finally moved out and got her own place. It was far enough away that she wouldn't have to put up with her ex coming over all the time. Besides, she knew she could get a job anywhere as a waitress or bartender. That was her plan. She had saved up enough money every week for the last seven weeks to finally have enough for a deposit and first month's rent.

But the next day, Chardonnay heard jingling so he went to look out the window. His new neighbor was crossing the parking lot, with her bracelets giving away her presence. She had just come back from Starbuck's, her daily ritual. As Olive sipped her Venti Carmel Macchiato with extra crème and three Splenda, she finally felt awake.

Chardonnay went out and greeted her.

"Hey there, new neighbor." He punched her lightly on the arm with a friendly greeting. "Do you still need that Bungee?"

"No, no, that's okay. I was going to strap down something we were moving last night so it wouldn't sway all around. I packed everything kind of hastily and didn't want my stuff to break. But thanks," said Olive.

"It was kind of late for moving," Donnay noted.

"Yeah, well I had to do it when my helpers were available, you know?" she replied.

"I see. Well let me know if you need anything. I can be quite accommodating," he winked.

"Well, actually, do you know any places that are hiring? I'm a pretty good bartender. Or for now I'd even go back to being a server. I mean, until I finish college anyway," she said.

"I'm a chef at the Nautical Knot. I'll see what I can do," he offered.

"Hey, that sounds great. I really appreciate it," said Olive. "Let me guess, that's a seafood spot?"

"It's the best around," Donnay added. "I'll talk to the manager. They're always hiring this time of year.

"Awesome, thanks!" she said. Chardonnay was cool. He was laid back and witty. She liked his style. However, she was definitely not interested in starting anything with him after just going through the big headache with her ex-boyfriend. Life here was a new start.

True to his word, Chardonnay talked to his manager on behalf of Olive. "Send her in, said the key holder. We need people for all shifts."

After she began working there, they got to know each other better. Not romantically, but as great friends. She enjoyed joking around with him if they were on the same shift together. Mostly she worked as a bartender, but she filled in as a waitress when they were particularly short staffed. She was great at both jobs and the management was happy to have her on board.

On their days off, sometimes Olive and Chardonnay hung out together. They both had some things in common, particularly a recent bad experience in relationships. Chardonnay enjoyed having a female companion to get things off his chest. Although he rarely complained, the ordeal with his ex-wife was eating him up inside. It was great to have someone to vent to. He also talked about his son.

Olive also liked getting the male perspective on her recent breakup. Her ex still tried to contact her frequently, trying to find out where she had gone. She had up and moved without much warning. He came home one day to find the place cleaned out of all her things.

Both Olive and Chardonnay dated occasionally. They often got together and laughed about some of their dates. "I just went out with this girl a few nights ago and she spent the whole night on her cell phone, texting away," said Chardonnay. "That's such a turnoff!"

"Ya, I agree. I saw a whole group of friends the other day at the coffee shop and all of their heads were buried in their mobile devices. I mean, what's the point of all going out together and hanging with your buds if nobody even talks to each other anymore?" Olive agreed.

"Well, needless to say, I nixed her off my second date list," he finished.

Olive said, "It's probably for the best anyway. I mean, what if you were making out and all of a sudden she got a text and said, '*Hey can you wait just a second I have to text this person back?*' Now that would be totally lame."

Both Olive and Chardonnay also loved to people-watch and make up hypothetical situations about the lives of those they chose in jest. They did it to make each other laugh. And they even had their own language of non-existent words. "CHA!" was often used at the end of an agreeing statement.

Olive thought nothing of it when Chardonnay offered to make her a dinner on one random Friday night that they both had off from work. They had been hanging out for months now, as well as living next door to each other. "Heck ya!" she said zealously when he made the suggestion for seared scallops and grilled asparagus. Being one of the best chefs in town, any meal prepared by "Chef Donnay" was sure to be gourmet.

"I don't usually cook anything fancy on my night off from work," he joked as he sprinkled some lemon pepper and garlic butter across the top of the asparagus.

"Wow, I feel special." Olive joked as she watched him prepare their dinner. She gulped down two glasses of wine out of the bottle she had brought over to share with him.

"Well, sometimes I just get tired of frozen pizzas," he kidded.

"So, what's on the agenda after dinner? Some reruns of Jeopardy!?" she asked.

"You know me too well," said Chardonnay.

But after dinner, things took a strange turn when all of a sudden they were sitting on the couch together and started making out. Maybe it was the wine, or maybe it was just the comfortableness of their relationship.

One thing led to another. Olive's bra went flying across the room and Chardonnay's pants came off as the kissing led to heavy petting and then more. Before either of them could protest, they slowly made their way to his bedroom.

"I hope you don't think that this means..." he said, just as he was about to remove the last article of clothing that had been hiding underneath her denim shorts.

"CHA!" she joked, breathlessly waiting for his touch in the perfect spot.

A few hours later, Olive got up and grabbed her clothes that were scattered all over his house. "Well, I have a long ride home so I better be going."

"Uh... do you need me to call you a cab?" he asked, kidding in return.

"Nah. I'm a big girl. I can handle it. Now you're just my FWB." With that, Olive walked next door to her own place.

He got it. "Friends With Benefits. I like it. So much easier than Match.com." Chardonnay gave her a quick kiss on the lips as he flicked off the lamp just before she closed the front door. It was 'awkwardly comfortable'.

As friends, they had great synergy. As lovers, too. Although there was some chemistry between them, both Olive and Chardonnay agreed that the timing was not so great considering both of their recent breakups and Chardonnay's still ongoing divorce.

The next day, it was a relief to finally know what it would be like to try the forbidden nakedness of friendship. But alas, they immediately dismissed the hot evening prior and went back to being friends. They played tennis, or they sat at the park lighting sparklers. Olive even brought him as a date to her friend's wedding, although both of them flirted with others at the reception. They had an understanding of what it was and both agreed that they didn't want to ruin a good thing by putting labels on it.

Occasionally whenever they were lonely or just wanted to fulfill their desires, Olive and Chardonnay crossed the line of friendship. Theirs was not a romantic relationship but more of a mutually beneficial arrangement. It was a quietly kept, understood arrangement. They did love each other, but only as friends. Most of all, they enjoyed each other's company.

Then about two years after she had moved in next to him, Olive got a new boyfriend. She had dated some, but this was different. It seemed as though she was falling for this new guy. Chardonnay saw less and less of her, especially after she moved in with her new beau. He hated to say it, but it bothered him. He didn't ever want to let on to that fact because he still wasn't sure if he ever wanted to be in another relationship again, at least not for a long time. But he missed his friend. His friend with benefits.

They still talked sometimes, even though Olive had moved on from her job at the restaurant and gotten an office job instead. He tried to be happy for her, but their conversations were quite brief now that they rarely hung out together. It was finally time for her to do something with her career. She had never aspired to be a waitress for her entire life, but it was a pretty good-paying job and had given her a lot of social contacts. However, the hours and the weekends and the other cons to working at a restaurant finally made Olive seek out a more stable position. Now it seemed she was looking for a more stable partner. It had been a great friendship with Chardonnay while it lasted, and now it was time to move on.

About eight years later, Olive went on a trip with her family to Disney World. She was with her husband, mother and two young sons, ages three and five. They were all looking forward to a getaway. One of the nights, her husband took her to the nicest, five-star restaurant in town while her mother stayed behind at the hotel to watch the little ones.

After ordering their meal, the waiter brought a bottle of wine to the table. It was her favorite kind. "Compliments of the Chef," he said.

"Oh, wow! What's the occasion?" she asked.

"He said he knew you," the waiter stated.

Now curious, Olive asked her husband to pop the cork so she could enjoy a glass. Next, the waiter brought out a delicious plate of seared scallops and grilled asparagus, prepared to perfection. Underneath her plate was a note that read, "*Sometimes the benefits of friendship last a lifetime in the memories they bring. – Chef Chardonnay.*"

Her heart started beating a hundred miles an hour and she knew that she had been spotted by her long lost FWB. "Excuse me," Olive said to her husband. "I need to go say Thank You to an old friend."

❖❖❖❖❖❖❖❖❖

# PROVISO

**Any woman that says she has never had a nice glass** of Chardonnay is most likely fibbing. Furthermore, deep down she will forever hide her true fondness for this delicious white.

The best part about drinking Chardonnay is that it is primarily about friendship. You care about it, but you're probably not interested in a full-blown relationship or commitment. And because you share a lot in common, you will enjoy the company of Chardonnay a lot. He is not going to "rock your world," but he is there for you and makes you feel comfortable in his presence.

There is something about Chardonnay that is attractive, yet in a different way than other wines that give you the warm tickles in your belly. Chardonnay has a sparkling personality. It's a wine that is plentiful around the world and is always enjoyable. Chardonnay offers convenience and flexibility, which can be beneficial at those low points, particularly after a breakup. In fact, why not celebrate your next divorce with a great bottle of Chardonnay?

You may try more than one type of Chardonnay in your life. Any time you're in a "single phase," it's nice to have that one wine you can count on to lift you up and listen to your deepest, darkest secrets or discuss the events of the world with. Chardonnay is familiar, and won't judge. It's a lighthearted, easy and fun wine to order without all of the complications of other wines. It's usually pretty smart, too.

On the surface, it might seem like Chardonnay represents the most ideal relationship. It is less worried about your character flaws and more about you as a person, making it tempting to commit to. You can put on your loungewear and fuzzy slippers to hang out with Chardonnay. While you're at it, why not order a pizza and watch reruns of Family Guy together? Chardonnay will still like you, whether you put on makeup or not. It is less "salesy" and gimmicky than other wines.

You can bring Chardonnay as a last minute date to a wedding without there being any strings attached. This clean, white wine can dress up and look debonair just as easily as it can be simple and casual. It's fun to drink, with all those sparkly bubbles amid swirls of tropical and fruit bearing aromas. It's the type of wine to vacation with if you want less hassles and more time to relax.

Chardonnay is there for you. It is likeable in every way and can be part of many other worthy wines as a blend. Yet, a fine line can develop between *'like'* and *'love'*. What's not to love about this wine is not obvious.

The FWB is a line to cross with caution. The hazy connection between lovers and friends can make the boundaries seem blurry, especially if you drink too much Chardonnay. Fortunately, since you have a solid foundation of communication together, it should be easy to expel any awkwardness. Besides, doing so will just make you look silly and vulnerable. If you form an attachment, it could ruin the friendship. Try not to develop any romantic feelings and keep your need for love elsewhere, because Chardonnay is not "the one" who will swoon you; such as that of more vibrant wines.

Some people do keep Chardonnay in a wine cellar for later on. It's always an option and good filler in between other more serious commitments. You can just grab a bottle of Chardonnay out of the cellar and it will still be just as good as it was the first time you tried one from the same batch, or maybe even better.

# About the Author

## Anne Violette

Author **Anne Violette** grew up in the northernmost region of Maine in Presque Isle and then lived in the Bangor area from her senior year of H.S. until 2004. During that time, she took on many hats as a professional photographer, graphic designer and account rep at an advertising agency, publisher, entrepreneur and writer / editor for several independent publications and New England-based papers. After moving to Delray Beach, FL, she was also a top regional seller for a national diamond store franchise but always continued freelance writing throughout her career. After launching AwesomeWriter.com in 2007, she began writing full time.

She has written 15 books as a ghostwriter and many more ebooks, marketing projects and more for clients around the globe in over 17 countries. MEN ARE LIKE WINE was born when Anne was researching her favorite wines and thought that the descriptions sounded quite like characters. Through the encouragement of her family and peers, Anne spent four years writing to make her debut fiction book a truly one-of-a kind creative project. Her goal was to encompass humor, relationships and the qualities of wine in an interesting way.

© Conrad Steward: Allure Photography

Personally speaking, Anne has done a lot of exciting things like skydiving, rappelling, snorkeling, traveling domestically and internationally, and bodysurfing, as well as having owned a motorcycle. However, after having three boys – Avery, a toddler; and twin babies Jasper and Chase – she has exchanged her adrenaline junky drive for motherhood.

Her key to success is living in the moment and not worrying about past laments or future uncertainties. She also believes that extending kindness to others cycles back to the giver. Anne loves writing both for herself and on behalf of her awesome clients.

You can reach Anne at: **www.menarelikewine.net** or **www.AwesomeWriter.com.** She has an author page on Facebook at: http://www.facebook.com/AwesomeWriter.

# Meet the Models

## Brittany Baldassari

The sexy cover model who graces the cover and promotional campaign of MEN ARE LIKE WINE is go-getter **Brittany Baldassari.** This Boston sweetheart has got the whole package from brains to beauty and a kind heart, too. Her "wicked" competitive nature began as a youth, where she always believed in good karma and that anything is possible through determination and an optimistic outlook.

Brittany is currently a full time model with numerous accolades. She's been featured in movies, reality shows, magazines, print campaigns, swimwear and clothing collections, makeup and cosmetics, and many more as a budding actress.

She inspires everyone to *dive for their dreams*. To get in touch for bookings or other,
email: bjabaldassari@gmail.com

© Conrad Steward: Allure Photography

# James Michael Sama

© Conrad Steward: Allure Photography

The handsome "face" of MEN ARE LIKE WINE is none other than **James Michael Sama**, born and raised right outside of Boston, Mass. He grew up in an entrepreneurial environment, where his parents have always encouraged him to pursue his dreams since day one. After earning a Bachelors in marketing from Suffolk University in Boston, James also became an entrepreneur, luxury brand liaison, and sales manager. James was in the Boston based movie "Angels Around Me", Style Network's "Wicked Fit" as a guest host of Bad Press with Extra TV's Steve Santagati, and featured in a commercial for George's Bakery in Methuen, MA, airing on major networks.

What makes James perfect for MEN ARE LIKE WINE is the fact that he represents so many of the greats – from Tempranillo to Shiraz; or Riesling to Chardonnay; Red Burgundy and Merlot; Pinot Grigio with a hint of Zinfandel – and for some lucky lady he may blossom into a fine Cabernet.

You can connect with James directly on Twitter at: @JamesMSama, as well as on Facebook at Facebook.com/JamesMichaelSama.

# Acknowledgements

**Family means everything to me, and that is because** I have one of the greatest. My parents had traditional values and raised us in a rural community in Northern Maine. We grew up simply, yet quite happily. We had our ups and downs, but mostly ups. My parents encouraged us to take action, make decisions, dream, learn and especially nurture our imaginations. Whether it was basketball camp or piano lessons, horseback riding or art classes, skating practice, swimming at the lake, building giant forts in tall snowbanks, or taking us on family vacations, my parents did everything to make sure that my sister and I had what we needed, yet without being spoiled. I would not have accomplished all of the many different endeavors, nor be where I am today, had it not been for their tremendous and tireless support. They have seen me succeed and fail. In both cases, they were always there and never turned against me when I was in need. They are exemplary role models and epitomic of how parents should raise their children. I am so blessed.

Now as a parent, I hope to pass on the same integrity and leadership skills that they have instilled within me and to encourage my sons to be anything in life; never to be hindered with the words "I can't"; but instead to know that if they try, they "can."

My sister is also someone special who I admire very much. She is a combination of confidence and sensitivity, generosity and wisdom. She tells it like it is. She has always been there for me and whenever we have experienced "sibling" quarrels, no matter what age, they never last long. That is because we love each other as only close sisters can understand. She has also been a huge supporter of this book and for that I am so grateful!

And my childhood BFF Elizabeth; there are few friendships that begin with playing together in a crib as infants and that can withstand the woes of childhood and high school and even after college when people move much further away than ten telephone poles. You're a wonderful mother and eternal friend who I will forever cherish.

There are others, too. The friends from Maine who continued to stay in touch even when the miles separated us. Alison, Meredith, Joelene, Shawna, Brandi, Steph, Heidi, April, Michele, Wes, and my friend Lil, who passed away last year without another chance to pay one last visit.

I am fortunate to have met some truly awesome friends in Florida. Especially Sheri, Becky, Julie, Mary, Kelly, Adrian, Matt, Brittany, Debbie and Amanda, Andres, Janine, Wendy, Sarah, Brian, Mike, Mei and Chris. Scott and Dan – you too – although you are both Florida and Maine friends from H.S., which most likely makes you a lifelong friends. To all of you: Whether we were able to spend enough time together or not, you have always made living in Florida fun and worthwhile. I can't wait to see you again!

Conrad from Allure Photography in Massachusetts is absolutely the best and most fun to work with. Look him up and hire him. You will not be disappointed by his stunning ability to capture people and their natural beauty. Not only have we been friends for going on 13+ years, I have watched him evolve as one of the most talented photographers in New England, whose passion for his craft is evident.

Jim "Bish"... how random you came into our life at just the right time and already have become such an important person! Some friendships are unexpectedly meant to be. I'm so excited to have you sharing in this dream, too.

Brittany and James, you are both very professional and fun to work with. As models these two have great on-camera synergy and are top shelf people in every way.

Andy, you were like a brother to me and one of the biggest supporters of this book. I will always remember all of the great times and football games and fun we used to have. Thank you for being there back in the day.

Leslie, as far as mother-in-laws go, you are the coolest ever. Jade and CJ, we've all been through a lot and I am excited to see what you both do with your lives. Thank you for helping with the kids from time-to-time. Love you all!

I must also acknowledge my beloved Maine Coon Cat, Kiki, who was more of an angel than a cat. She was faithfully by my side as the office mascot and beloved friend for 17 years. There have been very few creatures that have ever captured my heart so intentionally and with such loyalty.

I would also like to acknowledge new clients who have become great friends, like Nancy Oakley. You are an inspiration to women. Srey and Sovanna, I am fortunate to have been chosen as your voice for such a touching story. Everyone can find the miracles in your message. Rodney, even though we have just begun working together, I feel that we will be longtime friends.

Finally, my editor Raye Shelly was a last-minute that was meant to be. Her sense of humor meshed well with the style of this book and although there were heavy wine lingo terms in many places, she rose to the task like a champ and made suggestions that were both welcome and that made this book even more exceptional and perfect. You are the cherry on top of a delicious cupcake that was already tasty to begin with!

**"A great man is like a great glass of wine.
They both make you feel warm and tingly.
They give you goose bumps and make you giddy.
And just one a day is good for your heart."**

--Anne Violette

## MEN ARE LIKE WINE

**"Some are best right away,**
**but others need to be locked in the cellar**
**for a few years until they mature."**

--Anne Violette

71994188R10175

Made in the USA
Middletown, DE
02 May 2018